Praise for *The Millennium Matrix*

"*The Millennium Matrix* is a book for those who aren't satisfied with surface answers but want to rethink how culture impacts life and church."
—Dan Kimball, author, *The Emerging Church: Vintage Christianity for New Generations*, and pastor, Vintage Faith Church, Santa Cruz, California

"*The Millennium Matrix* is a fascinating approach to understanding the effects of communications media on social interaction and institutions throughout history. Congratulations on a fine contribution to futurist thinking."
—Cynthia G. Wagner, managing editor, THE FUTURIST magazine

"It is rare when clarity accompanies profound insight and deep thought. Rex Miller has accomplished this feat as he lays out for the reader an engaging review of our past, present, and future, primarily associated with the storage and distribution of information and how these various communication eras —oral, print, broadcast, and now digital—have transformed and are transforming our lives and our exercise of faith. Every serious believer should read this book as we begin to engage the digital age."
—William L. Thrasher Jr., general manager and associate publisher, Moody Publishers

"The uncharted path is more fearsome when you don't know enough about it to choose the right vehicle. Rex Miller does an amazing job of tracing history, revealing current culture, and sharing his view of the future so that the reader is ready to confront the growing world of postmodernism, pluralism, and globalism with a new sense of understanding and courage."
—Brad Smith, president, Bakke Graduate University

"Today more than ever we need leadership from people who are gifted to see beyond the present. Rex Miller blends technology savvy, business sense, and prophetic spiritual insight to create a unique manifesto that can help us chart our course in the twenty-first century. Leaders who want to break out of status-quo thinking must read this book."
—J. Lee Grady, editor, *Charisma* magazine

"Our nation is undergoing a profound cultural shift. The people we are reaching for Christ today are not the same people we need to prepare to reach tomorrow. The next generation is growing up immersed in digital communication. Their language, their tastes, and even their world view will challenge our paradigms and our current ideas about church and community. Leaders will have to change the way they think if they hope to speak to the emerging culture. I believe that *The Millennium Matrix* provides a mandatory survival guide for pastors and leaders."

—Tom Mullins, senior pastor, Christ Fellowship, Palm Beach Gardens, Florida

"*The Millennium Matrix* gives Rex Miller's unique insight into where our culture is and where is it going. Church leaders as well as thoughtful business leaders will benefit from reading and understanding the insights contained in this book."

—Pat Sullivan, founder, ACT Software and SalesLogix, and board member for the ministry Leaders That Last

"The changes in mediums of communication have each reformed the culture of the time. These reformations have brought new values to society including the Church. Rex Miller has presented and traced those changes well through the oral, print, electronic, and digital periods. New paradigms are needed to navigate through the new culture and new leadership style is required not only to be relevant and effective leaders but to help people understand what is going on. This book is a must for any person who leads others, whether parents or pastors, and those that want to know what is going on with their peers. I highly recommend this insightful and practical book."

—LaMar Boschman, author, *The Rebirthing of Music* and *Future Worship*, and academic dean, WorshipInstitute.com

"Rex Miller challenges us to think in a different way. He brings the scientific into the psychological. The change in thinking that he advocates will be essential to finding our way through the matrix. The digitalization of the individual is a key to facing the future successfully."

—Charles Simpson, pastor, Bible teacher, church planter, and senior editor, *One-to-One* magazine

"In great historical transitions, we need road signs that tell us where we've been and where we're going. For too long now, the Church has missed too many turns in the road. It's time to get back on track. Rex Miller clearly maps the way—no one will get lost here."

—Dr. Thomas Hohstadt, author, *Dying to Live: The Twenty-First Century Church*

"A sophisticated understanding of communications technology for today's church at the crossroads. *The Millennium Matrix* unveils history and the present

in a brilliant, new way for innovative ministry in the climactic days ahead."
—Clifford G. Christians, professor, Institute of Communications Research,
University of Illinois-Urbana

"This is a fascinating interpretation of modern society, based on the premise that the advent of our digital age has of necessity redefined how our cultures function. This is provocative reading for serious thinkers who are searching for ways the Church can fulfill its divine mandate in the midst of an ever-changing sea of technological advances. Thank you, Rex, for throwing out some markers that can help guide our paths through the complexities of this new millennium."
—Bob Sorge, author and teacher

"Our era has caught us all in a whirlwind of profound and rapid cultural change. Our parents didn't get us, and we don't get our kids. Pastors and congregations struggle to connect across the generations. In such times, we cry out for someone to make sense of our experience and to give us some bearings. Rex Miller's *The Millennium Matrix* does just that. He draws an analytic grid that sets our swirling experience in the larger context of the millennia. By doing so he helps us understand where the wind is coming from and where it might be going. Grasping his millennium matrix can help us find meaning in our experiences and direction for our individual, familial, and congregational journeys."
—Fr. Bob (Bernard R.) Bonnot, senior vice president,
special programming, The Hallmark Channel

"At last—a book about the Church that doesn't come from an ecclesiastical "Beltway Insider." Thoroughly researched, well written, and digitally aimed at our time, Rex Miller's *The Millennium Matrix* brings clarity for us on the future of the Church like the Hubble telescope brought the universe into focus for astronomers. Tomorrow is no longer another country; Miller has seen it, and he can take you there. Read this so future church history doesn't happen while you are looking the other way!"
—Gary Henley, director, International Outreach Ministries;
author, *The Quiet Revolution*

"*The Millennium Matrix* is a comprehensive look at our culture and church history, and provides an insightful lens through which to view the future. I strongly encourage pastors, music ministers, and worship leaders to read and study it because it provides a framework and a strategy for the emerging church. It provides insights to help make our worship both relevant and inspiring to our congregations. It also provides answers to traditional organizations feeling the crisis of change and offers vital perspective to new organizations that are providing fresh expressions of our faith.

—Don Cason, president, Word Music

"Rex Miller understands that world views change when information systems change, and his millennium matrix takes us through a rapid-fire review of the ways in which Christianity has been shaped by oral, print, broadcast, and digital communication techniques. Most important, he helps us to see what leadership will look like in our increasingly digital world, and how the Church can become a vital community by reclaiming lost virtues, giving priority to relationships, and approaching the future with open hands."

—Henry G. Brinton, senior writer, *Homiletics* preaching journal, and senior pastor, Fairfax Presbyterian Church

The
Millennium
Matrix

Reclaiming the Past,
Reframing the Future
of the Church

M. Rex Miller

A LEADERSHIP ❋ NETWORK PUBLICATION

JOSSEY-BASS
A Wiley Imprint
www.josseybass.com

Jossey-Bass books and products are available through most bookstores. To contact Jossey-Bass directly call our Customer Care Department within the U.S. at 800-956-7739, outside the U.S. at 317-572-3986, or fax 317-572-4002.

Jossey-Bass also publishes its books in a variety of electronic formats. Some content that appears in print may not be available in electronic books.

Scripture quotations marked (NASB) are taken from the New American Standard Bible®, Copyright © 1960, 1962, 1963, 1968, 1971, 1972, 1973, 1975, 1977, 1995 by The Lockman Foundation. Used by permission. (www.Lockman.org)

Scripture quotations marked (NIV) are taken from the HOLY BIBLE, NEW INTERNATIONAL VERSION®. NIV®. Copyright ©1973, 1978, 1984 by International Bible Society. Used by permission of Zondervan. All rights reserved.

Scripture quotations marked (KJV) are taken from the Holy Bible, King James Version, Cambridge, 1769.

Scriptures quotations marked (MSG) are taken from The Message by Eugene H. Peterson, copyright (c) 1993, 1994, 1995, 1996, 2000, 2001, 2002. Used by permission of NavPress Publishing Group. All rights reserved.

Credits appear on page 278.

Readers should be aware that Internet Web sites listed within may have changed or disappeared between when the book was written and when it is read.

Library of Congress Cataloging-in-Publication Data
Miller, M. Rex, date
  The millennium matrix: reclaiming the past, reframing the future of the church /
  M. Rex Miller.
     p. cm.
Includes bibliographical references and index.
  ISBN 0-7879-6267-8 (alk. paper)
  1. Church. I. Title.
  BV600.3.M55 2004
  270.8'3—dc22

Printed in the United States of America
FIRST EDITION
HB Printing   10 9 8 7 6 5 4 3 2

LEADERSHIP NETWORK TITLES

The Blogging Church: Sharing the Story of Your Church Through Blogs, by Brian Bailey and Terry Storch

Leading from the Second Chair: Serving Your Church, Fulfilling Your Role, and Realizing Your Dreams, by Mike Bonem and Roger Patterson

The Way of Jesus: A Journey of Freedom for Pilgrims and Wanderers, by Jonathan S. Campbell with Jennifer Campbell

Leading the Team-Based Church: How Pastors and Church Staffs Can Grow Together into a Powerful Fellowship of Leaders, by George Cladis

Organic Church: Growing Faith Where Life Happens, by Neil Cole

Off-Road Disciplines: Spiritual Adventures of Missional Leaders, by Earl Creps

Leading Congregational Change Workbook, by James H. Furr, Mike Bonem, and Jim Herrington

Leading Congregational Change: A Practical Guide for the Transformational Journey, by Jim Herrington, Mike Bonem, and James H. Furr

The Leader's Journey: Accepting the Call to Personal and Congregational Transformation, by Jim Herrington, Robert Creech, and Trisha Taylor

Culture Shift: Transforming Your Church from the Inside Out, by Robert Lewis and Wayne Cordeiro, with Warren Bird

A New Kind of Christian: A Tale of Two Friends on a Spiritual Journey, by Brian D. McLaren

The Story We Find Ourselves in: Further Adventures of a New Kind of Christian, by Brian D. McLaren

Practicing Greatness: 7 Disciplines of Extraordinary Spiritual Leaders, by Reggie McNeal

The Present Future: Six Tough Questions for the Church, by Reggie McNeal

A Work of Heart: Understanding How God Shapes Spiritual Leaders, by Reggie McNeal

The Millennium Matrix: Reclaiming the Past, Reframing the Future of the Church, by M. Rex Miller

Shaped by God's Heart: The Passion and Practices of Missional Churches, by Milfred Minatrea

The Ascent of a Leader: How Ordinary Relationships Develop Extraordinary Character and Influence, by Bill Thrall, Bruce McNicol, and Ken McElrath

The Missional Leader: Equipping Your Church to Reach a Changing World, by Alan J. Roxburgh and Fred Romanuk

The Elephant in the Boardroom: Speaking the Unspoken About Pastoral Transitions, by Carolyn Weese and J. Russell Crabtree

CONTENTS

ABOUT LEADERSHIP NETWORK

Since 1984, Leadership Network has fostered church innovation and growth by diligently pursuing its far-reaching mission statement: to identify, connect, and help high-capacity Christian leaders multiply their impact.

Although Leadership Network's techniques adapt and change as the Church faces new opportunities and challenges, the organization's work follows a consistent and proven pattern.

Although Leadership Network's techniques adapt and change as the church faces new opportunities and challenges, the organization's work follows a consistent and proven pattern: Leadership Network brings together entrepreneurial leaders who are focused on similar ministry initiatives. The ensuing collaboration-often across denominational lines-creates a strong base from which individual leaders can better analyze and refine their own strategies. Peer-to-peer interaction, dialogue, and sharing inevitably accelerate participants' innovation and ideas. Leadership Network further enhances this process through developing and distributing highly targeted ministry tools and resources, including audio and video programs, special reports, e-publications, and online downloads.

With Leadership Network's assistance, today's Christian leaders are energized, equipped, inspired, and better able to multiply their own dynamic Kingdom-building initiatives.

Launched in 1996 in conjunction with Jossey-Bass (a Wiley imprint), Leadership Network Publications present thoroughly researched and innovative concepts from leading thinkers, practitioners, and pioneering churches. The series collectively draws from a range of disciplines, with individual titles offering perspective on one or more of five primary areas:

1. Enabling effective leadership
2. Encouraging life-changing service
3. Building authentic community
4. Creating Kingdom-centered impact
5. Engaging cultural and demographic realities

For additional information on the mission or activities of Leadership Network, please contact:

Leadership Network
www.leadnet.org
(800) 765-5323
client.care@leadnet.org

Welcome to the Millennium Matrix

History becomes an astonishing succession of new media top-
pling old empires by repatterning perceptions of time and space.
—Michael Schrage, *No More Teams*

For the first time since ancient times, we have the percep-
tual capabilities to see the world not just as our little corner of the globe but as an interconnected multidimensional whole. Thanks to digital technology, text, sound, images, and data have all merged into one common language (zeros and ones) and one common medium of copper-etched silicon. Led by this new way of looking at things, our very perception of the world has changed.

> Most people sense that something is different or even wrong, and everyone seems to have a theory as to why. Few of these theories, however, offer a real framework for navigating change.

Most people sense that something is different or even wrong, and everyone seems to have a theory as to why. Few of these theories, however, offer a real framework for navigating change. In fact, the extraordinary number of theories and programs proposed to deal with society's weekly crises serves to reveal our deepening social fragmentation rather than heal it. Without a unifying theory, we chase every wind of crisis that blows through. Without a compelling unifying theory, this fragmentation will gain momentum and take on a devastating life of its own. The church will be no exception.

Seeking an alternate vision of our collective future has been the driving force behind the creation of *The Millennium Matrix*. Like you, I was raised in a world that changed more than it stayed the same, with the certain knowledge that tomorrow's news would bring some new jolting crisis or accomplishment. Today, as a businessman with a degree in theology and communications, I have a great concern about the world my children will inherit. I have wondered more than once where the rule book went that seemed to work so well for past generations. As I watch the world change before my eyes, I wonder how today's church, and the people who compose it, can respond to this changing cultural tide.

The Millennium Matrix

After twenty-five years of researching social change, I have designed the Millennium Matrix: a compelling framework that enables us to view ourselves, our times, and the church in a way that makes sense of the past, the present, and the future. The Millennium Matrix builds on the premise that when the primary means of storing and distributing information changes, our worldviews change. Here's how this works.

When our means of storing and distributing information change, our perceptions change. Changed perceptions create changed understandings and even changed psychology. Changed identity affects relationships. Changed relationships affect the traditions and institutions that support those relationships. These changes eventually reach a cultural critical mass, igniting a battle between old and new worldviews. Communication is the medium for relationships, community, and culture; so a more efficient or powerful tool of communication results in their restructuring.

This insight is not new. You may have read similar ideas in the books of a number of thinkers over the years, including Ivan Illich, Marshall McLuhan, Walter Ong, Neil Postman, Derrick de Kerckhove, Heidi Campbell, and others. Still, for some reason these important lessons have barely made it beyond the corridors of a few universities. What is new is this: for the first time, these ideas have been cataloged for easy access into a chart that spans more than two thousand years of human history and includes many insights into the history of the church, Christianity, and society through the millennia. If you spend some time walking with me through the Millennium Matrix, I believe you will never look at life—particularly your spiritual life—in the same way again.

The Church at a Crossroads

In my business of work place design and furnishing, we work primarily with firms that are growing or changing, so I've seen organizations attempt to integrate changing technology into their structures and cultures. I have viewed, from the inside, many of the leading companies of the new economy and have worked to support their efforts to anticipate and adapt to their roller-coaster industries. I have also worked with some of the bulwarks of the old economy and watched them convulse over the transitions they have had to face.

At the same time, I have remained active in lay ministry and have attempted to integrate my understanding of each of these different disciplines. Although I drew much of the material basis of this book from academic authors and thinkers, this book is not a theologically focused work or an organizational management text. Instead, I've filtered these complex studies into the practical language of the marketplace in a way that I hope will stimulate, strengthen, and challenge your faith.

Today the church is facing a scenario we find reflected in the business world. During the 1980s, for example, Royal Dutch/Shell—one of the largest corporations in the world—was at a crossroads. Its core business, oil and gas, had a questionable future. After a little over one hundred years of business, the company's future was threatened. Searching to redefine its missions and goals and remain vital during future radical transitions, top managers looked for companies that were equally large and had been around longer. They found only forty companies, of which only twenty-seven provided relevant comparisons.

But these companies had four critical elements in common that enabled them to prosper during times of economic, social, and technological restructuring. First, all of the companies externally integrated into the social and economic context of the times. Second, each one had a cohesive identity that gave it the ability to withstand the traumas of shifting circumstances. Third, they were risk takers; they understood how to take the kind of risks that allowed them to adapt. "These companies were particularly tolerant of activities on the margin: outliers, experiments, and eccentricities within the boundaries of the cohesive firm, which kept stretching their understanding of possibilities." Finally, they all enjoyed financial stability. They were financially conservative and maintained the kind of cash reserves that gave them "flexibility and independence of action."[1]

When we apply this analysis to the church, six problem areas rise to the surface:

- *Isolation:* Many churches and denominations are isolated from the realities of their community and the larger culture. In fact, they have moved to build support services and a culture cut off from the larger community. The strong reactions against society that some of these churches exhibit are the opposite of the cultural sensitivity that has allowed the companies Dutch Royal Shell studied to remain vital.

- *Fragmentation:* Many churches are so fragmented and activity-driven that they have little opportunity to develop strong relational bonds. One strong indicator of this problem is the churn rate that churches experience. *Churn rate* is a business term for the number of people who enter, leave, or change roles within an organization. A high churn rate inside an organization results in damaging client turnover and in the case of churches, congregants. A company with a yearly churn rate of more than 15 percent, for example, has a serious and quantifiable problem. Many expanding churches reflect similar and even higher churn rates.[2] What does it mean to have a completely new church every five to seven years?

- *Lack of identity:* Part of this lack of cohesion stems from a lack of clear identity. Community and corporate identity are not the same as being purpose-driven or having a mission statement. Leaders and members have to spend time together in meaningful fellowship and service in order to develop both identity and cohesion. Meeting once a week on Sunday or for hit-and-run activities do not provide the context for building community.

- *Lack of innovation:* Many churches do not tolerate fringe or eccentric elements, due in large part to their emphasis on the Sunday event. They would no sooner introduce a fringe expression of faith on Sunday than you would serve sushi to your Italian in-laws on their first visit to your home. However, you might create an internationally themed buffet for your extended family, allowing them to experience new things and choose what they like. In the same way, churches can provide forums and permission for people to try new things then incorporate those elements that show promise.

• *Central leadership:* The leadership structure of many churches can prevent adaptation. Many churches maintain a tight rein on what they approve and reject. They operate like a central command post, when a more decentralized and federation form of governance might actually be more beneficial.

• *No margin for error:* Many churches confuse running lean with being fiscally conservative. They are so highly leveraged (extending resources beyond a safe limit) with both their time and their finances that they have little margin for error or the flexibility to change directions.

So the question is not only "Can we adapt to the near future?" but "Can we adapt to major social change?"

The Millennium Matrix: A New Way of Seeing Solutions

"The problem is never how to get new, innovative thoughts into your mind, but how to get old ones out. . . . Make an empty space in any corner of your mind, and creativity will instantly fill it."

—Dee Hock, quoted in M. Mitchell Waldrop, "Dee Hock on Management," *Fast Company*

Since about 1960 churches have gravitated toward adopting more business and entrepreneurial models. Although this has brought promise and results to many churches, a downside has yet to manifest. The average lifespan of corporations, including Fortune 500 corporations, is between 12.5 and 40 years.[3] Many of our rapidly growing nondenominational churches have neither stood the test of time nor exhibited the qualities of enduring communities. At the same time, several long-established and revered corporations have been unable to endure the recent business upheavals of deregulation and global competition.

Similarly, traditional church institutions, some lasting centuries, are declining. The pressures of deep change are felt everywhere.

Consider another warning sign—the rising hunger for spiritual connection in our increasingly technologically driven world. More than one thousand nondenominational churches launch every year. Religious books are being published at four times the rate of business books.[4] So isn't this a good thing for the church?

What are we to do? We need to begin by seeing the world in a whole new way. And it is here that the Millennium Matrix opens a whole new window of perception and possibility.

Not when you consider that many of the growing churches represent a collection of some of the most driven people on the planet. We focus on sermon techniques, worship techniques, youth techniques, small group techniques, growth techniques, evangelism techniques, Bible study techniques, prayer techniques, and devotional techniques. We cannot seem to wean ourselves away from reaching for the quick fix in order to experience something more individual and vital. But rather than quench the thirst, we only make it worse. As one preacher said, our efficient delivery of Christ's love (an oxymoron in itself) is turned to an offering of saltwater to the thirsty. What are we to do?

We need to begin by seeing the world in a whole new way. And it is here that the Millennium Matrix opens a whole new window of perception and possibility.

The Millennium Matrix chart clearly shows how the world and our way of perceiving it have changed over the last few millennia and how key elements of church theology and practice have changed in response to our changing worldviews. From a design perspective, the Millennium Matrix lays the foundation by developing necessary criteria to build appropriately for the conditions of a particular environment. You can take a few moments to look at the chart now to get some idea of where we will be going, or you can reflect on it later, after you have had some time to absorb some of the issues we'll be touching on (see the abridged version on page 225 and the complete version beginning on page 95). When you understand the dynamics of this simple chart, you'll find that your way of viewing the world and your place in it will never be the same.

By the time you finish this book,

- You will see infinitely more clearly where culture and the church have been; where we are; where we're going—and why.

- You will have a practical framework for understanding the historical church in a new way.

- You will be able to recognize the root causes of many of the present conflicts and crises that concern church leaders, and you will be able to use that knowledge to generate real solutions and invigorate leadership.

- You will be able to use the Millennium Matrix to bridge old barriers within the church and to find a common language and a common point of reference to lower these barriers.

- You will find ways to reclaim and recontextualize lost or ignored virtues that once played a vital role in our expressions of faith.

- You will understand the shaping forces within the emerging medium of digital communication and create new cultural and organizational design criteria that better fit the new realities.

The first part of this book is a journey through changing world-views: from the oral culture of Jesus' time, to the print world ushered in by Gutenberg's Bible, to the broadcast era of television, and finally to the emerging digital culture that is rushing to meet us. The chapters in Part Two use the lens of the Millennium Matrix to provide a fresh perspective on the foundations of our culture and the church. They also address the practical implications for you and your church, and provide suggestions for moving forward.

I invite you to come with me now on a journey through time and spirit. Our destination is an exciting new vision and vista for you, your family, your church, and all of us.

May 2004

M. Rex Miller
Dallas, Texas

Acknowledgments

One of the messages of this book is that we live in a time of continuous change, creating an ever greater need for significant relationships. Our best work and fulfillment increasingly will come from the strength of our collaborations. Writing this book has confirmed to me that this trend will continue to grow. I want to thank some of my collaborators and also provide a brief context for how they've contributed to this work.

I have to begin with Professor Clifford Christians, who captured my imagination during his introductory class on communications theory at the University of Illinois. Professor Christians helped to shape my framework for viewing history and anticipating change by guiding me through the works of thinkers such as Jacques Ellul, Walter Ong, and Marshall McLuhan. He has been a friend and my sounding board for more than twenty-five years.

Well before that, my extraordinary eighth-grade teacher, Mr. Rubidoux, set me on a quest to find my purpose in life by lifting me in the air and shaking me until I turned to putty. He said, "Miller, you have too much going for you for me to see it go to waste." I've tried to live up to that challenge ever since. I wish he were still alive to see one more student he sent forward to make a difference.

Mrs. John Kraft is an amazing woman whom God somehow sent to me. She had no idea who I was, but she gave me a scholarship to attend a Fellowship of Christian Athletes camp when I was in high school. I gave my life to Christ at that camp, and Mrs. Kraft has kept an ongoing interest in me.

I learned so many of the fundamentals of life and relationships through the influence of Pastor Charles Simpson. In addition to the value of spiritual family, mentoring, and personal pastoral care, I learned that spiritual truths need to produce practical realities. You will find that balance throughout this book.

I don't know Eric Clapton, but his "Unplugged" performance on MTV was the catalyst that led me to propose the idea that the growth of new media was changing the way we were relating to the world and spurred me to start sharing my thoughts with others to hear their reactions.

Lamar Boschman has an incredible ministry and institute helping churches and leaders create cultures of worship. I was asked to advise his ministry in the early 1990s, and in the process he gave me a public forum to begin teaching about how communication revolutions change society and the church.

Carol Childress is a maven when it comes to the church world and the people who are shaping it. She attended one of my seminars and afterward asked if I would provide an interview for the Leadership Network newsletter. The response to that interview opened the door to providing a book proposal to Jossey-Bass.

Soon after my meeting with Carol, I attended a writing seminar and sat in on a class by Lee Grady, executive editor at Charisma. He provided a roadmap and encouragement to develop my concepts into a book proposal, and made the generous offer to stay in contact.

Brian McLaren played an invaluable role in my development of the ideas for this book. His book *Finding Faith* was one of the first Christian books that I felt comfortable giving to a friend who was searching for spiritual answers. I called Brian, asking for input on my ideas, and after a few meetings he invited me to give a seminar on the topic to his leadership group. The critique his team provided, not to mention the patience, was instrumental. Hearing my thoughts expressed in a live setting was even more valuable.

After Jossey-Bass accepted the book proposal, I met acquiring editor Sheryl Fullerton, who has led this project. My focus and confidence came from her patience, pruning, and setting of firm bottom-line requirements, beginning with her distillation of my twenty-page book proposal into an outline of less than a half-page. Sheryl provided whatever resources she felt necessary to help me complete the job.

Nancy Caine is a wonderful friend and professional editor whom I've known since high school and who edited the first chapters I submitted to Jossey-Bass. Nancy helped me develop a structure and a voice and simplified my efforts greatly.

Naomi Lucks is the editor that Sheryl hired to help me create the final draft. She was more than an editor; she was my coach and close adviser. There would be no book without Naomi's talent and her personal interest in the subject. My goal is for you to come away with the same response that Naomi gave me when I asked her what effect the book had. She told me that once she got "into" the matrix, she could picture it at work everywhere she went.

Ray Hollenbach is another close friend from high school. He's a pastor in Campbellsville, Kentucky, and a college teacher. More important, he was the person I called almost weekly to ask a question of or for help when I got stuck.

I would also like to mention some others who provided ideas or who helped refine the text: Rich Thiessen, Steve Peifer, Don Hammond, Rich Raad, Ed Chinn, and Joe Ryan.

I have been extremely fortunate to arrive at this completed book because I cannot take full credit for the path that has led to it. I am grateful to everyone who has played a part, but most especially to my mother and father. Thanks to my father, Morris, I have developed a fascination for finding creative connections, for setting high expectations, and for taking risks to meet those expectations. My mother, Dolores, provided me with the discipline and persistence to complete what I start and to keep my commitments. She also taught me to question conventional wisdom no matter what the source.

My wife, Lisa, is my perfect complement. She has supported my time away from home to work on this project and her critiques helped me to visualize who I was writing to. Finally, our children, Michelle, Nathan, and Tyler, have provided motivation, daily object lessons, and a window into the future.

The
Millennium
Matrix

Vertigo

Ready or Not, Here Comes the Future

> Vertigo . . . a reeling sensation; feeling about to fall. A sensation
> as if the external world were revolving around an individual . . .
> or as if the individual were revolving in space.
> —WordNet 1.6., Princeton University, 1997,
>   www.health-dictionary.com

When did the unfamiliar become more common than the familiar? During the last forty or fifty years, it seems, our culture was transformed; the dynamics of our relationships shifted; our brains got rewired. Shouldn't we have adapted to a world of continual change by now?

We've been hearing about this perpetual motion lifestyle since at least 1970, when Alvin Toffler first described the damaging effects of constant and unrelenting change in his best-seller, *Future Shock*. He argued that the pace of change was racing faster than our psyches and society were able to digest, and he predicted that we would all burn out if the world did not find a way to alter its course. "Unless man quickly learns to control the rate of change in his personal affairs as well as society at large," Toffler warned, "we are doomed to massive adaptational breakdown."[1]

> The future is now.
> Our world has changed.
> Even the dynamics of change
> have changed—and like it or not,
> we are all along for the ride.

Well, as we so often hear, the future is now. Our world has changed. In fact, even the dynamics of change have changed—and like it or not, we are all along for the ride.

For most of us, it's a roller-coaster ride of slow climbs, fast drops, and spinning turns that leave us breathless and disoriented—and then picks us up to start all over again. To use Davis's and Meyer's term, the "blur" of the present is keeping us off balance;[2] and the increasing complexity of our technological present is confounding our efforts to gain solid footing. Attempting to recover from future shock, we are hurtling headlong into a new condition: vertigo.

Hurtling Headlong into Vertigo

> You are here because you know something. What you know you can't explain but you feel it. You felt it your entire life. There is something wrong with the world but you don't know what it is. But it's there like a splinter in your mind.
>
> —Morpheus to Neo in *The Matrix*

My good friend Ed Chinn has a great description of vertigo that I would like to share with you:

Certain conditions or dynamics are known to induce vertigo: *Fatigue* slows the cognitive process and leaves people or institutions vulnerable to disorientation.

Moving too quickly seems to upset the body's balance mechanisms and leads to *coriolis vertigo* (disorientation associated with operating physically free from the earth's movement).

Pilots know that anytime they experience a *loss of horizon* (such as when flying at night or in clouds), they are in danger of vertigo.

Too much *noise and vibration* in the environment creates a mental overload, which very often leads to vertigo.

Finally, *fixating* on a particular item or issue can cause one to eliminate or deny other essential information and thereby lose the panoramic command of the environment.

Another—psychologically brutal—form of vertigo is induced by flickering light (such as disco strobe lights or sunlight oscillating through helicopter blades).

Those suffering vertigo lose all sense of vertical and horizontal orientation; they literally lose their alignment to, and placement in, the real world. Pilots suffering vertigo have flown their planes full throttle into the earth.

Because it represents the tyranny of the subjective, the only effective recovery from vertigo is an absolute, resolute, focused reliance on objective reality (such as an airplane instrument panel).

But the same disorientation strikes organizations, businesses, movements . . . even civilizations! All of us lose our alignment to . . . or placement in . . . the real world. And the speed and fatigue of life simply hasten the process. Then, like pilots ignoring their instrument panel, our tunnel vision—our denial of reality—is a crash waiting to happen.[3]

The endless noise and vibration of experts on every issue adds to our sense of vertigo with conflicting opinions and analysis. The media compound the problem by bombarding our attention with the flickering strobe light of daily crisis all day, every day. We are caught in the waning gyrations of a vicious cycle.

So what's on our instrument panel? What reality can we hold on to in order to regain our balance? Step one is to understand the basic nature of the changing world in which we now must operate.

Life Acceleration 101

> Society [and the church], therefore, is out of control because we are systematically destroying all of the authority and all of the control that our institutions once had.
>
> —Peter Senge, *Rethinking the Future*

Future Shock's analysis set a benchmark for understanding the effects of technology and change on society. The assumptions that Toffler used in

1970 were based on a new dynamic: the relentless change in every area of life brought about by technology, a reality captured in the constant flow of televised images. With the advent of digital media—computers, cell phones, file sharing, personal digital assistants—the pace of change has changed again.

Digital networks create simultaneous interactive events that cycle thousands of times per second. Each time information loops through the system, it changes slightly because the system is fluid. Each little change, magnified over hundreds of thousands of cycles, can produce major shifts in the system. The iterations amplify to create a kaleidoscope of possible outcomes.[4] What may take decades to surface within natural systems can show up within minutes in a digital environment. In this new reality, known as systems thinking,[5] the threat of terrorism, a single word from our Federal Reserve chairman, an outbreak of a deadly disease—reverberates globally, systemwide.

We can describe the dynamics of the onrushing events of the new millennium in these seven qualities, all inherent within digital media: interconnection, complexity, acceleration, intangibility, convergence, immediacy, and unpredictability. As the Millennium Matrix makes clear, these seven qualities are also affecting the life of the church.

Interconnection

Instead of living in a domino world, where one change logically causes the next, we have entered a chain-reaction world of exponential outcomes. In this brave new world, interdependent relationships can exhibit extraordinary cohesion or, if destabilized, spiral out of control like a nuclear reaction. We know firsthand how hard it is to predict the outcomes of natural and economic systems, whether it is the effect of a particular pesticide on the environment or the behavior of the stock market or the weather.

This interconnection means that our problems and opportunities are intimately tied together. Rapidly changing and improving telecommunications—broadband, cell phones, portable devices—are making instant access to anything and anyone a not too distant reality.

And emerging networks (virtual communities of common interest)—which seem to have a collective intelligence that defies our old logical or sequential decision-making processes—have already begun to level our hierarchical organizations.[6]

Complexity

Complex systems behave not as a collection of separate parts but as a whole. When you cut down a forest, divide a family, change a line of computer code, or protect a threatened industry with tariffs, you set in motion an invisible ripple effect. Old analytical tools fail to anticipate potential consequences of action and policies within complex systems of relationships. Using linear logic and deductive analysis is like using a bulldozer to cultivate orchids.

Simulation, aided by digital tools, gives us a way to understand complex, delicate, and volatile environments. These tools already aid our understanding in disciplines from surgery to economics, from the military to the environment.

Acceleration

Change accelerates with each new technology and concept. These changes have a compounding effect within a complex and interconnected system, sending out an exponential ripple that drives additional change and accelerates the pace of life. We all get caught up in this acceleration. Many already feel that accelerating change has taken on a life of its own.[7]

We all know about the feedback effect: we see it when rock stars puts their electric guitars right next to the speakers to create a chaos of noise, amplifying and accelerating the sound. This creates a feedback loop. Kept up interminably, something will blow. As our lives become more interconnected—through e-mail, television, phones, the Internet—our actions get cycled back through our living and technological networks and become amplified and accelerated.[8] We all feel out of control from time to time, and sometimes our lives do blow up.

Intangibility

We're moving away from a tangible world we can touch and hold to a world that operates on intangibles like information, potential, and reputation.[9] In our hyper-mediated world,[10] we have little or no connection to the original source of the things we buy, use, and rely on. Do you know who grew the apple you ate the other day, who sews your clothing (and the nation she lives in), or the person who printed your family Bible?

We're also moving away from tangible and rational measures of value. The recent saga of Arthur Andersen's fall from grace is a perfect example. When clients hired the accounting firm, they were receiving some tangible service—accounting, audit, process integration, and so on. But they were also buying intangibles: Andersen's credibility and its reputation for being the best. When its client Enron imploded in scandal,[11] Andersen's intangibles went up in smoke.

Convergence

Convergence is an inherent property of our digital medium of information and communication. Print, graphics, sound, and data can all reside in a single medium—such as a CD or DVD—reproduced through a common digital language of bits and bytes, zeros and ones. Digital data makes no distinction between *Romeo and Juliet*, that snapshot of you on a pony when you were five, geological calculations, or the sound of a Bach cantata—except for the sequence of those zeros and ones. The digital environment is thoroughly integrated. That means we will no longer process these sensory experiences separately. It also means that the past boundaries of knowledge and organizations will blur, crumble, and eventually integrate.

The boundaries that once separated disciplines of knowledge—physics, poetry, metaphysics—are also beginning to blur. Nanotechnology is emerging as one of the world-transforming sciences of the new millennium—converging physics, chemistry, and biology. One book calls this "the convergence of infrastructures."[12] This confusion in categories is also working its way through organizations. For example, AT&T, AOL, and Time all began as separate technologies (phone company, Internet service provider, and news magazine) based on separate technologies (telephone wire, cybertechnologies, printing press) operating as separate industries, and controlled by separate government regulations.[13] But digital technology essentially provides all with a common platform, and they all know it. So as AOL buys Time Warner and Comcast acquires AT&T Broadband, all are preparing for the day when the government regulations catch up to the technological reality: it's all the same bits and bytes.

Immediacy

The time it takes us to absorb and adjust to digitally paced activities grows ever shorter. As the interval between question and answer, request and fulfillment, grows narrower (the other day Google found the answer to my search in 0.19 second!), we are asked to respond to the world with an immediacy similar to that required by fighter pilots in combat. Colonel John R. Boyd recognized that the context for air warfare involves such high speeds that it requires the F16 fighter pilot to master a different set of rules for decision making. How do we function in an environment where reality leaves us little or no time for reflection but "changes ceaselessly, unfolding 'in an irregular, disorderly, unpredictable manner,' despite our vain attempts to ensure the contrary"?[14]

How do we function in an environment where reality "changes ceaselessly, unfolding 'in an irregular, disorderly, unpredictable manner,' despite our vain attempts to ensure the contrary"?

Unpredictability

Complex and highly interactive systems are unpredictable. Kenneth Boulding, renowned economist and scholar, says that "the search for ultimately stable parameters in evolutionary systems is futile, for they probably do not exist."[15]

In the old physics, every action has an equal and opposite reaction. When you drop a rock from a window, you can predict with accuracy when it will hit the ground and with what impact. But each factor, player, condition, issue, or option, when interconnected, exponentially multiplies the number of outcomes. Within complex systems actions often create unintended consequences.

Rob Norton, former economics editor of *Fortune* magazine, cites this example: "In the wake of the *Exxon Valdez* oil spill in 1989, many coastal states enacted laws placing unlimited liability on tanker operators. As a result the Royal Dutch/Shell group, one of the world's biggest oil companies, began hiring independent ships to deliver oil to the United States instead of using its own forty-six-tanker fleet. Oil specialists fretted that other reputable shippers would flee as well, rather than face such unquantifiable risk, leaving the field to fly-by-night tanker operators with leaky ships and iffy insurance. Thus, the probability of spills will increase and the likelihood of collecting damages will decrease as a consequence of the new laws."[16]

We see this reflected in many organizations today. Creating efficient health care systems in an increasingly complex and changing world has confounded health care experts. As our means dramatically improve, the number of patients who die or become worse is skyrocketing—so much so that the condition has its own term, *iatrogenic*, meaning an illness that the doctor (*iatros*) induces (*genic*).[17] New laws enacted to correct a problem actually exacerbate it; solving a problem in one area creates five more in other places, and new innovations bring with them a whole list of side effects.[18]

Society's Dam Is Cracking

> The Christendom paradigm is coming apart at the seams.
> All the institutions and patterns of life that grew up during Christendom are having their foundations shaken. . . .
> We live in the memory of great ways of understanding how to be a church and to be in mission. Those memories surround us like ruins of an ancient . . . civilization.
> —Loren Mead, *The Once and Future Church*

If you sometimes feel like the little Dutch boy who stuck his finger into the dike to hold back the waters, you're not alone. Society's dam is leaking! Our major institutions—along with our ideas about how the world should work, relationships, and civil society—reveal irreparable stress fractures. When the final breach inevitably comes to pass, what will the floodwaters of change wash away and what new fertile soil will they wash ashore?

This much is clear: the great powers of technology, politics, science, economics, culture, social causes, ethnicity, morality, and religion are all jockeying for the lead position in framing a new order once the retaining walls of our current institutions give way. Over the past fifty years or so, hundreds of cultural battles have been fought locally and nationally; but we are now beginning to witness a convergence of these battles into a global cultural war—thanks to digital media. When the dam protecting insulated organizations and thinking bursts, there won't be much left of the nice and neat world we designed.

Institutions—including the church—approach the world from the vantage point of their unique historical beginnings. But successful habits for one context do not easily translate into another. Over the millennia, the church has adapted to changing social conditions by taking on different forms: the liturgical church was designed to unite a world of tribes and oral communities; denominational churches grew out of the soil of intellectual grounding and the continuity that a rational worldview provides; less structured nondenominational churches fit a world of changing novelty. Yet despite this proven ability to adapt and survive, none of the church's previous forms will survive long in the emerging digital culture.

What used to work—and worked well—won't.

Some counter this argument. "Wait just a minute," they say. "Maybe this is all just a sign that we need to pull up our bootstraps and soldier on. Maybe these challenges are simply a sign of declining morality."

To the contrary. Declining morality is not the cause of a war of worldviews but evidence of it. During times of titanic cultural upheaval, central moral battles rise to the surface. As the old order passes and a new order rises up, the old moral restraints begin to fall away before the new boundaries have stabilized. Paul dealt with this issue in the Corinthian church. As the restraints of the old Jewish law collapsed under the new freedom in Christ, many took license and were rebuked or excommunicated.[19] The church resisted numerous abuses and heresies for the next three hundred years. The revolution of the Reformation resulted in conflict not only within the Catholic Church but against numerous sects and radicals. The Jesus movement was part of the larger countercultural revolution of the 1960s. On the secular side, we saw a wave of drug use, sexual experimentation, and civil disobedience. On the religious side, we witnessed a rise in cults, alternative forms of worship, and a rapid growth of more fundamentalist churches.

During any transition the rules of life are unclear and shifting. We feel that we have lost our boundaries and our compass. Some throw themselves headlong into extreme behavior to push the limits of freedom, while others clutch to the security of order and control. Only those with transcendent faith and an exercised moral compass are able to navigate such waters. We see our true moral condition in turbulent times.

Life Is Like an Oil Tanker

> All crises begin with the blurring of a paradigm and the consequent loosening of the rules for normal research. As this process develops, the anomaly comes to be more generally recognized as such, more attention is devoted to it by more of the field's eminent authorities. The field begins to look quite different: scientists express explicit discontent, competing articulations of the paradigm proliferate and scholars view a resolution as the subject matter of their discipline.
>
> —Thomas Kuhn, *The Structure of Scientific Revolutions*

An executive for one of my former clients—one of the largest oil companies in the world—helped me understand the underlying nature of the emerging culture. I spent several hours with a director in charge of the design and construction of the company's oil tankers. This helped me reconstruct my own mental picture of how to build for an environment of turbulent change.

Building an oil tanker is an amazing feat. The number of details is mind-boggling, and the obstacles are incredible. Each tanker is designed differently, depending on its purpose and destination. North Atlantic tankers experience the most treacherous environment— remember the *Titanic?* These oil tankers have to be able to withstand a direct hit from an iceberg at seven knots. They have to be able to locate and attach to a floating mooring in the middle of a turbulent sea. Without dropping anchor, they must maintain a stable position while buffeted by fifty-foot waves. They must remain relatively stationary so that the large hose bringing oil to the tanker does not get ripped from the mooring and gush oil.

These tankers rely on satellite tracking systems to hold their position. They have tremendous stabilizers that keep them positioned, even with waves crashing over the sides of the ship. Multiple redundant systems act as safeguards and backups. These ships are one-third the size of regular tankers but cost three times as much—more than $250 million to build just one.

What a phenomenal metaphor for the church to consider as it builds a vessel to navigate the turbulent sea of social change! The church has been building the spiritual equivalent of vacation cruise liners: large, slow structures made for calm balmy seas and friendly ports of call. We may be trying to make these ships a little faster, a little more up-tempo and with a mission statement, but we are still expecting calm seas and a sunny horizon.

Here's the catch: the church has long since left a stable, homogeneous, and predictable culture. The design criteria for North Atlantic oil vessels included the following: smaller scale (highly agile and faster), redundancy (extra capacity), geopositioning (external awareness), powerful stabilizer engines (counterbalance), double hulls (buffer) and the ability to quickly disconnect from destabilizing conditions. These ships were also much smaller than traditional oil tankers and required fewer crew members to keep them afloat. Is it time for the church to build differently for a different future?

Understanding Where We've Been and Where We're Going

The church is not losing ground. On the contrary, we're simply awakening to our true condition. We have an opportunity to uniquely stand in the middle of opposite poles to provide a prophetic moral compass in a time of profound contradictions. Change and turbulence don't create today's problems; they bring them to the surface. We don't need a change in models but a model for change! Today we need a church that knows how to craft a new ethic, an ethic based on a reality of change rather than a fiction of stability. The church must now, and quickly, learn to build seaworthy vessels that can handle cultural turbulence as challenging as the North Atlantic.

> The church is not losing ground. On the contrary, we're simply awakening to our true condition.

And the church, as we know, is people: the body of Christ. That's us. As we rush headlong into a world of interconnection, complexity, acceleration, intangibility, convergence, immediacy, and unpredictability, just trying to keep our ship afloat, we will be aided greatly by a broad knowledge not only of where we're going but where we've been. In the next four chapters, we'll slow down a bit and take a leisurely tour of four cultures: the oral culture of Jesus' time (the birthplace of the liturgical church), the print world ushered in by Gutenberg's Bible (the birthplace of the reformation church), the broadcast era of television (home of the celebration church), and finally the emerging digital culture that is rushing to meet us (and where we will meet the convergence church).

Bon voyage!

PART 1

Stopping Time

The Medium Is the Worldview

> I have remained steadfast to [Marshall McLuhan's] teachings that the clearest way to see through a culture is to attend to its tools for conversation.
>
> —Neil Postman, *Amusing Ourselves to Death*

Our communication tools have changed over time: from the spoken word, to the written word, to the broadcast-image word, to the digital multimedia word. With each change has come a new and different way of seeing the world. Here's what happens:

- When our communication tools change, our perception changes.
- Changed perception creates a changed understanding.
- Changed understanding changes our psychological makeup.
- Changed psyches change our interaction with the world.
- Changes in our interaction with the world change our relationships to one another.
- Changes in our relationships lead to changes in the institutions that facilitate those relationships.

- Our psychological makeup changes, and we reshape the world in our own image.

Communication has been with us since the beginning, but communications theory was developed during the first half of the twentieth century. Individuals like Lewis Mumford, Ivan Illich, Walter Ong, and Marshall McLuhan laid much of the foundation. Their research began as an analysis into the interwoven relationship of modern culture and technology—that is, tools. If the wheel is an extension of the foot and the hammer an extension of the hand, then communication tools extend the personality and being. Sometimes our tools become so pervasive that we take them for granted. These communications pioneers brought them back to our attention by exploring the expanding nature and effectiveness of different tools and their implications.

In the 1960s Marshall McLuhan provided an accessible and popular way to view this method of analysis through attention-grabbing visual commentaries, humor, and his famous aphorism "The medium is the message."[1] McLuhan concluded (along with others) that even though we create these communications tools after our own image, at some point they reshape us. In the mid-1980s Neil Postman restated and updated the argument in *Amusing Ourselves to Death*: "The medium is the metaphor."[2] William Stringfellow provides a spiritual bridge that exposes the underlying principality that drives tools to take on a life of their own, eventually inverting their original intent.[3] And Jacques Ellul developed a painstakingly thorough examination of technology's dominating nature in each of his books, concluding that the technological principle represents the dominating spirit of the age.[4]

Chapters One through Four explore the inherent nature of history's dominant tools of communication: the spoken word, print and publishing, broadcast, and digital networks. Understanding how these four tools get their work done will help you see their influence on people, society, our worldviews, theology, and the church. Using these four tools, the Millennium Matrix provides a fresh understanding of where we've been, where we are, and where we're going. This book makes the case that the medium is the worldview. Chapter Five begins a deeper understanding of the worldviews created by the four major ages of communication and their implications for the church.[5] This understanding will ground you in a way of seeing change you may never before have considered. It will also give you a practical framework for understanding our changing world and exciting new directions in which the church—and your church—must consider changing.

As you will see, the oral world, the print world, and the broadcast world experience life in different and distinct ways. When you can begin to feel and perceive the interplay of these senses, you will have gained a vital skill for the coming digital age: the ability to think and work in a multisensory and multimedia world. These initial chapters are more than a chronicle of historical, theological, and cultural differences. They are providing you with the grammar and syntax to allow you not only to analyze the traits of each era but to synthesize them as a new expression of a convergent church and convergent community.

CHAPTER 1

Oral Culture–Liturgical Church

The Living Word

Circa ?B.C.–1500 A.D.

> In the beginning was the Word, and the Word was with God, and the Word was God.
> —John 1:1 (NASB)

God spoke the universe into existence.

Our first culture was oral, based in the spoken word. The air was filled not by radio waves or the instant connections of cyberspace but by human voices: person to person. Oral communication is not only about speaking but also about hearing: not reading the printed word, watching television or movies, or visiting a Web site. In fact, the ancient Hebrews considered understanding to be a type of hearing.[1]

Jesus lived and spoke in an era so profoundly different than ours that we can miss the full meaning of his teachings. It's not the content we're missing, however; it's the context of the living word. His world was not our world. As Walter Ong explains, "The strongly oral cast of the Hebrew and Christian Scriptures bespeaks a culture not only temporally but temperamentally quite different from ours, with a sense of the world and a psychological structure which is different not merely by reason of position in time and of social institutions generally but also specifically by reason of the way in which it is oriented toward the word itself."[2]

GETTING INSIDE THE ORAL MIND-SET

Have a Sound Experience

Sound is magical. You receive it through your ears, but you can feel it working on every cell in your body. If you don't know what I mean, try the following exercise.

Visit your local stereo retail store—preferably a retailer that caters to people with a lot of disposable income. (Don't worry, you're not going to buy anything, you're just after an experience.) Ask to have a demonstration in their best sound room. In order to get the most out of this experiment, bring some of your own CDs. I recommend bringing some live performances, including classical music with solo strings, a live concert with acoustical guitar (like Eric Clapton's *Unplugged* or Eduardo Eguez's *The Lute Music of J. S. Bach*), and something that sounds best loud—loud enough for you to feel the vibrations.

If the room is designed correctly, sound from all the speakers will converge at one spot in the center. You will know you are in the right spot when you close your eyes

This world of sound was also largely silent—or at least it lacked the sounds with which we are so familiar today. Close your eyes for a moment and just listen. Even if you are in a quiet room, you probably still hear some of these sounds: your computer's fan humming, the printer printing, a CD playing next door or in another room, a plane flying overhead, one driver honking at another. Now think about the world Jesus lived in, a world of silences and natural sounds: the wind blowing, the rain spattering, people talking, animals calling. A world intimately connected to nature: the feel of the hot sun on your back, the and cannot tell from which direction the sound is coming. You should feel surrounded by sound, immersed in it.

Ask your salesperson to show you how to change the CDs yourself, and explain that you simply want to listen undisturbed. If possible, turn off the lights in the room. The goal is to limit any other sensory distraction so that your ears can make the most of the opportunity.

Now get in the most comfortable position you can, close your eyes, quiet your thoughts, turn on the music, and just exist inside it. Feel the sound vibrations—not just in your ears but in every part of your body. Are you in a different world yet?

Experience Silence

Find the quietest place you can find. If you can go to the country or camp in a forest, go there. If not, just find a quiet room in your house at a quiet time of day.

Now close your eyes, breathe slowly, relax, and just let your ears receive the silence. Let the silence wash over you like a tide. Stay in this space as long as you like.

Can you sense the penetrating power of a word fitly spoken?

cold night air filtering into your home, the sand blowing in your face, the refreshing cool water from the well or river. A world covered over at night by the constellations, whose stories and relationships you knew so well you could navigate by them. When a stranger entered your world, he or she really was a stranger. When someone in your community was born or died, your relationship to that person was by blood or shared experience.

So when Jesus' miracles shattered the continuity of daily life, they did not need to get people's attention with pyrotechnics, mood music, colored lights, voice modulation, or special effects. His words were so connected to the composition of the universe that they calmed raging seas, gave sight to the blind, and raised the dead.[3]

Emotional Space: Intimate and Connected

Who has ears to hear, let him hear.
—Matthew 11:14 (NASB)

The magic of oral cultures lies in intimate connection. Word and spirit, spirit and being, words and essence, words and things: all are interrelated. The dividing lines—between art and religion and science and literature—don't exist in the same way they do in our visually mediated, rational world. This synergism—this circle of life—falls far outside our current experience, but it is this intimate relationship that makes the difference between the amazing and miraculous stories we read about in the Bible and our daily reality in which seas do not part on request.

What is the nature of revelation, truth, faith, time, space, relationships, and institutions in a world centered on the spoken word? When God creates by speaking, sound is *now*, time is *present*. We have a world in which burning bushes, parting seas, miraculous battles, and resurrections are entirely plausible.

Social Cohesion: The Covenant

Covenants exemplify the legal and sacred tie between two or more people. Hebrew culture, for example, trusted God to protect the integrity and cohesion of covenant agreements, to surface breaches, and to supercede human frailties and failures. The serious implications of oral covenants tied fortunes, personal and family destinies, and even life and death. Covenant represented the character and nature of God and His dealing with humans.[4] God's words are reliable; God's words are effective; God's intentions are merciful; and God's words are immutable. Covenant, by design, extends beyond human capabilities; and at the same time, we as humans are called to behave as God's representatives, covenant people. We see again the seamless link between heaven and earth within oral culture through covenant. Covenant enables us to deal with one another in the same way God deals with us.

The Bible illustrates several covenants beginning with Adam, Noah, Abraham, and Moses.[5] These all reflect the highly relational interaction and character behind these agreements. They were bonds of mystical love.

In oral cultures a covenant not only had the spiritual bond of one's word but also called upon God's power to hold each party accountable. Covenants included ceremonies to formalize commitments and invoke God's presence. Covenants represented an extension of God's own character and appealed to God to bless the union and curse any attempt at division. The mystical sacred link that covenants provided would later be replaced by a more rational mind-set that called on conscience, recognizing in the abstract that covenant reflects God's character and that therefore we too should adhere to the covenants we make.

> The magic of oral cultures lies in intimate connection. Word and spirit, spirit and being, words and essence, words and things: all are interrelated.

This intimate tie between essence (word) and being is no clearer than with Jesus' incarnation: the Word becomes flesh (John 1:14). Jesus later confirmed this cohesion between word and substance when he said: "I am the way the truth and the . . . life" (John 14:6, NIV). A person's word was a sacred bond.

Teaching and Learning: Discipleship

People in oral cultures taught by mentoring and learned through discipleship or apprenticeship; they did not go to school to decide what job they should hold. In these cultures a man inherited a calling from his family or was called to perform a task or responsibility, a vocation. Names often reflected that calling—John the Baptist, for example.

Masters, people respected for their skills and knowledge, were living embodiments of wisdom. They passed along the secrets and skills of their culture, religion, wisdom, arts, crafts, and trades to those who were willing and able to put in the years watching the master at work and performing menial tasks. In this way master and apprentice made a highly relational connection. In many ways they were replicating a heavenly model on earth. The apprentice could experience a powerful transformation simply through the invisible dynamic of abiding for many years in the presence of a master.

Jesus was such a master. Even the experts of his day admitted that he spoke with a level of "authority" they lacked.[6] The humor and sadness underlying many of the encounters of Jesus and his disciples cuts to the heart of our own awkward attempts to touch the transforming reality within Jesus' words. We in the church, along with many scholars, have done our best to decipher the literal meaning of Jesus' words, hoping to recapture their power. The writings capture the lasting substance of his statements; but the momentary, contextual encounter with a word made flesh—the living essence—remains both elusive and alluring.

Essence: The Living Word

The spirit (Latin, *spiritus*), we remember, meant the breath, the vehicle of the living word in time.
—Walter Ong, *Presence of the Word*

Why were Jesus' words so powerful that we still know them today, more than two thousand years later? Because they contain the living essence of Jesus' presence. Peter's encounter with Jesus was within a real living context, which created a moment of truth. Peter saw the Father through Jesus, and Jesus gave us this pattern to present the Father to others. Although God may choose and has chosen to act unilaterally, there is a particular power when a transformed, transcendent being in a living relational encounter raises the dead spirit in another.[7] Jesus touched others with his living presence and told his faithful to go and do likewise.

The power of God's love is the transforming power of one transformed life standing in front of another. In such a context, every encounter is charged with meaning and possibility.

In a world like this, God's word permeates our every action. In a world like this, a lie before God has real consequences. What do you conclude, for example, when you read the story of Ananias and Sapphira (Acts 5:3–8)? This couple had contributed property to the local church but misrepresented the portion of their offering. The Holy Spirit revealed this to Peter, and when Peter asked Ananias and then Sapphira, they lied—then died. Think about it: Have you ever seen anyone drop dead in front of a church elder because they lied to the Holy Spirit? A person may cry or feel guilty and ashamed, but in modern life nothing comes close to what happened to Ananias and his wife![8]

Consider also Paul's critical letter to the Corinthians (10:27–31, NASB) regarding communion, when some Corinthians approached the communion table in a casual manner, leaving some sick or dead: "Therefore, whoever eats the bread or drinks the cup of the Lord in an unworthy manner will be guilty of sinning against the body and blood of the Lord. A man ought to examine himself before he eats of the bread and drinks of the cup. For anyone who eats and drinks without recognizing the body of the Lord eats and drinks judgment on himself. That is why many among you are weak and sick, and a number of you have fallen asleep."

Paul is clear: if you come to this sacred gathering ill motivated, you put your life in jeopardy. Why did this event make such a difference then, and why not now?[9] There is a fundamental divide between worldviews then and now: one in which words and being are intimately linked and one in which words live and extend outside our being.

Turn the pages back to the Old Testament, and consider Abraham's attempt to sacrifice Isaac (Genesis 22:2). Abraham clearly had a relationship with God that we moderns can't pretend to imitate—what church today would allow a member to replicate this story?

We relate to these stories, like so many other stories in the Bible and other ancient texts, by calling them mysteries or reinterpreting them in a modern context. But there is no modern context in which a reasonable person can imagine a father preparing to kill his child because he heard God's voice.

TRY THIS: LIVE IN A DIFFERENT WORLD

Imagine yourself living in a time when everything you know, including your identity, depends entirely on the verbal communication of trusted intimate relationships. You have no television, no radio, no Bible, no pavement, no cars, no planes, no watch, no knowledge of world events, no computers, no phones, no malls, no ATM, no credit cards, no electricity. Imagine a world that moves at the speed of walking.

Imagine knowing intimately every corner of your village. Imagine actually paying attention each day to what's happening around you. Imagine knowing not only who lives in your village but all of their interconnections, stories, histories, and extended families.

You are just as familiar with the rhythms of the natural world: when it rains, when the sun beats down, when the cold drives you indoors, when the moon rises, when the sun comes up. You know the intimate relationships of the stars in the sky. Now put yourself right there and pay attention: with this kind of direct connection and daily contact, can you know the imprint of destiny in someone's life?

Now imagine Jesus looking at you and saying, "You aren't hiding a thing." Imagine taking part with him in one of many legal debates with the Pharisees over technicalities, as he cuts to the chase to expose underlying motives. Imagine you are performing an act of kindness with Jesus and he turns to chastise bystanders because he "heard their cynical thoughts" (Matthew 9:3–5, NASB).

How different is this world from the world we live in today?

The Roots of the Church

As we try to find our way back in time and space through the layers of mechanically mediated communication that surround us—print, broadcast, and the emerging computerized world—to find an ancient universe with which we are intimately connected and in which everything is tangibly real, we can begin to recognize the reality that Jesus and we are words and worlds apart.

Truth Is Relational

Truth is relational in oral cultures. The truth and the truth giver are intimately connected. The credibility of the message was based entirely on the credibility of the messenger. In those days killing the messenger who brought the bad news was more than just a metaphor.

When the Pharisees commented that Jesus spoke with a level of authority they had never before encountered (Luke 4:36), they were implying more than that this man was a compelling speaker. People in oral communities feel the sacred tie between oneself and one's words, a feeling we experience only rarely today.[10]

> Truth is relational in oral cultures. The truth and the truth giver are intimately connected.

Faith Is Trust

Faith equals trust in oral cultures. It is not an internal voice or act of conscience but an invasion through God or God's messenger.

Each patriarch in the Old Testament had his day with God or one of his messengers, and their encounters reveal a relationship with God that is difficult for us to understand today. The Bible says that Abraham was ready to sacrifice his son Isaac because he trusted the promise that God gave him. Abraham took God at God's word. He knew God would raise Isaac up from the ashes if necessary to fulfill it. Abraham did not hold this conviction because he reached a conclusion based on evidence or an understanding of God's nature or because he read it in a holy text; he held this conviction because perfect trust was implicit in his faith. David's relationship with God began at an early age, when he was a shepherd protecting the flock from lions and bears. He spoke personally and passionately to God his whole life. He approached God as both an intimate friend and as a holy God. God answered David's prayers; God hid his face; he rebuked David; God protected him from harm and raised him up to lead and conquer.

The New Testament also says, "Faith comes from hearing . . . a word from God" (Romans 10:17, NASB). *Rhema*, the Greek word used in this passage, means "a spoken word."

Faith, like truth, has a different orientation for oral cultures and consequently is foreign to us.

The Community of Faith

Oral cultures centered on the community of faith, one of the enduring contributions of the liturgical church. Early Christians lived in hostile and often foreign cultures. To survive and maintain the integrity of its beliefs, Christianity became a cohesive subculture.

The process of inclusion involved a period of preparation and a final initiation. Sons and daughters of believers were also required to express a disciplined understanding of their faith and go through different forms of initiation. Jews used circumcision as the sign to determine whether a man had accepted the covenant—not something to be undertaken lightly. For Christians public baptism became the sign of inclusion, an act that was often performed at risk to all involved until Emperor Constantine adopted Christianity in the fourth century.

Consequently, one did not join such an organization simply out of loneliness or boredom but because one seriously desired to became a member of the faith community. The oral tradition of discipleship reinforced these tight bonds and intimate connection to the fathers of faith. Here orthodoxy is secondary to faithfulness and loyalty. Leaving such a tradition can be more psychologically difficult because it very likely means severing most existing relationships. (Today excommunication is a very real severing for many Catholics. For Protestants, who have separation at the root of their tradition, changing churches is often simply an administrative and financial transaction.)

Worship Service: Liturgy

The term liturgy did not enter our vocabulary until the 1500s, but it describes the structure of worship for the early church. Liturgy is a ceremony centered on ritual and using symbols, sacraments, and signs to create a mystical event.

The Eucharist for the Catholic Church is the weekly mystical celebration of communion with Christ. The liturgy is a sacred reenactment that transforms the place, time, and participants from ordinary to extraordinary. The event is sealed with the sacrament of communion, in which the transforming power of Christ's body and blood is transmigrated into the bread and wine. The liturgy is also expressed in an elaborate calendar of prayers, devotions, and remembrances providing an active daily revelation of God's kingdom on earth.

The early church fathers, along with the rabbinical tradition, held that heaven and earth were intimately connected.[11] Rabbis worked tirelessly to interpret heaven's pattern, attempting to recreate it on earth. Jesus prayed, "Your will be done on earth as it is in heaven" (Matthew 6:10, NASB). The rabbinical order believed that when they fulfilled the law, God's kingdom would come. The Hebrew word for law, *halakah*, actually means "the Way"—the way things should be done according to the heavenly pattern as Moses passed it down orally to the seventy elders.[12] If we critically judge the intricate detail of Jewish law, we miss the radical revolution that Christ posed. When Jesus said "I am the way" (John 14:6, NASB; the Greek *hodas* (way) has the same sense as the Hebrew *halakah*), he hit a deep nerve.

The Catholic Church developed a tradition similar to that of the rabbis. When you read through the liturgy, explore chant, or examine cathedral architecture, you find the same theory operating: life on earth is a direct reflection of life in heaven. The goal was to translate the heavenly pattern into spiritual expressions that would create a sacred union and revelation for the believer.

Worship Styles: Chant and Psalm

Religious music in early Christian culture took the form of chant (within the priestly orders) or simple psalms and folk music for the common population. Chant provides another fascinating insight into the ancient oral mind.

Beneath the chant's deceptively simple surface is an intriguing degree of intricacy tied to the art of numerology. Oral culture saw the universe as equally constructed through word and number. Oral and print cultures alike have believed that numerical relationships and symmetry reflect the cosmic order. Searching out or reinforcing these relationships helped to restore harmony in the routine of daily life to the sacred. For example, the number three represents the mystery of the synergy and strength of the Godhead, and a cord of three strands cannot be easily broken. Six represents the human being as the incomplete reflection of the Godhead. Seven represents perfection, fulfillment, or completeness, as in the seventh day or the year of Jubilee, which is seven cycles of seven years. Even our seven-note musical scale came about as a means to express musically the laws of God's harmony.[13]

Chant creates a mystical algorithm using overt and covert meanings of words along with their relative position on the musical scale to formulate a coded expression of worship. Worship was a means of restoring harmony with God. Experiment for a minute to feel the different qualities inherent in a scale by singing *do, re, mi, fa, so, la, ti,* and *do.* Now go back and slow down to feel the nuance of these differences in relation to the other notes to catch a glimpse of what these monks were attempting to capture.

Do, the beginning, provides a confident foundation. When you move to *re,* you feel the need to move on. *Mi* has a pleasing sound and allows one to linger or come back, but it is not a final destination. *Fa* stands balanced in the center, able to proceed either up or down. Moving down from *fa* provides a smooth closure as in the *Amen* sung at the end of many hymns going from *fa* to *mi.* Moving up to *fa* provides a platform for a more dominant *so,* the most energizing note on the scale. After *so* we reach *la,* another transition note similar to *re,* seeking to move up or down. *Ti* reaches for the next progression. *Do* provides an octave from the initial journey. You can actually sense how the different notes make you feel motion or rest, resolution or conflict. You can also feel these notes resonate in different parts of your body: head, throat, chest, and stomach. The individual characteristics of these notes and their relationship in song to one another script a secondary layer of meaning that express heavenly truth.[14]

Each repetition unfolds a similar but unique layer of the divine revelation. In one sense those who understood the art of chant were tuning themselves to heaven's chords. Transformation still came to all who willingly participated, not just to those who understood the content or divine choreography.[15] I recommend that you listen to the recording *Chant*,[16] or go to the Vatican Web site (http://www.vatican.va/phome_en.htm) and listen to the on-line recordings.

Church Architecture: Sacred Patterns

In oral cultures sacred places are physical expressions of heavenly reality. They are built according to a revealed sacred pattern, with the intention to reconnect and relive the sacred moment.

One example of this relationship is showcased in early Gothic architecture, when the common culture was still primarily oral. Cathedrals were intricate constructs designed to bring heaven's story, order, awe, and mystery to earth. Imagine that you are a peasant standing for the first time in front of a massive cathedral: you would very likely be overawed, feeling both insignificant and fortunate to have such a bridge out of your mundane existence (see Figure 1.1).

Everything within the cathedral was designed not only to engage all the senses but also to overload them, bringing about a sacred transformation. The spires, dome, windows, carvings, altar, incense, acoustics, aromas, pews, aisles, and entrance: everything communicated the story and created a focus that distinctly departed from the individual's profane existence. Sacred architecture, whether grand or simple, provided a centerpiece for oral societies.

Numerology was central to ancient and medieval thought. The sacred mathematical relationships of the universe were also carried through into cathedral architecture. When we look at the floor plan of

Figure 1.1. Interior of Washington National Cathedral.

The Millennium Matrix

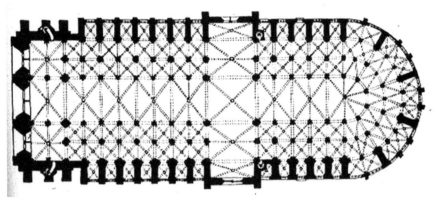

Figure 1.2. Floor Plan of Notre Dame Cathedral.

Notre Dame Cathedral, even the uninitiated immediately see an intricate structure with a cross as the central shape. Looking closer, we see several dimensions of sevens and threes. Look particularly at the number of spaces between columns. Standing inside one of these cathedrals inspires awe in most people. Imagine the impact on people who understood the interwoven language that permeates every stone and fixture (see Figure 1.2).

Shifts in Morality: Wisdom

Wisdom is the keyword for oral cultures.

Teaching in an oral culture was much different than today. When a rabbi asked Jesus, "Who is my neighbor?" Jesus told the story of the good Samaritan (Luke 10:30–37), which would be like telling an Irish Republican Army soldier the story of the good Irish Protestant. Jesus told the story to wake the rabbi out of his complacency and knee-jerk responses. Such a story was designed to circumvent the logical process and go straight to wisdom.

Moral teaching finds its roots in the oral soil of family, neighbors, and strangers—three very clear and distinct categories. Morality is tied to the mystical bonds of reciprocity and, like covenant, is relationally and situationally specific. Encountering truth was ultimately an encounter with the Creator through the presence of the messenger. Integrity—the complete merging of person, spirit, and message—had everything to do with the impact of the message. That is why even the best experts of the law found themselves speechless when Jesus spoke. It was the power generated by this unison of word and being, not simple mastery of the law or a skilled gift of persuasion. The truth and the truth giver were inseparably linked.

• • •

The people of the oral world—the people of the Old and New Testaments, the prophets, Jesus—lived in a time when "an eye for an eye" was common practice. They experienced life directly, inhaling the breath of God every moment. With the advent of print—and paradoxically the dissemination of the word of God to the masses of Christians—that visceral world would be subsumed by the world of logic and the mind.

CHAPTER 2

Print Culture–
Reformation Church

Separating the Message from the Messenger

Circa 1500–1950

> Reading maketh a full man; conference a ready man;
> and writing an exact man.
> —Francis Bacon, *Of Studies*

When Gutenberg set the Bible in movable type around 1454 and created the first mass-produced book, it literally spelled the end of oral culture's dominance and the rising of print culture. Until then the word of God was passed from mouth to ear; now it was available for everyone who could read. This changed everything. Gutenberg's converted wine press compressed the time needed to reproduce texts like the Bible from years to weeks. By the time Luther posted his Ninety-Five Theses almost seventy years later, more than one thousand printers had sprung up throughout Europe.

The development of the printing press signaled the world's first step into mass communication, arguably the most profound cultural dividing point in history. From this one invention, the general population could now have access to the same thoughts and ideas once reserved for religious, academic, and government elites. The general population stood on the same informational foundation as kings and popes.

In the West the print revolution coincided with an age of exploration, the Renaissance, mapmaking, enlightenment, the Reformation, and the quest for truth. Artists and painters, notably Leonardo da Vinci, literally began seeing things in a new perspective. We still recall the innovators of this time as geniuses, masters, and pioneers: da Vinci, Michelangelo, Luther, Aquinas, Columbus, and Shakespeare.

The ability to rightly divide, discover, and understand the truth has been the key to the success of Western culture and Reformation theology. None of this could have happened without print—and more important, the linear and logical mind-set that living in a print world creates. The thinking and mechanics that lay behind composition, printing, and reading require a different kind of human being, different kinds of human relationships, and different supporting organizations and institutions.

From the Messenger to the Message

In oral cultures knowledge was transmitted from master to apprentice, person to person, as a holistic learning experience. With the advent of movable type and the availability of knowledge encased in books, our basis for understanding came to live in letters on paper. Lines of type and words on a page are by nature linear: they disconnect word from spirit, spirit from being, words from essence, essence from things.

> Lines of type and words on a page are by nature linear: they disconnect word from spirit, spirit from being, words from essence, essence from things.

The implications of this would alter the direction of Western civilization and society's worldview. The West exploded with new discoveries, and Christianity found a new and powerful vehicle. The church stabilized its dogma, extended its influence, and released believers to a new level of responsibility and opportunity. The inherent rational laws within print communication create a rational mind that largely leaves mystical vision behind and sees the world as orderly, discernable, and within the grasp of reason.

From Context to Content

Oral cultures, ruled by sound, fashion an intimately connected and fluid world. Print cultures, led by what they can see, create an abstract, detached, and structured world. Print, a powerful and efficient medium, soon left behind a world it viewed as undisciplined, subjective, and backward. Print ripped the curtain that protected the mystery of the living word, creating a divide that remains at the center of many of our religious and cultural conflicts. The Apostle Paul expresses the same sentiment that many felt during the advance of the Reformation: "The letter kills, but the spirit gives life" (2 Corinthians 3:6, NASB).

The question of which way of perceiving is better is not the point. At the bottom of these feelings is a fact: the shift in the balance of power from ear to eye creates a shift in the balance of how our senses receive and interpret information. Our perception is no longer tied to the messenger—the context. Now it is fixed on the message—the content. The print world finds its new power in the content of the message.[1]

The ancient human carriers of information and understanding—elders, priests, bards, teachers, and community members—are superseded by a more durable and efficient medium, the printed word. With literacy, says Walter Ong, "the individual finds it possible to think through a situation more from within his own mind out of his own personal resources and in terms of an objectively analyzed situation, which confronts him. He becomes more original and individual, detribalized."[2] This cascade of adjustments in perception and a psychological rewiring changes the rules of relationships and the organizations and institutions supporting society. Historians describe this rewired person as modern: rational, autonomous, and self-made.[3]

Here is a brief catalog of the trade-offs that becoming modern brought:

- Understanding through analysis replaces understanding through dialogue.

- Individual autonomy replaces community allegiance.
- A conceptual understanding of God replaces a relational orientation toward God.
- A progressive view of history replaces a cyclical view of history.
- Reading about the gospel in a book replaces experiencing the gospel through ceremony and ritual.
- Ethical principles replace moral choices.
- An objective worldview replaces a participant worldview.
- Pedagogy replaces mentoring.
- Logical reasoning replaces dialectic exploration.
- Rational design replaces symbolic art and architecture.

TRY THIS: GET INSIDE THE PRINT MIND

What does the process of reading and writing do to the mind? Try this.

Sit with a pencil and paper and take some time to compose a paragraph.

Now tell a friend or family member the same thought you just attempted to put into words on paper.

Do you feel a difference in process and product?

The superior economy, flexibility, and breadth contained within the alphabet are nothing less than miraculous. Writing is like drawing a map: you want to lead your reader to a thought destination as efficiently as possible. (Writers can also provide you with a scenic tour, but they still lead you down specific thought paths to arrive at a designated destination.) Reading and writing develops the left or logical side of the brain. Dialogue, on the other hand, is anything but linear. Its power lies within its open-ended flow and interaction. Oral cultures retain a bias toward the right or poetic side of the brain.

Print Silences the Living Word[4]

Francis Schaeffer examined the influence of key figures in the formation of the modern worldview. If we look at some of his work through the lens of the Millennium Matrix we can see how the shift from an oral orientation to print helps explain how the work of the great masters of this age converged to create a radical new worldview. Shaeffer's book *How Should We Then Live*[5] primarily addresses the great divide between oral and print worldviews.

During the late thirteenth and early fourteenth centuries, people like St. Thomas Aquinas, the poet Dante Alighieri, and the painter Giotto breached the sacred boundary of oral thought to explore the implications of how visual perception might refashion our idea of a living messenger. Even though it would be another hundred years until Gutenberg created the tool that made the final break from an oral worldview, the foundations for the shift had been laid centuries earlier.

These three pioneers of modern thought helped define the new Western person's sense of autonomy—another way of saying disconnectedness—as one piece in a universe of other autonomous pieces. Aquinas began by separating the natural from the spiritual; Dante elevated philosophy to the level of revelation; and Giotto swept away Byzantine symbolic artistic representation to allow us to represent what we actually see. You might say that the world shifted from "Believing is seeing" to "Seeing is believing."

Written Words Dis-Integrate Nature and Spirit, Reason and Will

In our scientific world, we are used to taking things apart to see what makes them tick. But in the centuries before the Renaissance, this was brand-new thinking, and what these thinkers did was revolutionary. Aquinas, for example, dis-integrated humans into will and reason, the universe into nature and spirit. Our will was part of our fallen nature, but (for Aquinas) reason fell outside sin's influence. He held reason to be universal and separate from our idiosyncrasies. Our will fell outside reason's control but could be influenced by it. Therefore, our will was subject to and in need of God's revelation and grace.

Reason, however, provided a morally neutral tool that could aid salvation by counterbalancing our baser instincts. Reason alone could provide a compelling understanding of the benefits of virtue, and virtue then raises us above our animal instincts. Revelation and grace, on the other hand, dealt with issues of the spirit and will as well as areas that reason could not answer. Revelation and grace could bring us to repentance and sacrifice in the service of God.

Once Aquinas established this dis-integration, the territory of reason would expand and continue encroaching on the receding boundaries of revelation and grace. In essence, this created a separate world for the intellect.

The Power of the Eye

> The system of perspective became universally codified. . . .
> it developed into a strict scientific process and became
> the "method" par excellence, the language lying at the
> heart of Western visual culture. . . .
> —Sandro Sproccati, *Guide to Art*

Like Aquinas, Renaissance artists used new tools of perception. Instead of using their art to transmit religious stories only through well-understood symbology, they relied on the power of their eyes and their imaginations to reveal a degree of humanity within the biblical stories that artists had never before expressed.

The word *imagination* is built around the very idea of recreating an image held in the mind's eye. For modern viewers especially, Renaissance paintings come alive and inspire a new depth of insight. The artist's use of geometry and the science of optics created an objective means for judging and comparing elements of realism, proportion, lighting, detail, and composition. That is why Renaissance-era art is the easiest for us to appreciate and understand.

When you look at paintings from the two periods, the contrast between ancient and Renaissance art is clear. The shift to print, with its

Figure 2.1. This thirteenth-century Madonna and child (left) is meant to be symbolic, whereas Raphael's sixteenth-century version (right) is drawn from life.

emphasis on logic and linearity, created an art that sees the world as orderly and rational. The rationalistic person begins with what is seen and then works outward. The artist does not layer multiple flat dimensions of reality as ancient art does (think, for example, of Egyptian tomb art or medieval depictions of the Madonna and child) but separates them and focuses on the detail of a character, a scene, or a story. For example, in Figure 2.1 compare the flat, iconic planes of the Madonna and child painted in the oral culture of the Middle Ages with Raphael's fully human and empathetic portrait of the same subject, placing the viewer at a particular angle of view in the foreground of a pastoral scene. Raphael's realism is a by-product of expressing what he saw as visual truth.[6]

Perspective Changes Worldview

If I were to select one driving idea behind the transforming forces of a visually oriented world, it would be the concept of perspective.[7] That concept is the very foundation of early Renaissance art and the new era, and it reigned supreme until cubism blasted it apart early in the twentieth century.

Perspective is the artistic technique of creating a three-dimensional effect (depth) on a two-dimensional medium (such as paper or canvas). Perspective brings unity to a picture by taking an outside vantage point and arranging the scene using completely rational geometric ratios. The laws of geometry and optics now govern the painter and empower these paintings with a sense of symmetry, depth of field, and volume. In other words, it makes them look real (Figure 2.2). With perspective, art—and the world for the next seven hundred years—becomes the unique vantage point of the outside observer: a metaphor for the new age.[8]

Essence: The Rational Mind

Print creates a rational mind, a mind that sees the world as parts assembled in an orderly whole, like words in a sentence. The print mind is analytic. It separates the whole into its constituent parts. The print mind uses the principles of logic to disassemble and reassemble the whole. Logic, from the Greek word *logos,* means a written or fixed word. It also means reason.

The print mind held that the world is orderly and reasonable. Because logic provides the structure of pure reason, then logic also provides the tool to understanding the universe. It's only logical![9]

The foundation of Western thought and empiricism is built around two simple formulas: "A is A" or "A is not non-A."[10] In other words, something is not anything other than what it is. This is the starting point of Western understanding and the origin of our notion of absolute truth. These express the complete visual, linear, solitary orientation of the print mind, quite different from the meandering, mystical, communal discovery process of the oral mind.[11] It is interesting to note

Figure 2.2. "Marriage of the Virgin," by Raphael. Lines of perspective make this painting look real.

that Proverbs 9:10 (NASB) states that the beginning of wisdom is relational, the fear of God: "The fear of the LORD is the beginning of wisdom, And the knowledge of the Holy One is understanding."

The Birth of Autonomy

Here is the cultural significance of the impact of print's dominance: the Renaissance worldview is not possible unless you can first disconnect the message from the messenger. Reading does that. Reading also creates a buffer from collective thought and dialogue (*dia logos* means "penetrating words"). You need this separation before you can conceive of outside thoughts and an outside vantage point.

> The print mind held that the world is orderly and reasonable. Because logic provides the structure of pure reason, then logic also provides the tool to understanding the universe.

More significantly, the integration of reading creates a different psychological makeup. It desensitizes the eye to the interactive integration inherent in oral communities. The eye signals the brain to discern (mentally separate) and analyze (break up the whole). By contrast, the ear seeks harmony and synthesis. When there is conflict, sin, or something that seeds disharmony within oral cultures we often see it acted out in dramatic fashion through violence or rituals of restoration.[12] These worlds could not be more different.

The Centerpiece of Reformation Theology

Here is the spiritual significance of the impact of print's dominance: it established the written word as the ultimate standard of authority. Luther probably stated the premise of print culture more eloquently than anyone else in his testimony at the Diet of the Worms in 1521: "*Unless I am convinced by Scripture and plain reason—I do not accept the authority of the popes and councils, for they have contradicted each other—my conscience is captive to the Word of God.*" Print's inherent characteristic of drawing distinctions also propelled the ongoing protest and debate within the church, resulting in numerous denominations and sects—a characteristic that continues to this day.

A Cascade of Changes

Here is the spiritual significance of the impact of print's dominance: it established the written word as the ultimate standard of authority.

Other significant shifts include replacing symbolic architecture with simple and functional buildings. The ritual of reenacting the Last Supper is replaced by a retelling of the gospel. The focus of the service shifted from the Eucharist to the preaching of the word. Communion is no longer a mystical union but a soul-searching remembrance of Christ's sacrifice. Hymns carry much more content and are melodically more complex, taking advantage of polyphonic scores.

The Reformation tradition developed a rational systematic theology. Leaders did not carry a symbolic authority, as the pope did, but instead provided theological expertise. The central importance of the Bible led the church to develop an education system in order to provide every person the opportunity to understand and receive salvation. The print paradigm also led the church to focus on the cause-and-effect relationship of applying God's laws to everyday life. The Protestant work ethic promised prosperity to those who were diligent in their vocations.

How We Experience the World: Reading Objectifies Thinking

When in the Course of human events, it becomes necessary for one people to dissolve the political bands which have connected them with another, and to assume among the powers of the earth, the separate and equal station to which the Laws of Nature and of Nature's God entitle them, a decent respect to the opinions of mankind requires that they should declare the causes which impel them to the separation.

—The Declaration of Independence

Words are properly thought of as sounds that originate inside the body and exist for a fleeting moment in the air. Alphabetic writing, on the other hand, recreates that sound in the mind or mouth of the reader. It gives words a permanent life outside the body by altering that essential inward pathos and external fleeting quality. Written words become objects—fixed in space and motionless over time. That permanence can act as an anchor or can reveal new meaning as the reader returns to the words from a new vantage point.[13]

Print's objectification of thought removed the exclusive ties that family, community, and tradition had in forming one's identity and worldview. Print takes away the personalized filter of community. The very means of writing requires a clear, sequential, rational development of thought. Print reorients us away from the imprecise beliefs and opinions of others toward detached scrutiny.

The Declaration of Independence could never have been written in an oral culture. The opening paragraph provides a clear example of the conflict between changing worldviews, from oral patriarchal sensibilities toward a rational objective orientation. Print creates a sense of autonomy—detachment. In this case print enabled the colonists to compare and contrast their condition in the colonial context with the context and condition of their masters in England. Print also gave them the means to articulate a sequential and rational case to separate from England.

Such statements as "We hold these truths to be self-evident" express the natural objective conclusions of a rational process. The entire document presents a logical argument for a new nation. The American Revolution drew its power as much from the autonomous mind-set that print created as from the shortcomings and injustices of the English monarchy. It established a new means for association based on reason and mutual self-interest. This is the same fuel that fired the Protestant Reformation and has provided the foundation for our individualistic, progressive American culture.

Emotional Space: Detached

Seeing is distant and detached. If you walk down the street and just observe, your eyes treat what they see—whether people or trees or buildings—as fundamentally alike. If the act of hearing is an immersion experience, the act of watching separates us from it.

Devoid of any other sensory interaction, simple watching tends to create a world of objects or things from which we are separate. We learn quickly to discriminate between different types and categories of things: tree things, building things, people things. From this point of view, we are no longer members of one great creation but more like assistant gods, creating our own rational universes as we go along. This is one of the key shifts away from oral sensibilities.[14]

Social Cohesion: The Contract

Contracts represent a transaction between two or more people. Although most contracts neither include nor imply any spiritual consequences, there are practical consequences for breaking a contract.

Handshake agreements (oral contracts) work in connected communities, but written contracts are necessary in a world of strangers. Contracts do not tie together mutual welfare or destiny; they do not deal with motivation. Contracts may be recorded and upheld by governmental authorities, but the signing parties certainly do not submit nor expect divine intervention when a breach occurs. This is the work of covenants within an oral context.

Contracts rely on explicit detail regarding expectations and obligations. Contracts enumerate the benefits each party brings to the other, whereas covenants often add divine blessings if they are fulfilled and curses if broken. Contracts, because they focus on the letter of the law, reflect both limited liability and gain. Covenants, on the other hand, go directly to the heart or spirit of the matter, creating consequences that can be more extreme. We no longer carry the mystical links that bind us as individuals or communities, but print compensates for that bond with its explicitness.

Teaching and Learning: Instruction

As we have seen, teaching in ancient times centered on dialogue, or what is called dialectic instruction. Dialectic teaching is also referred to as the Socratic method. Socratic teaching is akin to an interview: the teacher asks questions and students provide answers, which the teacher questions further.[15] The students strive to keep up with their mentor and continue the game. Reaching a hard conclusion is a secondary objective to the exercise of reason and thought.

The advent of the printed word released learning to a wider audience: with a book one master could have many apprentices, and the master did not have to be present in order to teach. This moved learning from personal immersion in the experience to the more impersonal world of instruction. Although some might argue that the learning experience lost some quality with this trade-off, we can also argue that it enabled more people from a wide variety of backgrounds to absorb knowledge that previously had been limited to a privileged few.

Books also created the professional instructor. Teachers provide a systematic exposure to the principles of many disciplines of learning. Teachers are able to expose students to the greatest thinkers and ideas of history as well as the current understandings. In this regard the teacher is both the door and the filter for the student but is not necessarily the model or the mentor. Many students still find a teacher who becomes, for a brief time, a mentor. However, the teacher's primary role is to teach the student how to learn and take responsibility for his or her own educational progress.

The Roots of the Church

As the church changed from being a space of intimate connection to a place of rational detachment, the premises of the individual's relationship to God necessarily underwent a fundamental shift. This shift made the Reformation inevitable.

Truth Is Based on a Principle or Proposition

Print makes the message more important than the messenger. Truth, in print cultures, shifts from its relational foundation to principle (elementary) or propositional truth: we rely on the content and construction of communication as the sole means for validating the message. The Bible replaces the church as the source of authority and truth.

This shift creates the foundation and engine for the Reformation, and it sets thinkers free from the rules of tradition and authority to pursue observation and experimentation to further science. It releases the Renaissance to explore a human-centered universe, transforming the arts and reordering civil government. A wave of revolutions and reforms challenged divine authority and secular tradition with the power of written documents—a manifesto, stated grievances, or a constitution.

Faith Is Belief

Print shifts the experience of faith away from a living messenger (or tradition) to the bedrock of the printed word (*logos*), the Bible. Reformation theology established the Bible as the sole authority of revelation, *sola scriptura*. This not only placed the Bible above tradition and authority but altered spiritual sensibilities as well. The visual orientation that resulted from relying solely on the printed word created an emphasis on reason, analysis, systematic understanding, and a rational explanation of doctrine. This difference in sensibilities from oral to visual has as much to do with the schism between Protestantism and Catholicism as do differences in doctrine.

> Print shifts the experience of faith away from a living messenger (or tradition) to the bedrock of the printed word *(logos)*, the Bible.

The "Fact, Faith and Feeling Train"[16]

Reformation teaching creates a linear progression to faith. The following key elements in the Reformation presentation of the gospel can be heard in some similar form throughout thousands of Protestant churches on any Sunday:

- We are sinners, and sin is part of our nature.
- We can't overcome sin on our own to reach God.
- God came to earth in the form of a man, born to a virgin.
- Jesus lived a sinless life and is able to make a bridge for us to God.

- Jesus offered his life as an act of obedience and sacrificial payment for our sin.
- He rose as Christ, validating his sinless life and his power over death.
- We can experience rebirth and resurrection life by accepting our condition and Christ's payment.

Protestant churches teach that any person who follows this progression of thought and accepts the final conclusion can become a Christian by acknowledging agreement or faith. The form of agreement varies between denominations, but the rational formula is basically the same. Compare this to the description of the call to faith experienced by people in oral cultures. Abraham's reliance on a personal conversation with God is worlds apart from reaching a conclusion or belief about Christ through a series of propositions. In a somewhat similar fashion, Catholic liturgy extends God's voice in a call to faith, and the church, not the individual, validates that faith through the Rite of Acceptance leading to the Rite of Election.

The Priesthood of the Believer

The Protestant mind favors an individualistic and analytical approach relying strictly on the Bible text. This foundation for rational reductionism made the oral approach feel inefficient, imprecise, and indirect. Catholics would criticize the autonomous and private orientation of Protestants as divisive and dangerously adrift from the balancing context of the community of faith.

Protestants, on the other hand, see themselves as individually standing before God, neither spiritually tied to family or tradition nor requiring mediation through a sacred priesthood. The believer is a priest with direct access to God through Christ. "But you are a chosen people, a royal priesthood, a holy nation, a people belonging to God, that you may declare the praises of him who called you out of darkness into his wonderful light" (2 Peter 2:9, NIV). The trade-off brings a greater burden of responsibility, but it also brings greater freedom of conscience. Education, rather than initiation, becomes the primary tool to guide the Reformation believer toward a realization of vocation and fulfillment.

Worship Service: Orderly vs. Ritualistic

Protestant churches, like the Presbyterians, Methodists, Baptists, and other nonliturgical denominations, reflect the more rational and objective characteristics of the print medium. The service divides into a consistent and logical order building up to the preaching of the word. These church services are designed to inform and reinforce God's truth. It is designed to provide a logical explanation of our need for Christ, a systematic retelling of Christ's ministry and ultimate triumph, and then a prescribed response for those who need to reconcile their current state or situation with the gospel. We make a decision and voice our need for and allegiance to Christ. We join in with the assembly instead of being coactors in a divine play.

Worship Style: Hymns

Without question the development of movable type radically shifted the form of music. Sacred music was no longer relegated to the world of the professional religious who were trained in the arcane traditions of chant and liturgy—it was for everyone. This also meant, however, that music shifted from the mystical to the explicit. Composers could now write complex melodies with the assurance that musicians could follow the score. This expanded the number of musicians who could perform in concert with one another. The new science of developing individual music scores that when played together creates a synergistic sound (symphony) took the form of orchestrations.[17] Prior to this, musicians relied on what they could imitate and improvise from one another. For congregants print communicated content-rich theology in the vernacular lyrics of hymns.

Worshipers could now express the content of their faith in their common language. They could listen washed by the harmonic sounds of choirs and feel the notes of many instruments vibrate in their bodies. When the congregation approached its final verse and the massive pipe organ shifted to an otherworldly pitch and volume, they could feel the cosmic drama drawing to a climax. When I was a child, I remember sitting through most of the songs we sang in our large Presbyterian church, basically uninterested and pretending to sing the words—until we reached the last verse. Then I sang to feel my chest vibrate to the different notes within the chords, attempting to match my vibrations to the different frequencies of the organ. The fourfold amen seemed the perfect and satisfying ending to these songs.

We are historically well past the context in which we can fully appreciate the power of these songs, with perhaps one exception, Handel's *Hallelujah Chorus*. Here we see the best in content, orchestration, and drama contained in one nearly perfect score.

Church Architecture: Functional

In the print culture, the building no longer embodies the story, as the cathedral did with its spires reaching to God and its nave in the shape of a cross. Instead, the church building provides a more neutral space in which to tell the story written in the book. Protestant churches place the pulpit as the focal point because that is where God's word is read.

As Figure 2.3 shows, the comparison between the Gothic-styled cathedrals and Protestant churches is quite dramatic in the move away from the symbolic to a rational and linear construction. Reformation churches provide a forum for people to assemble and hear the word of God. The setting inside a Reformed church is ideal to address an audience and make a rational case on behalf of the gospel.

Shifts in Morality: Ethics

When Jesus told the story of the good Samaritan to his oral audience, the Pharisees were shocked into a moment of truth that required a choice—a moral decision. But when we read or hear this story within a print mind-set, it derives its power in a completely different way: through analysis. The principles and precepts we derive from this analysis define a Christian perspective of right and wrong behavior toward strangers.

We begin by drawing parallels between our general condition and that of the Pharisees, concluding that we are likely insensitive, too

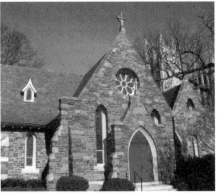

Figure 2.3. The oral-period cathedral (left) reaches toward God, whereas the Reformation church (right) reflects rationalism.

busy, or worse—bigoted. We contrast this with the behavior of the good Samaritan, who defies reason to help an enemy. We reconcile this universal challenge by exploring the implications of the gospel. We are then led either to the ethical implications of living like a good Samaritan or recognizing our inability or unwillingness to do so. This linear logical process not only provides an explicit understanding of the elements of a good Samaritan but also produces the compelling imperative to become one.

• • •

When we compare print's ethical imperative with the oral paradigm's moral moment of truth, we can see the distance that reading imposes on the way we see the world. We have now traveled through two distinct worldviews, gaining insight into their differences and the reasons they were so different. As we explore the broadcast paradigm in the next chapter, we will see how the sights and sounds that continually wash over us today have irrevocably changed the way we experience Jesus' words and the way we express that experience.

CHAPTER 3

Broadcast Culture– Celebration Church

Watching the World Go By

Circa 1950–2010

> The television environment was so total and therefore invisible. Along with the computer, it altered every phase of the American vision and identity.
>
> —Marshall McLuhan, *War and Peace in the Global Village*

Bob Dylan put it succinctly: "The times they are a-changin'."[1] When an army of youth took over the culture in the 1960s, it was more than a generational turf battle: it was spiritual war of genuine Pauline dimensions (Ephesians 6:10). The young adults and adolescents who stood on one side and the confused, befuddled, and even scared adults on the other might as well have been from different planets.

No one reading this book was around to witness the end of the oral era and the beginning of the print era, so we can't really understand what happened then. But many of us have experienced firsthand the social upheaval that occurs when a new mind-set replaces the old. If you grew up during the 1960s and early 1970s, or were raising teenagers at that time, you were at the epicenter. Those younger have seen and felt the continuous aftershocks of this social revolution. While the old guard attempted to keep culture inside the boundaries of its neatly defined, homogenous paradigm, their kids sought not just to break out of the box but to blow the box to smithereens.

In a fundamental sense, the broadcast age began to erode print in the mid-nineteenth century with the invention of photography and overturned it with art movements like cubism and surrealism. Broadcast began to gather speed with the advent of movies and radio. But it was television that really kicked it into high gear, and that is what we will use as our metaphor here.

Television: The Contemporary Altar of Communion

> As the influence of print wanes, the content of politics, religion, education, and anything else that comprises public business must change and be recast in terms that are most suitable to television.
>
> —Neil Postman, *Amusing Ourselves to Death*

When my generation was growing up in the 1950s, the media were trying to answer the question "Why can't Johnny read?" The answer, they claimed, was television. As it turned out, that answer was on target.

By the 1960s most American homes had televisions. Television became the victor and centerpiece of the home—an altar most kids scurried to sit in front of after school, absorbed in a secular form of worship. These kids, raised in the language of television but schooled in the language of print, labored each day in the restrictive world of school. Three o'clock brought relief from the rigors of an oppressive print regimen. Television, on the other hand, demanded nothing but instead gave a continuous stream of pictures to entertain them and open the world. School had their bodies, but television captured their hearts and minds.

Television creates a kaleidoscopic world of dramatic and changing images. Individual programs have plots and narratives, but taken together—image on image, show after show, punctuated by commercials—there is no overarching perspective, no narrative to give these image fragments a cohesive meaning. In fact, the very act of watching television creates a psychological phenomenon called *gestalt*: when several related but disconnected pieces of a picture or an event suddenly merge in the mind as a whole. This is sometimes called an "aha" experience—even a psychedelic or mind-expanding experience.

Just how does a generation with this kind of perspective react to a generation raised on an abstract, print-based worldview?

Storming the Gates of the Establishment

When my generation came of age in the mid- to late 1960s we reacted by storming the gates of the establishment and throwing out everything we could not validate for ourselves. We saw the world as impersonal, unfeeling, mechanical, and shallow. We thought people (which we defined as everyone over age thirty) were in bondage to external rules, rules they did not really believe in but that the system imposed on them anyway.

By *the system*, we meant those in power who took advantage of our naive belief that they knew best and had our best interests in mind. The good citizens of the dying print world believed in the power of a rational authority, decreed and documented: "Ours is not to question why, ours is but to do or die." The print world, which spent its youth revolutionizing Western civilization, seemed to be spending its senior years asking everyone to read off the same page and prizing order and conformity. Neatness counts.[2]

> Television was the ideal medium to reveal the inconsistencies between the well-reasoned and well-written plans and actual life.

But television took my generation on a quest down the yellow brick road. Like Dorothy, who exposed the Wizard of Oz as a con man (in a movie faithfully presented on television once a year when I was growing up), we wanted to tear down the curtain. And television was the ideal medium to reveal the inconsistencies between the well-reasoned and well-written plans and actual life.

Television quickly blew the lid off print's nicely colored and drawn Norman Rockwell image of life—especially as the daily news brought John F. Kennedy's assassination and the war in Vietnam into our living rooms, with television journalist Walter Cronkite telling us, "And that's the way it is."

Television showed us that life and history were far messier, and more interesting to watch, than the nice neat stories we were used to reading. Even *Life* magazine began to carry images of war and the psychedelic world. We no longer bought into the (historical) legacy handed down by a "bunch of dead white guys." We sought to revalidate everything we were told. Some understood more literally than others that culture was undergoing a mind-altering shift, and they accelerated the eradication of the print paradigm with mind-altering music, drugs, and meditation practices. In the end the existential medium of television produced an existential generation that grew up to become the dominant culture.

Television gave us our daily reality, and it also taught us to doubt the justifications of the past. Print didn't tell the whole story—at least not the way television seemed to. We found that the establishment hid many of its dark secrets by printing positive propaganda. Television exposed the contradictions in the government's portrayal of the Vietnam War, the bigotry of Southern politicians, the deadliness of chemicals, and the scary fanaticism of Senator Joseph McCarthy. It exposed us to previously invisible cultures within our own nation. White kids adopted black and Latino music, fashion, and attitudes. These helped to break down old and engrained barriers of separation. Television also created contentious and violent confrontations between those who wanted life to stay the same and those who wanted radical change. In *The Medium Is the Message*, Marshall McLuhan put it this way: "[Television's] message is Total Change, ending psychic, social, economic, and political parochialism. The old civic, state, and national groupings have become unworkable. Nothing can be further from the spirit of the new technology than 'a place for everything and everything in its place.' You can't go home."[3]

Dismantling Modernism

> It may be that, ironically, the sacramental power of images in society has been most effectively taken over by television.
>
> —Marshall McLuhan, *The Medium Is the Message*

Broadcast dismantled modernism and every single one of its presuppositions. The world was no longer orderly and predictable. Reason no longer provided the only effective language with which to address reality. Postmodernism, the new worldview, unraveled and unnerved those still loyal to the modern paradigm. No amount of logic or reason will put things back in order.[4] We no longer control our destiny. As Buckminster Fuller put it, we're simply along for the ride on "spaceship earth," spinning through space at sixty thousand miles per hour, and we'd better hang on.[5]

Artists, scientists, and many academics readily experimented in the early twentieth century with the implications of this new worldview, but most of the church marched in the opposite direction, committed to preserving the paradigm of an absolute objective and knowable reality. Television, presenting a fluid and fragmented experience, provided the perfect medium to channel this new worldview to the masses. This open-ended medium was the antithesis to modern sensibilities of closure. As more people began to see the world differently, fewer people listened to the church.

The Subatomic Metaphor Is the Message

Television can only exist in a world far different from the orderly cause-and-effect world Newton described centuries ago. In Newton's print world, matter was stable. In Einstein's world—the broadcast world—matter is energy. Everything is in motion. Time and space are not fixed but relative. What we have called reality for thousands of years is actually made up of small subatomic what-ifs with paradoxical properties. This is not a world made up of waves and particles but a world made up of packets of energy that may be either waves or particles, depending on how they are being observed. In fact, the very act of observation changes the reality.

Television is the perfect delivery system for this new worldview. It structures how we see, experience, interpret, and express our world. Living inside what has become a ubiquitous environment, it can be difficult to tell where the medium ends and the world begins. As Neil Postman says, "Television has achieved the status of 'meta-medium'—an instrument that directs not only our knowledge of the world, but our knowledge of ways of knowing as well."[6]

Television: The Perfect Medium for Our Contemporary Metaphor

> I learned that it is possible to speak through media directly into people's heads and then, like some other-worldly magicians, leave images inside that can cause people to do what they might otherwise never have thought to do.
>
> —Jerry Mander, *4 Arguments for the Elimination of Television*

Television is fluid and continuously reconstructing itself. It retains no memory. Television reaches beyond physical and conceptual boundaries and unites people through common experience. It synchronizes cultural emotions and perception (which is different from understanding). Television—at least as it is expressed through mass media—reconstructs the complexity of life and creates clear and simple visual images. Television's powerful images replace millions of written words. For example, each December all of the major television networks provide their collage retrospective on the year. They select the compelling images from many of the headline events, add music, and create what has become a ritualistic broadcast memorial. This has also become a common way to recap major sporting and political events. Journalists usually add their comments, but their words are quickly flushed from

Television is fluid and continuously reconstructing itself. It retains no memory. Television reaches beyond physical and conceptual boundaries and unites people through common experience.

memory while the poignant images and the emotions they generate linger. Broadcast has replaced public discourse with a collage of layered reality that evokes a visceral response.

The culture has assimilated and integrated the television metaphor, and in return television has recontextualized our common myths. In a highly complex society, television has begun to perform one of the oldest, most traditional functions of images: to visualize common myths (success, the good life, tolerance of diversity, heroes and hero-ines) and to integrate the individual into a social whole.

Broadcast: The Secret Behind Contemporary Church Growth

Most of today's successful and growing churches are what I call celebra-tion churches (primarily nondenominational). From the parking to the ushers to the stage set, the refreshments, and the performance, these churches are designed to take full advantage of the television studio model. Reformation era (print-based) churches suffer in this kind of world because they were set up to deliver a deliberate, structured, and rational presentation of God's word. George Barna's research further confirms this dramatic changing of the guard. Protestant denominations peaked in membership in 1950 (with the exception of the Southern Baptists) and have been in decline since. In contrast, the celebration churches have been steadily growing.[7]

When we view these differences through the lens of the differ-ent communication eras, we can see what happened: celebration churches are built like theaters or studio sets, whereas Reformation church sanctuaries are like large lecture halls with the pulpit (which holds the written Word) as the focal point.

The primary music in celebration churches is rhythmically complex and up-tempo, and the message is usually simple and to the point. Traditional hymns, although simply structured, often carry com-plex themes and content in the words and don't carry over well in the vignette format of celebration services.

The typical celebration pastor delivers the message from an out-line and uses theatrical techniques to connect with the audience. Their preparation focuses heavily on delivery and dramatic moments to create audience impact. Scripture is usually a launching pad; the pastor uses stories, humor, anecdotes, and summary slogans to aid in the broadcast art of persuasion. Classic Reformation preachers, on the other hand, typically deliver prewritten sermons. The nature of the message is more like a legal argument or a lecture, with reason, evidence, and scriptural validation providing the basis for an argument in favor of the gospel. Evidence and the structure of the argument take priority over connecting with the audience.

Finally, the atmosphere for most celebration churches is casual and enthusiastic. Sunday services are events, and people come anticipating something new and exciting. Denominational services, in contrast, have a tone similar to a class or civic meeting. The atmosphere is more formal and serious. Congregants generally know what they can expect.

From Content to Event

Books or television? Is one really better than the other? Most people—caught as we are at the end of a period of transition—have some pretty strong judgments on this question. And of course it's foolish to claim that we have all thrown over the print world in favor of broadcast—you're reading this book right now! And this book is not debating the wisdom of change but underscoring its inevitability.

So each medium's power to change the world from the inside out is unquestioned; there are just some differences in the way they work. Again, as we saw in the transition from oral to print cultures, the transition from print to broadcast cultures inevitably involved some trade-offs:

- Broadcast's epistemology of immediate experience replaces print's reliance on rational analysis.

- Broadcast's collective awareness replaces print's sense of individual autonomy.

- Broadcast's existential understanding of God replaces print's abstract orientation.

- Broadcast's chance-driven view of history replaces print's linear progression.

- Broadcast's dramatized presentations replace print's structured oratory.

- Broadcast's "Be all that you can be" replaces print's "Do the right thing."

- Broadcast's emphasis on process replaces print's emphasis on outcome.

Essence: Being There

Broadcast, far from providing a perspective, absorbs us into the larger context. Whether we are watching a war, a tropical romance, or reality show, we feel as if we're there. This is the premise behind Jerzy Kosinski's novel *Being There*, the story of Chance, the gardener, a person so void of perspective and personally validating experiences that he becomes the ideal everyman, able to adapt to any circumstance: "He could . . . change as rapidly as he wished by twisting the dial. . . . he could spread out into the screen without stopping, just as on TV people spread out into the screen. . . . Thus he came to believe that it was he, Chance, and no one else, who made himself be."[8]

Broadcast culture disconnects the world from its context and feeds it back to the viewer as an edited, moving collage. It creates a collective experience of stimulated images and sound that reformats life as a state of mind. It deconstructs and reconstructs reality, as cubism did. Cubism attempted to take all aspects of a subject—all angles and dimensions, as well as its soul—and represent it in a two-dimensional plane using simple and universally recognized symbols. This compression of reality was intended to create a visceral, nonrational response. Television's multilayered reality communicates the entire form and essence of the subject, reflecting the profound shift in worldview. It bypasses rationality with an all-at-once message, the deconstruction and the arbitrary reconstruction of meaning.

Television is a self-contained representation of reality that requires no analysis, no historical perspective, and no connection to any other event. It requires only your attention and reaction. These unique qualities are woven into the grammar and syntax of our current worldview.

Closure vs. Open-Endedness

The print mind drives toward closure; it wants to reach a conclusion or to have a perspective. The broadcast mind drives toward keeping an open mind, considering the options, and going with the flow. Written words lock in meaning and create linear furrows of thought, whereas broadcast images leave information open to many meanings.

Many artists of our time reflect this worldview. Some people find it difficult to appreciate contemporary art because they are still looking for the rational world of art that burst onto the scene in the Renaissance. It's important to remember that when linear perspective first appeared (images that appeared larger or smaller in geometric proportions to their relative distances and angles to one another) on the scene—for us the very epitome of rational, understandable art—viewers who came of age in the oral world found the new paintings incomprehensible.

Contemporary art basically says that life is unpredictable and random. Some artists go so far as to try to dismantle any illusions of order and meaning, whereas others—such as Jackson Pollock—attempt to find some larger unifying force.[9]

Pollock is famous for his splatter paintings, which broke the barrier of direct contact between painter and canvas. He unrolled his canvas on the floor, opened his cans of paint, and then did something different: he poured paint right out of the cans and splattered paint from brushes (Figure 3.1). He used gravity instead of friction to transfer paint to canvas. Paradoxically, Pollock felt this provided him with control by reducing the constraints between impulse and expression.

Musicians like John Cage celebrate the tolerable or intolerable limits of chance. John Cage is known for concerts in which he would sit onstage in silence for half an hour because that was his impulse at the moment. Some of his musical scores are simply random noise—and again, that is his point.

I could catalog many other broadcast-based art forms: surrealism, conceptual art, and of course video installations. These artists, breaking the bonds of the rational print-based world, are expressing the new world of uncertainty that Einstein and Heisenberg described and that the explosion of the atomic bomb at the end of World War II made manifest.

Figure 3.1. Jackson Pollock used gravity to create his paintings.

Most of us still don't comprehend what physicists discovered a hundred years ago and have been trying to describe ever since. Most of us still have a hard time getting the point behind most contemporary art. In many ways physicists and artists are both claiming what the broadcast paradigm has already achieved, as summed up in the closing lines of *Being There*: "Life is a state of mind."[10]

The challenge for visual artists is that the viewer stands outside their works. Because we are outside the art, we attempt to analyze it. But we automatically experience television. Broadcast naturally creates an altered state. It penetrates the subconscious in ways that contemporary artists can only dream of achieving. In doing so, broadcast provided an everyday tool for everyman that has exceeded the efforts of all the contemporary artists combined in destroying the paradigms of rationalism and our Newtonian sense of an orderly and meaningful world.

A Shift to Right-Brain Thinking

Even though the shift from print to broadcast has been going on for a good many years, many people are still having trouble making it. One reason is how our brains have been wired. Put simply, the left hemisphere of our brain handles rational thought, whereas the right hemisphere handles nonrational thought. Living in the print world for so long has predisposed us to left-brain thinking. We know how it works, and we're comfortable here.

But broadcast is an open spigot from which information flows in a never-ending stream of images that the left-brain's linear thinking cannot process. The right side of the brain, associated with creativity, spontaneity, and pattern recognition, is far better equipped to deal with this kind of information.

Living in a right-brained culture is still a relatively new condition. Print wrenched us out of our more integrated oral world, and its five-hundred-year dominance naturally developed a left-brained rational culture. Now broadcast's rise to dominance has made right-brain capabilities more valuable and necessary.[11] The barriers are down; information, it seems, is flowing freely between left and right. Perhaps as a result, our culture is coming out of its rigid emotional closet—a confusing state to some, a welcome state to others.

For those raised in the world of traditional religion, this less formal, more fluid, openly expressive, theatrically presented atmosphere in the celebration world can be threatening.

For those raised in the world of traditional religion, this less formal, more fluid, openly expressive, theatrically presented atmosphere in the celebration world can be threatening. It feels like emotionalism and manipulation—a bit narcissistic overall. But this brings us to the heart of these two very separate worldviews. In the debate between these traditions, it helps to first recognize that "reformers are from Mars and celebrationists are from Venus."

Reflexive Thinking

Print makes reason king and stimulates reflective thinking. Broadcast elevates desire and emotion and stimulates reflexive thinking—the kind of thinking that fighter pilots, emergency room workers, cops on the beat, and you driving your car do.

Many popular television shows—ER, Alias, 24, The West Wing—represent broadcast's move toward a more intense and reflexive experience. They create a feeling of perpetual motion, stress, and high energy. The characters on these shows encounter numerous unplanned situations and crises and must juggle multiple priorities while handling ambiguous circumstances, all of which require a judgment call—now! The characters move fast, and the shows run two or three story lines at a time, jumping from story to story to maintain that sense of intensity.

That same intensity is reflected in real life. Recently, I had breakfast with a man who has spent many years working in the White House. We were talking about how hard it is to find time to have quiet thought and reflect. He began sharing what some of the atmosphere is like in the White House and why there is such a high staff turnover. During a fifteen-hour day, he is fortunate to see a newspaper, let alone read one. Instead, the staff receives a daily summary of all of the top news headlines along with a brief synopsis—and most staff members are hard pressed to flip through that. At the same time, he must deal with as many as fifteen major national and international crises, and he is expected to provide immediate feedback. "And you know," he said, "people make decisions in that environment, and for the most part incredibly good decisions requiring a lot of detail and flawless execution. But that is one reason why there is so much burnout. The pressure and the stakes are so high."[12]

A less benign and more disturbing illustration of reflexive thinking can be seen in the wave of random shootings with which we are all too familiar. A psychologist speaking about fourteen-year-old

Michael Carneal commented on the clinical way the boy carried out his murders at a school in Paducah, Kentucky, in 1997. Normally, he said, a young boy—or any untrained killer—would show a high level of anxiety reflected in a scattered and random shooting pattern. But in this case each victim was killed by one accurate shot—there were no wasted rounds. Investigators discovered that Carneal liked to play a particular video game that required shooting "human" targets. The psychologist compared playing this game to the kind of training soldiers receive. The rapid interaction required to play the game bypasses rational thought and taps into that reflexive level of consciousness.[13]

Blurring Private and Public

Broadcast also blurs the line between private and public. During the Vietnam War, for example, the American public saw events that no other population so far removed from the battlefield had seen before. The effect of actually seeing the war being played out live in our living rooms had a profound effect on the country's consciousness. As journalist Ed Murrow used to say in the early days of television, "You are there." In previous wars, the government could censor the information that went out to the public at large. But broadcast made it much more difficult for the government to control its message.

And it's not just war. The private (covert) behavior of governments and individuals is often visible because of broadcast. In the 1960s the brutalities of state governments against civil rights marchers radicalized a nation. Perhaps the most dramatic example of television's power to bring down print-reinforced barriers was the rise of the Solidarity movement and revolution in Poland during the 1980s. The ideological walls of print came crashing down through the power of public exposure and galvanized the Polish population.

Television has also exposed the scandalous behavior of many secular and religious leaders. Television allows no hiding place. And once exposed, the damage is usually terminal—unless the person exposed understands how to use television to fight back. Here is just one example of spinning the spinners.[14] This classic case of how potentially bad news can be well managed involves CBS news correspondent Lesley

Stahl, who put together a long report showing the gaps between Ronald Reagan's carefully styled news images and his actual policies in office.

Stahl was nervous about the piece because of its critical tone and the practice the White House Communications Office had of calling reporters and their employers about negative coverage. After the report aired, Stahl received a call from a "senior White House official." She prepared herself for the worst. In her own words, here is what happened:

> And the voice said: "Great piece."
>
> I said: "What?"
>
> And he said: "Great piece!"
>
> I said: "Did you listen to what I said?"
>
> He said: "Lesley, when you're showing four and a half minutes of great pictures of Ronald Reagan, no one listens to what you say. Don't you know that the pictures are overriding your message because they conflict with your message? The public sees those pictures and they block your message. They didn't even hear what you said. So, in our minds, it was a four-and-a-half minute free ad for the Ronald Reagan campaign for re-election."
>
> I sat there numb. I began to feel dumb because I'd covered him four years and I hadn't figured it out. Somebody had to explain it to me. Well none of us had figured it out. I called the executive producer of the Evening News . . . and he went dead on the phone.
>
> And he said, "Oh my God."[15]

More recently, the blur has shown up in the form of so-called reality programs. *Cops, Survivor, Big Brother, The Bachelor, Fear Factor*, and other shows now provide a large part of prime-time television. The hidden camera is supposed to be capturing the spontaneous and supposedly natural behavior of these subjects. In fact, these shows are edited for maximum emotion, drama, and suspense. When do we all begin to wonder whether or not we are living in the television-created world of *The Truman Show*?[16] When does our diet reach the point when we think and behave more like Chance the gardener?

Social Cohesion: No-Fault Agreements

Covenants and contracts have given way to agreements that reflect a shift toward no-fault arrangements of mutual benefit. Our language has shifted from the oral context of mystical covenant bonds to a print context of principle-based contractual bonds to a broadcast language of potential and fulfillment. The broadcast paradigm assumes that greater freedom leads to exceeding expectations without the downside pressure of obligation. Contracts in the print paradigm, by contrast, restrict that freedom and are inherently inflexible, despite changing circumstances.

We now live in a world in which arrangements seem to last only as long as they appear to be mutually beneficial. Our social bonds gyrate between the poles of fragile goodwill and ever present litigation.

Teaching and Learning: Edutainment

Learning in a broadcast world has shifted toward a more specialized, topical, and pragmatic focus. The first children's television shows—*Ding Dong School* and *Howdy Doody,* for example, reflected the more static images of the waning print mentality.[17] These were quickly replaced, however, with the purposely fragmented *Sesame Street,* which presented the alphabet one letter at a time and rarely in the correct order.

Schooling shows similar changes. History lessons have become specific, covering narrower time frames or even a specific event. English courses divide into multiple categories, including journalism and film study. Math now covers the extremes of calculus to mundane personal finance. Textbook assignments are heavily supplemented by in-class movies, documentaries, and videos. Education has become more pragmatic and conscious of different means to engage student interest. In many ways educators are applying mass marketing disciplines to reach their audience by assessing needs and providing attractive choices.

One by-product of this research is *edutainment,* a combination of education and entertainment that promises to hold the interest of our increasingly shorter attention spans.

The Roots of the Church

The church is as fully immersed in the broadcast culture as any other institution. The changes we see in today's church, whether we like them or not, reflect the world we live in.

Truth Is Validated by Experience

Print asks us to accept the truth as written. But in broadcast cultures, truth has to ring true for us. We have to be able to feel a visceral connection to it.

Consider, for example, the hundreds of thousands of people who every year attend religious revivals, from those of Billy Graham to Benny Hinn. Many come curious and perhaps skeptical, drawn by the spectacle of the event. Sitting in a sea of bodies in a large auditorium of ten thousand and more, they are anonymous to others in the audience and to the speaker. Cloaked by anonymity, they are free to relax and suspend their earlier apprehensions—no one's judging them. The music and worship help to create a mood of anticipation. Once the crowd reaches a point of collective synchronization, the speaker leads everyone into a vivid description of the promised destination. Little by little, people proclaim reaching that promised land, filling the auditorium with an atmosphere of expectation until it reaches a critical mass and breakthrough for scores of individuals who suddenly "feel the truth."

> In broadcast cultures, truth has to ring true for us. We have to be able to feel a visceral connection to it.

In this way many individuals see, feel, and encounter God in transforming ways, even though they may not understand the theological justifications or protocol. When asked for an explanation, they are just as likely to respond by saying, "I'm not sure what happened, but before I was blind and now I can see!"

For some Christians the very idea of these emotional appeals is abhorrent. In fact, it is a great source of controversy in the church, especially for those who have a print worldview. Whatever our worldview, however, it's clear that the broadcast medium changes how we perceive and experience truth.

Faith Is Conviction

In our broadcast culture, faith comes by experiencing the presence of God or a change of heart. Both television and celebration services are at their best when stirring the emotions of guilt and spiritual hunger. Sermons present a vivid word picture or dramatize the road of sin and its consequences and the promised solution—often with personal testimonials. But these preachers make their offers for a limited time only.

Advertising explicitly understands the broadcast medium, and success within this medium requires following this ethos. Many of the most successful evangelists stick with the script: they keep the message simple, tie it to emotions, create a visual image of the benefits (promises), create dissatisfaction with the way things are, use the power of music to set the mood, boil it all down into a single image or story, make it easy to follow through, paint the painful consequences of letting the opportunity slip away, protect everyone's anonymity, and finally ask for a response. Once the early responders break the ice, the evangelist leverages their experience to induce those still holding back.

Church Era: The Presence of God

The broadcast medium is experiential. It is no coincidence that most of the growing churches place an emphasis on having a personal encounter with Christ. Many point out how we can see God's hand in examples like answered prayer, through interactions with others, and in the daily challenges and crises of life.

On the one hand, broadcast Christians criticize their print-oriented brothers and sisters as sterile intellectuals or legalists. Print Christians also criticize liturgical (Catholics and some Protestant denominations) brothers and sisters for going through ritualistic motions and maintaining spiritual community at the expense of requiring moral accountability. Print and liturgically oriented Christians criticize broadcast Christians for wanting God to perform for them, just as they expect their pastors and worship leaders to perform on Sundays. The way we interpret God's presence within community, orthodoxy, or personal experience reflects some of the media filters our faith traditions operate with. These filters have created disconnects and misunderstanding between one another. Knowing this and knowing why provide a means for those within a liturgical, Reformation, or celebration tradition to reengage with one another.

Worship Service: Program

Celebration churches design their programs around a theme or desired results. Although their programming adheres to a basic structure, the themes can change weekly, as can the order and choice of events. They adjust their programming to meet their audience's needs. Reformation churches, on the other hand, stick to the agenda and follow the classic themes of church history; and liturgical churches stay true to the divine script. Celebration churches take a more pragmatic approach, centering on evangelism, which gives them greater flexibility to adapt new means to achieve their desired results. For example, if the need arises to help members better connect with one another, the church can insert a "series" that allows people to join small groups or attend some church sponsored mixers or other forums for people to meet.

Worship Style: Songs

The music of celebration churches is rhythmically more complex but lyrically more simple than hymns. The medium favors the amplified sound of a smaller cluster of musicians playing more fluid and up-tempo music. The content in hymns is difficult to convey through this format. Songs expressing feelings and conversations with God fit better.

Compare the lyrics of traditional hymns with most of today's songs. "When I in awesome splendor consider all the works thy hand hath . . . wrought" is replaced with "I'm in awe of you, awe of . . . you."[18] One catalogs the reasons for awe, and the other expresses the feeling. One carries content well; the other carries emotion well.

Church Architecture: Promotional

The larger celebration churches use their buildings to draw attention and attract the curious. Buildings provide the public face of the large, anonymous congregation. They are designed to be warm, impressive, and convenient.

The auditorium is typically designed to optimize the broadcast format (Figure 3.2) and may even include large-screen televisions.

Figure 3.2. Broadcast-paradigm architecture is built for the big event.

Acoustics are critical, with elaborate soundboards to mix and balance input from the numerous microphones. The setup crews work on the lighting, adjust the monitors, run through the projections, place the props, and rehearse what goes where during the different transitions. These are sophisticated studio productions. Most church members are unaware of the amount of work and expense that goes into each weekly production. But that is the point: all of these tools and props remain relatively invisible to provide focused attention on the stage performance.

Shifts in Morality: Pragmatics

The parable of the good Samaritan, first a shock of truth and then a story to be analyzed, is something else again: something of a how-to guide to behavior. The celebration pastor might begin with a contemporary story that parallels the good Samaritan. We may even hear how the pastor once acted like a Pharisee and how God faced him down over behavior or attitude. Then we will hear ways that we all act like Pharisees or priests on our busy roads of life. We will hear about the seven conditions of a modern-day Pharisee and the seven steps to change. We can then compare the pastor's checklist against our self-assessment and figure out where we fit on the continuum of good neighborliness. Then we can think about how we might apply some of the pastor's seven steps on the road to good neighborliness and be on our way.

Logic, reason, and the ethical imperative of print take a secondary seat to persuasion, emotional connection, and the specifics of one's current circumstances. Broadcast's goal is to stimulate action—now or soon—in response to a change of heart. Instead of ending with a conceptual understanding of the ethical roots behind the good Samaritan and how this fits into our lives, we receive an urgent appeal to make an immediate life change and are provided with action steps to do so.

• • •

The oral worldview occupied humanity for a long time before print came along, and we had centuries to adjust to the print world before broadcast's new paradigm knocked us off our feet. In comparison the time between the advent of broadcast and digital culture's explosion on the scene is only a blink of an eye—hardly time to assimilate the old ideas, let alone adjust to the new. But as we will see in the next chapter, the essence of digital is its ability to synthesize. Thus, we can find the best of what the oral, print, and broadcast paradigms have to offer made new again in this onrushing new world.

CHAPTER 4

Digital Culture— Convergence Church

Reconnecting Word with Spirit

Circa 2010–

> The ability to communicate—readily, at great distances, in robes of light—is so crucial and coveted that in the Bible it is embodied only in angels. . . . When anyone can transmit any amount of information . . . at any time, instantaneously . . . the resulting transformation becomes a transfiguration.
>
> —George Gilder, *Telecosm*

T he oral world trusted in God's hidden wonders: the coterminous reality of heaven and earth lay just beneath its ancient languages. The print world was confident in its ability to know, through reason, the *what* and *why* of the world. The broadcast world is interested in what we don't know, as a flood of fresh images blurs our once fixed and stable thought boundaries. The work of the coming digital world—whose birth we are now witnessing—will be in synthesizing our past into our desired future, shaped and influenced by the integrated character of digital media.

The digital language can create virtually any kind of information using two symbols—the numbers zero and one—encoded on silicon and moving at a speed of several million cycles per second. Computer code is both the most rigid and restricting environment and the most adaptable and diverse—able to convert text, images, sound, and data into a new universe of possibilities. Our shift to a coming digitally defined culture is more than a change in technology, attitude, and understanding. It is a sensory change with revolutionary implications. In the digital era, change is not only the constant, it is the organizing principle and the foundation from which we build. No wonder we feel the turbulence of vertigo!

Future Perfect

As we have seen, oral culture's time is the continual present; print fixes the past in place; and broadcast lives in the future. Digital culture's time is future perfect: a verb tense that conveys the sense that a future event has already taken place. Digital technology is changing our sense of time and history, both pulling the future into our awareness and drawing in the best of the past. It treats time as malleable, to be compressed or expanded as needed.

> In the digital era, change is not only the constant, it is the organizing principle and the foundation from which we build.

The limits of our culture reflect the limits of our communication. We hold in awe and fear those areas of life and the universe that we cannot experience, translate, and express. Occasionally, we transcend these limitations—in what some call epiphanies and others call gestalts. But whatever the description, at the boundaries of our social order, we glimpse new realities. These glimpses are becoming clearer as we begin collectively to peek through the door into a digital universe. Not only has its hyper-reality brought new insights, but its interactive nature has sparked a thirst for deeper connection.

We now have the means to allow our desires to journey virtually anyplace, to consider anything we choose. Our imaginary games of fantasy can for the first time achieve virtual reality leading to a corresponding physical expression. There are theoretically no boundaries or restrictions within this environment.[1] We are transcending the gravitational pull of our traditional worldview, and we are experiencing a social and moral weightlessness as a consequence.

In the not-so-distant future,

- Digital's desire for direct, unmediated, hands-on experience will replace broadcast's passive gestalt.
- Digital's reliance on networks and personal relationships will replace broadcast's bias toward collective main-event experiences.
- Digital's open-source technologies, organizations, and thinking will replace broadcast's branding and proprietary claims.[2]
- Digital's ability to reframe the past will replace broadcast's tendency to discard the past.
- Digital's paradigm-based approach to complex issues and conflicts will replace broadcast's political approach.
- Digital's multimedia language will replace broadcast's visual language.
- Digital's integration of right- and left-brain processes will replace broadcast's reliance on right-brain thinking.

Our World Is Already in Flux

My first language is broadcast; my second is print; and my most recent is digital. The difference between my approach to using the computer and my children's approach is obvious: I use only a portion of its capabilities. I use it for specific functions and do so self-consciously. My children, on the other hand, find new applications every week and solve technical challenges that I quickly give up on. I work with my computer, but my children live with it.

The number of people using digital communication as their primary source of information and exchange is growing at such a rate that soon a series of revolutions will ignite as institutions and organizations are forced no longer just to accommodate but to adapt. More than 50 percent of U.S. households (and more than 70 percent of households with children) have computers. At some point in the near future, children raised primarily in a digital environment will rise up and push aside both the broadcast rules and structures and the remaining residual print mind-sets.

Our basis of knowing and understanding is shifting to an interactive, global, anytime, anywhere, multimedia experience with countless sources to explore and test. The experience will be unlike the intellectually passive experience of watching television or the emotionally distant experience of reading. Our minds and bodies will undergo yet another rewiring to support this different sensory experience.

To the uninitiated a person who can write computer code seems like a modern-day Mozart—a musical genius who was said to have been able to compose elaborate and technically perfect scores without correction or error. Writing computer software is far from a flawless endeavor; however, this direct connection between thought and execution is commonplace for many computer programmers.

> Our basis of knowing and understanding is shifting to an interactive, global, anytime, anywhere, multimedia experience with countless sources to explore and test.

Now, through familiarity with computers, this capability is also becoming available to the rest of us. As we begin to understand how digital media integrate print, graphics, sound, and data into a new multisensory interactive experience, and as we experience the medium's speed and access to information and people, we begin to work with instantaneous responses on multiple and simultaneous interests. Many people regularly describe themselves as *multitasking*: doing several jobs at once, such as talking on the phone while cooking dinner and keeping an eye on their children, sending e-mail while taking a phone call, listening to a book on tape while jogging and running the dog. As I'm writing, for example, I've sent several e-mails on topics the writing stimulated me to think about and paused to research a few sources for this chapter. I find that I am no longer working sequentially, but in a hyperlinked manner, able to jump from topic to topic and back again.

Kids as young as elementary school regularly communicate with their friends through instant messaging, download MP3 music files from the Internet, know how to use Google or other search engines to find information almost instantaneously, and put together multimedia presentations for class projects. They get their information from peers or networks rather than from institutions or authority. Connectivity is quickly eliminating traditional boundaries, forming new relationships intimately tied together through webs of information.

Young people are in the forefront, but we are also beginning to see a digital mind-set change the workplace. Increasingly, it's your contribution to the organization that tells how significant you are, not the placement of your office. Events and decisions are seen as occurring continuously, without bureaucratic time lags, reducing the need to go through channels of departments, and phases are shortened due to collaborative efforts and structures. Talent and information are often more highly valued than the commodity or product involved in a transaction.

Traditional manufacturing, for example, focuses on a linear process. Manufacture of a product begins with market research and feasibility studies; it then proceeds sequentially through engineering, creation of prototypes, tooling (building the manufacturing equipment), creating the sources of supply, testing the product with selected clients, training, and eventually sales. For many companies this process can take years. We are moving, however, toward integrated teams that work simultaneously on all of these elements using on-line collaborative tools. When the Boeing 777 was designed and engineered, a new kind of software called CATIA (Computer Aided Three Dimension Interactive Application) allowed virtual testing. The 777 was the first commercial plane flown without the testing of a built prototype. This new approach significantly shortened the time and cost of building a plane. The capability of CATIA allowed the engineers to work as a collaborative team instead of as independent elements.

Creation and innovation of manufactured goods will experience the kind of time compression and growth that Gutenberg brought to books and writers.[3] Celera Genomic, a private company, mapped the human genome in approximately two years—a project the National Institutes of Health, a print-based government agency, had projected originally would take more than fifteen years.

The times they are a-changin'.

Systems Thinking

The digital generation will filter the world through a set of dynamic models that describe the general behavior of complex systems. As we discover and map the behavior of these systems, we will be able to apply them to our situations and relationships. This discipline is called systems thinking. When we talk about the weather in terms of patterns or systems, we are using archetypal or systems language.

MIT professor Peter Senge has developed a hierarchy of different archetypes for organizational behavior.[4] For example, the Middle East conflict reflects an archetype or system that Senge would term as a reinforcing loop. It is a vicious cycle—and we've all seen people or organizations caught in vicious cycles. One party misinterprets or overreacts to cues, eliciting a similar misinterpretation and overreaction from the other party, ultimately leading to either a blowup or a meltdown. In the case of the Middle East conflict, Israel's steps to increase security threaten the goal of freedom for the Palestinians, and Palestinian terrorism threatens Israeli civilians, causing the Israeli government to increase security. Each party views the other's attempts to forward its position as a threat leading to inevitable escalation. There is no unraveling who started what and who's to blame for what. That is an old and ineffective linear, logical approach. Stopping the vicious cycle requires shifting to a different archetype. Shifting to a different archetype requires a change in paradigms. Our best intentions using the old paradigm are no match for the new conflicts of a highly complex, rapidly shifting world. This next generation will major in paradigm thinking and paradigm shifting the way earlier generations majored in Cartesian logic.[5]

Here's to You, the Virtual Good Samaritan

Increasingly, we will have contact with countless people we never meet face-to-face. Without the solid conceptual (ethical) boundaries of print or the relational (moral) connections from oral cultures or even the weak vicarious (pragmatic) relationships created in broadcast, we will encounter no perceptible consequences, positive or negative, in the way we treat strangers. The virtual boundaries of an Internet world will prove too fluid and too ephemeral to restrain human nature. Even with the many random acts of kindness over the Internet, good will continues to weaken and our trust levels lower with each new spam or scam we encounter. If the rampant proliferation of unsolicited pornography and spam on the Internet offers any projection toward future social behavior, we quickly need a model that promotes a virtual civil code of behavior.

Intimacy must coexist with greater openness. The protection of that intimacy and vulnerability will directly influence whether we become a more connected civil society or fragment into bunkers of narrow self-interest and survival. This is a question of social maturity. According to Walter Ong, "It is distinctive of matured technological man that he must and can maintain a large number of contacts, which are decently personal and yet relatively noncommittal."[6]

Emotional Space: Absorbing

Interaction on a computer is both distant and connected. Watch an accomplished kid play a video game at an arcade. Her experience and yours will probably be quite different. She will fly through the game with amazing ease and speed. You and I, on the other hand, usually get stuck on level one. Why? Because we try to figure it out. We get bogged down in the specifics—that strategy is too intimate to succeed.

Those who are most proficient at video games maintain a high degree of detachment and play almost as if they are an extension of the game. They are able to turn off their subliminal dialogue and enter an intense state of kinetic reaction—a reflexive state of mind. That is one reason why computer simulators have become such a valuable tool for training pilots, soldiers, and doctors.

Social Cohesion: Weblike Connections

Weblike connections provide both the hold and flexibility to create cohesion and freedom. The complex, decentralized, and fast-changing environment of digital culture will require a new form of social and economic commitment.

One reemerging concept is the idea of intentional communities. These go beyond our homeowners' associations, church affiliation, or other community structures. Intentional communities provide a digital remake of communal living. They do not require some of the impracticalities of the kinds of communities that developed in the 1960s and 1970s. Digital technology allows groups to reconstruct the components of an extended family and community. Businesses are discovering the possibility of forming virtual organizations.

I travel monthly to Washington, D.C., to facilitate a network of about twenty companies that have formed an intentional community. Each of these companies serves businesses that are moving or expanding. That is our common community. This association began as a network of companies that helped each other identify more business opportunities. Over time, however, it has become a committed community.[7]

Digital technology provides the means to organize and develop cohesive communities across, between, and around current organizations. In the future deep connections that range beyond the immediate geographical community will become more and more common.

Teaching and Learning: Self-Directed Learning and Guides

We are beginning to see the dramatic difference in how our children learn and at what pace. They no longer grind out their lessons by rote memorization. They no longer sit passively in front of a television and say "Huh?" when asked what they learned. Children are absorbed in an interactive-game environment, pursuing treasure hunts of knowledge over the Web. They integrate what they learn, expand far beyond the assignment, and retain a high level of enthusiasm.

There is also a danger to this new form of learning. What happens when our play allows us to simulate and rehearse reality? We applaud simulation for pilots or physicians—in fact, we demand it. We want them to be able to handle the chaos of a crisis with veins of ice. However, when this simulation technology seeps into our youth, we can unwittingly create cold-blooded killers (as we saw with fourteen-year-old Michael Carneal). Grossman explains in his book *Stop Teaching Our Kids to Kill* that the video games our kids play provide a highly effective form of rehearsal for the real thing. This cautionary tale not only raises issues about the pushers of exploitative content but must force us to examine the entire context of digital learning and simulation. We are no more prepared for the implications of what this technology will bring, both good and bad, than we are to see a fourteen-year-old become a deadly marksman.

This new generation of children approaches the world of knowledge in a unique way. They naturally challenge common assumptions, conventional boundaries, and accepted authorities. In *Growing Up Digital*, Dan Tapscot explains, "Child development is concerned with the evolution of motor skills, language skills, and social skills. It also involves the development of cognition, intelligence, reasoning, personality, and, through adolescence, the creation of autonomy, a sense of the self and values. . . . all these are enhanced in an interactive world. When children control their media, rather than passively observe, they develop faster."[8]

The early childhood education innovator Maria Montessori may have been a hundred years or so ahead of her time. She believed that people could better reach their potential through the educational environment rather than through the content or process. The focus on context or environment is a key shift toward a digital mind-set. Montessori also held that children learn best through meaningful play and coaching versus rote instruction, and I would venture to add, through edutainment.[9] Children (and adults) are naturally curious, and they explore that curiosity if allowed to do so. If they have the tools, the coaching, and a well-designed environment, they have the potential to learn more, learn more quickly, and develop a passion for learning. That brings us to the entry point in our embryonic digital culture: the computer.

There is no question that the computer provides a dramatic shift for learning possibilities. It not only transforms the tedium of learning dry fundamental skills into play, it also allows for more individualized rates of learning. The Internet enables the curious to follow hyperlinks connecting diverse topics and ideas. The almost limitless access to resources allows students to cover a topic comprehensively and find helpful material.

Multimedia provides a layering of experience so that one can read a text, listen to a lecture, see pictures of referenced examples, test assumptions, conduct virtual experiments, work through complex calculations, interact with peers, read what the experts say, and so on. Online group discussions about a specific topic allow yet another angle of discovery.

Our educational models are beginning to shift in this direction—and for good reason. So many of the challenges schools currently face—including teacher-student ratios, rising costs, tailored curriculum for special educational needs, assessment, parental involvement, depth for noncore subjects, expansion of curriculum options, flexible schedules, diverse learning modalities, cohesion for time-stretched families—all have promising possible solutions both in the new technologies and in the new paradigms behind this interactive medium.

In the future self-directed learning will become more and more the norm. Teachers will move away from being grade specialists to becoming general facilitators handling several grades at a time. In a virtual little red schoolhouse, technology will afford a shift back to the teaching relationship. Continuity will lead to greater effectiveness, and that effectiveness will create opportunities for mentors and higher levels of fulfillment for all concerned.

Essence: Interaction Integrates

Interactive digital media connect multiple modes of experiences into one, combining text, sound, data, and images onto one common platform and into one language. Digital media reconnect touch, thought, and expression; they connect one person to another or others; and they encourage interaction. Digital media creates a simultaneous multimedia, multisensory encounter (virtual reality). It is the most fully engaged, broad-based, explicit, and calculating medium of expression ever experienced.

The potential is that people will become far more engaged and involved specifically where they can make the most difference. They will be less likely to apply either-or standards that might end in polarized factions. Instead, they will enter into ongoing dialogues committed to the exponential effect of incremental improvement over wholesale change. This new freedom of expression is and will continue to be tested by those who go to excess. Virtual communities are learning how to establish guidelines and values to filter in and filter out people who become disruptive or even destructive. And there are forums that appear to have no boundaries for expression. The power and potential of collaboration will remain attractive and lead to a collaborative ethos.[10] The digital medium creates a mind that is more ecologically oriented rather than being either the master or the center of the universe.

The Roots of the Church

By means of all created things, without exception, the divine assails us, penetrates us and molds us. We imagined it as distant and inaccessible, whereas in fact we live steeped in its burning layers.

—Pierre Teilhard de Chardin, *The Divine Milieu: An Essay on the Interior Life*

The emerging digital culture will reconnect word (content) with spirit (source) and disconnect spirit from flesh. It will reconnect words with their essence (original intent) but separate essence from things. This virtual reconstruction will ignite a quest for meaning, voice, and substance searching for new forms and expressions.

As the word takes on this new form, the world will change to reflect the seven realities we introduced at the beginning of this book: interconnection, complexity, acceleration, intangibility, convergence, immediacy, and unpredictability. Virtual reconstruction creates intriguing implications to Jesus' words: "They are not of the world, even as I am not of it. Sanctify them by the truth; your word is truth" (John 17:16–17, NIV).

Truth Is Collective and Contextual

Digital cultures will continually reach for the wisdom of the ages and seek to recontextualize it within their community and setting. Print provided a conceptually cohesive foundation for truth. Broadcast provided an appealing package for it. The digital world, however, provides a swirl of truth for collective reassembly. It is a passionate environment in which to work out one's salvation with "fear and trembling."[11]

The interconnected digital environment provides a proving ground (feedback loop) for truth. It provides elements of oral culture by engaging and testing the source of information. It follows elements of print culture with its deductive process for discovery (search engines and file directories, for example, follow a logical structure) and through text. Hyperlinks add an inductive texture, allowing one to pursue related topics or go deeper into a subject matter. The real-time nature of hyperlinks along with these other elements of discovery changes the quality of one's pursuit for understanding and truth.

> The emerging digital culture will reconnect word (content) with spirit (source) and disconnect spirit from flesh. It will reconnect words with their essence (original intent) but separate essence from things.

Some of our prescriptive approaches to truth (rational and detached) have acted somewhat like chemotherapy: we hope to kill the disease before we kill the person. We are beginning to see smart drugs that are able to kill the disease without harming the rest of the body. In a similar way, we are seeing companies offering "smart" goods and services tailored to the person's needs instead of taking a one-size-fits-all approach. The clothing retailer Land's End, for example, sells blue jeans tailored to your unique body dimensions—without you ever walking into a store. They do this by guiding you through a series of body measurements over the Internet. Gone are the days of small, medium, large, and extra large. Collective collaborations are beginning to express truth tailored to their context in what we might call smart truth. Online forums search the vast memory banks of the Internet, debate the findings, and merge their insights, producing alternative solutions that challenge conventional wisdom from health to public policy.

Faith Is Faithful Skepticism

Digital kids start out questioning. They tend to seek and find for themselves. More than one teacher has taught a lesson, only to have a child return the next morning to challenge the story. It's a game, and it's survival.

Digital kids are learning that many of the truths and promises from past generations aren't necessarily so or that they no longer fit the way they used to. They learn at an early age that the authorities in their lives don't know everything. And unlike my generation, which thought the established order was full of hot air, this new generation has the means to figure out whether and why that's true. They are more willing to accept realities outside their microuniverse. In other words, they are far less loyal toward established groups. They fiercely defend their current views and also hold the right to change their position. This is a generation that says passionately, "I believe, help my unbelief" (Mark 9:24). In other words they are profoundly spiritual yet profoundly disillusioned with traditional religion—the so-called authorized source for their faith.

The Body of Christ

A hologram is a projected image—say, of a person—that appears fully three-dimensional and real. (The MIT Museum currently has the world's largest collection of holography.) The wonder of a hologram is in its structure: any slice of a hologram contains the entire, three-dimensional image. The hologram provides a working metaphor for the future convergence church. This metaphor finds its power in the nature of digital media, in which print, sound, graphics, and data integrate in a common medium through a common language, creating an integrated sensory effect. It will carry forward, dissolving and integrating previous walls of separation including national origin, race, age, income, and doctrine. Each of us carries with us—individually and collectively—a unified expression of Christ's character.

Within oral cultures the fatherhood of God provided the framework for the family of faith and the mystical union of believers. Print cultures shifted that focus to the saving grace of Christ, the priesthood of the individual believer, and the irresistible and unerring written word of God. Broadcast cultures awakened to the person of the Holy Spirit and discovered the power of collective praise and worship tied to a tangible presence of God.

The convergence church will combine several of these characteristics and adapt them to each congregation: extended spiritual family, knowledge of the word, and expressive praise. In addition, however, we will likely see a renewed emphasis on a broader expression of community, beyond congregation and beyond denomination. The inherent nature of a digital environment allows for a diverse and unified global expression of Christ's body—a fourth tangible expression of the Godhead. This very real capability falls more in line with Paul's description of "the body" to the Corinthian church (1 Corinthians 12). It sheds new light on Jesus' prayer and final instructions in John's Gospel that we become one so the world might know Him. Finally, it animates Paul's goal, the universal church.

For the first time, humankind is moving into an environment with the means and a developing mind-set to behave both collectively and individually on a global scale. This may not lead to the ultimate expression of Christ's body on earth, but one can see why even secular thinkers like George Gilder draw religious parallels to what is emerging.

Worship Service: Assembly

His intent was that now, through the church, the manifold wisdom of God should be made known to the rulers and authorities in the heavenly realms.
—Ephesians 3:10 (NIV)

Convergence churches will develop skills to create a collaborative experience. You might think of this as a techno-Quaker meeting, a jazz ensemble, or improvisational theater. All of these are highly interactive, and even newcomers quickly get oriented and participate.[12]

These interactive assemblies transcend the challenge of trying to choose the right style for the service—whether contemporary, traditional, youth, or blended. They will also transcend age barriers and be more inclusive of youth and elders. This happens as a result of the shift away from stage performance as the center of the event to personal interaction and group dynamics as the new center. With this new center these gatherings might be "unplugged," or multimedia to the max.

Interactive assemblies are not limited to a Sunday church service. They have the potential of carrying over into homes and small groups. They can take a large burden off the pastor, worship leader, and core staff and allow full participation in the body of Christ.

Worship Style: Tailored Contextual Songs

Music for the convergence church will likely incorporate and better integrate elements from past traditions, in the same way that today's music is showing the power and creativity of sampling parts of disparate recordings, remixing them to create wholly original music that still reflects the strengths of the past.

There also seems to be a trend of returning to psalms that reflect the local congregation and its experience. Many churches have musicians writing and recording their own music. The broadcast barriers of quality and cost are dissolving. A lot of this initial product is still oriented toward performance, but a growing number of artists are creating music that expresses specific stories not meant for mass consumption. Recently, one of the sound technicians at our church handed me a CD he had written and performed. When I listened to it, I was not only impressed by its quality, but I recognized the story behind the story because I know him. That connection point adds context to the words, meaning that broadcast songs cannot create.

Younger members of the emerging digital culture tend to reject pop hits in favor of more creative and challenging alternative music. They burn their own mixes on their own CDs and give them to friends. The implications for the church are similar to those for the music business.

First, technology is lowering the threshold for those who want to be musicians, in terms of both technique and cost. There will be an explosion of new artists. Second, commercial music distribution is at a crisis point. The Internet has created the means to bypass the record companies. Print-based laws to prevent free access to recordings simply represent fingers in a dam ready to burst. Third, music will come home to connect with the local church. Fourth, families will be able to enjoy and participate with music together. Finally, we will create our own tailored music anthologies.

Church Architecture: Accessible, Interactive, and Flexible

Convergence churches will view the idea of the church building from an entirely different perspective than ever before. Most of today's church buildings sit idle during the week (unless they contain a school) and then get 90 percent of their use on Sundays. This adds to the compartmentalized and fragmented lives we live. If we think about the life of a community, we think about frequent comings and goings. The local coffee shop, for many, is becoming a secular sanctuary and community center. By contrast, most churches between Sundays seem cold, quiet, and dead. Other accessible and interactive facilities—some large, some small—will develop.[13]

We will see a shift away from mega-churches to smaller-scale facilities that fit well within their neighborhoods. Congregations will shift back toward being more rooted in the local community, connected perhaps to a larger assembly. Interactive church services will require a change in sanctuary design. The barriers of platforms and the configuration of seating need to communicate that this is an interactive and safe environment in which all can participate.

Greater collaboration between congregations can free up resources, which greatly affects the design and use of a facility. The freed resources may be clerical staff, financial managers, sound technicians, or other functionaries that handle the operational side of a church. One church may also collaborate with another in areas in which it does not have experience or expertise. By freeing its resources, a congregation can emphasize its interests and unique strengths instead of diluting itself by attempting to cover every ministry base. Churches do not have the funds to address their congregation's every need or desire—no organization does. It is better to excel at strengths (ministering to youth, providing music, teaching, counseling) than to offer half-hearted and mediocre programs or services. It may be better for your congregation to partner with a congregation that excels in areas that yours does not. Overbuilt and underused facilities and overstretched budgets are luxuries that will not survive in the future.

Architects, pastors, and leadership boards would do well to begin now to reconsider the vital and symbolic role buildings play in church life and to examine the enormous resources our current models require. Architecture provides a field ripe for a new paradigm. We will explore this new paradigm more in the final chapter.[14]

Shifts in Morality: Root Understandings

The emerging digital generation is passionate about two seeming opposites: returning to root understandings and creating original experiences. These youth recognize the power of ritual reenactment by virtue of computer simulation and virtual reality, and they are suspicious of using other people's experiences as their foundation for acting. They understand that universal principles govern behavior, but they also want to understand these principles in the current context.

These youth do not trust nicely wrapped truisms like "Hate the sin, love the sinner." Instead, they are attracted to people who have been through the fire, taken a stand, worked through failure, learned how to love the sinner and express themselves in their recognizable voice—not a borrowed, schooled, rehearsed, or clichéd voice. They want to dig deeper and find the fundamental why behind people's convictions and the ancient stories.

Next-geners seem to be more interested in small acts of charity than my generation was. As a true broadcast product, I have gravitated toward causes and efforts to change the world. I can talk the talk of a good Samaritan with full conviction, and I'll send my money to those who can do the work better than I. I often find myself at a bit of a loss, however, when dealing with a real stranger in my path. In contrast, the digital generation possesses a self-sufficiency, a confidence, and a dynamic to do something now. Instead of preparing a compelling sermon about the good Samaritan, they are more likely to go out, help a stranger in need, and then share their experience. The digital environment strips away pretense and reconnects good intentions with true good works.

• • •

Right now, in the United States, we have for the first time in history three generations raised under the influence of three different dominant communication tools. I see this reflected in my parents, my children, and myself. Each of us sees and experiences the world in such different ways that it's a miracle we can communicate at all!

The authority of books and television are giving way to the authority of digital networking, but that doesn't mean we do not need to understand these media that seem to be falling by the wayside. This transition has already created a time of conflict and turmoil, but it can also be a glorious opportunity to understand and take hold of the time we live in and the times that made way for it. Once your print or broadcast self really comprehends the world that nurtured it and sees and experiences some of the potential hidden just below the surface of the onrushing digital universe, your mind and spirit will be taken to places that you could not have imagined possible before, and you will see them in ways you may not anticipate.

Understanding our own time—right smack on the fault line between broadcast and digital communications—requires seeing it in context. To this end I have built a consolidated comparison of these historical periods in the form of a chart, or matrix, a unifying theory of time and communications. This tool, the Millennium Matrix, will be an invaluable guide to understanding the three-dimensional nature of the paradigm in which you were raised, in which your parents were raised, and in which Jesus lived and taught.

The Millennium Matrix is easy to understand and easy to use. The four columns are the four eras: oral, print, broadcast, and digital.

The rows list various categories of thought and sensibilities, from worship, truth, and understanding to production, and medium of exchange. If you read each column from top to bottom, you will get a comprehensive idea of how that worldview shaped every aspect of life and thought, and you will build a deeply layered understanding of the worldview and mind-set for that medium. If you read each row from left to right, you will see how a particular concept—such as sense of identity, for example—was transformed through time.

I believe that you will come away from the Millennium Matrix understanding why you, your parents, and your children look at the world in such specific and very different terms. You will also see the church you belong to as a product of one of these columns. The matrix provides a kind of understanding that goes much deeper than studying your church's history or doctrines, providing a context for all of that historical and doctrinal content you have stored away. I hope that reading and studying the Millennium Matrix will create an awakening in you, that surprising new picture that appears when all the pieces of a jigsaw puzzle come together.

THE COMPLETE
MILLENIUM MATRIX

	Oral Culture—Liturgical Church ? B.C.–A.D. 1500	Print Culture—Reformation Church 1500–1950	Broadcast Culture—Celebration Church 1950–2010	Digital Culture—Convergence Church 2010–
HOW WE BELIEVE	**Ancient**	**Modern**	**Postmodern**	**Convergent**
Worship	**Liturgical:** A mystical, experiential ritual reenactment. The ceremony centers on a mystical ritual reenactment of sacred and eternal events. It creates the context for leaving the common world to enter into a sacred time and place. For example, the ritual journey of the Catholic mass prepares one to enter the sacred moment of the Eucharist, where the wine and bread are transformed into the spiritual body and blood of Christ.	**Meeting:** An orderly reinforcement of the principles of faith and presentation of the gospel. The service, centered on preaching, provides an orderly reinforcement of the principles of faith and presentation of the gospel. The worship portion centers on singing hymns that confirm scriptural and doctrinal truth. Content is more important than style. The sermon is the focal point of the service.	**Event:** A dramatic presentation and celebration of the gospel. The service centers on praise and follows a large-event entertainment format. The worship team or leader energizes the audience. The songs center on an up-tempo praise style of worship. The worship leader or team defines the worship experience. The audience responds to that direction. The pastor uses stories and personal experiences in the sermon to connect to the audience.	**Gathering** An interactive, intimate, multisensory, improvisational, immersive, mystical, highly engaged experience. A spiritual conductor creates an open-ended experience, exploring a wide range of ways to express worship. The ritual, preaching, and praise of earlier eras are used as elements to create a highly engaged and unique experience.

	Relational	Principle	Existential	Contextual
Truth	**Relational:** The message and the messenger are one. For ancient Hebrews understanding was a kind of hearing.[1] Truth and the truth giver were intimately connected, so truth's credibility was tied to the messenger's credibility. Jesus also connected one's being with one's speech: "The mouth speaks out of the overflow of the heart" (Luke 6:45, NIV).	**Principle:** Truth is based on the content of the message alone. The written word makes understanding a kind of seeing.[2] Truth is embodied in the statement or the concept. Truth is based on the content of the message alone. Written language developed structure and rules (logic, history, analysis, expert opinion, and other tools of deduction) to determine meaning. Truth becomes embodied in the creeds of faith and through logical theorems.	**Existential:** The truth of a theory is in your mind, not in your eyes.[3] Truth is validated through experience, the force of conviction, or some tangible outcome. The concrete reality of the moment takes priority over distant and abstract concepts. This defines the current existential context for truth. The search for truth and understanding takes the path of deconstructing past norms and experimenting with eclectic sources of understanding.	**Contextual:** Truth is malleable and relevant within particular contexts of meaning. Context becomes the simulator for our understandings of reality. Community (virtual or otherwise) tests and validates reality. Seekers in a digital world, like computers, do not possess rational attachment, objective certainty, or an emotional feeling about the truth. Like Gulliver in *Gulliver's Travels*, everyone will journey through numerous micro-worlds that behave and operate from different paradigms. Future generations will be willing and forced to construct truth from the ground up using bits and bytes of their encounters with others from "other worlds." We will experience the new reality of Paul's admonition to the Philippians to "work out our salvation with fear and trembling."

(continued)

THE COMPLETE MILLENNIUM MATRIX (continued)

	Oral	Print	Broadcast	Digital
HOW WE BELIEVE	**Ancient**	**Modern**	**Postmodern**	**Convergent**
Understanding	**Insights:** The goal of understanding is to find the internal nature of a person, an event, or the world. The mysterious nature of the world came by revelation, observation, and insight. Early Greek medicine, for example, looked at the nature of four internal fluids as the basis of behavior, health, and well-being.[4]	**Facts:** The tangible, permanent nature of print creates a world that relies on facts. This imperative is part of our presuppositions. For example, "We hold these truths to be self-evident, that all men are created equal and are endowed by their creator with inalienable rights."	**Selective awareness:** Bathed in a continuous stream of news, images, and information, we filter in what we are familiar with or in search of and filter out the opposite. This is not an age of facts because that assumes the ability to find the source, test the assumptions, and verify outcomes.	**Recontextualizing:** Our ability to take information from separate disciplines and mediums and work with different data on a common platform leads to an explosion of innovations. Breakthroughs in genetic research, nanotechnology, and communications are just three examples of innovations that grow out of recontextualizing.
Faith	**Trust:** Believing is seeing. "Those who have eyes to see let them see" (Matthew 11:15, NIV). Faith originates out of the spoken word: "Faith comes from hearing the message,	**Belief:** Seeing is believing. Faith is based on the accepted authority of the Bible, its propositions and facts. For example, the Bible states that people are sinners and Christ redeemed us through his death	**Conviction:** Feeling is believing. Faith is based on realizing or experiencing something bigger than oneself. This basis of existential attachment can lead to a passionate pursuit of	**Pragmatism:** Belief resides in the medium of digital community. Faith begins with the context of a community, both physical and virtual. The community narrative creates a

and the message is heard through the word of Christ" (Romans 10:17, NIV). It relies upon the one who speaks—the messenger (for example, Abraham's relationship with God).	and resurrection. A person who accepts these assertions as true receives salvation.	Christ or many blind alleys. The broadcast medium provides a context of larger-than-life experiences, which explains the popularity of all kinds of events.	microworldview expressing origin, points of validation, and destiny. Doctrinal differences blur, yet microworldviews separate. For example, faith communities emerge centered around sustainable living, traditional family values, or alternative lifestyles, each with its own genealogy of thought, filtering process, and rites of initiation.
Gospel **Reenacting:** Reliving the gospel as a divine drama.	**Retelling:** Remembering the gospel as an event in history with eternal implications.	**Reselling:** Using persuasion, drama, and demonstration to present the gospel as an appeal to one's conscience and soul.	**Recontextualizing:** Unprecedented individual access to church history, traditions, and styles creates a desire to freshly encounter past traditions and gospel truths, sampling and synthesizing them into new expressions.

(continued)

HOW WE BELIEVE	Oral	Print	Broadcast	Digital
	Ancient	Modern	Postmodern	Convergent
Godhead	**Father:** God is a father, Someone to fear and Someone who will protect. Leadership reflects this orientation. Priests require special training and discipline to qualify to act as intermediaries for their people. They may approach God only through elaborate ritual.	**Son:** The Godhead is expressed in the Son and his forgiveness and redemption. Believers become joint heirs, a holy kingdom of priests. Jesus removes the need for intermediaries or ritual in order to approach God. All believers are able to stand blameless before God's throne.	**Holy Spirit:** The Godhead is expressed through the revelation of the Holy Spirit and an elevated awareness of his role and being. Leadership uses the language of spiritual discernment ("The Holy Spirit revealed to me") as a validation for authority. At one extreme the manifestations of the Holy Spirit are necessary to validate one's experience with Jesus. Most churches that reflect this position feel that the Christian who has not had a direct encounter with the Holy Spirit is living a limited Christian life.	**Body or church:** The Godhead will be expressed with a new awareness of the church as the Corpus Christi, Christ's tangible expression on earth. Leadership acts as a catalyst for members of the church to minister to one another and to the community (sometimes known as body ministry) in acts of healing, confession, correction, and charity.

	Up/Face	Out/Mind	In/Hand	Everywhere/Heart
God's location	**Up:** God is above us and looking down as a caretaker or a judge (Ephesians 4:6). We can speak with God directly. Before Moses (when God wrote down His laws), Abraham was God's friend (James 2:23); Job debated and Moses negotiated with God (Exodus 32:31).	**Out:** God is somewhere out there. He is the great architect who designed our creation and watches it function. Prayer to God replaces dialogue with God.	**In:** God is in our heart. He enters and guides our thoughts through the Holy Spirit. We have internal conversations with God.	**Everywhere:** All creation is a reflection of God. In this holographic paradigm, the entire image is intact in each and every fragment. Because God is everywhere, we can access God through many means.
Connection with God	**Face of God:** We behold his face. "I shall behold thy face in righteousness" (Psalm 17:15, NIV). This is an act of intimacy.	**Mind of God:** We see God's mind expressed in the physical world and its processes. *"The Mind of God* begins with physics, looking at different theories of the creation of the universe, the nature of physical laws and the possibility of a theory of everything."[5]	**Hand of God:** We focus on the tangible acts and evidences of God, whether in miracles, natural disasters, news events, or answers to our prayers.	**Heart of God:** We see God's heart expressed in a yearning for connection and community and getting back to something simpler. This anthem is expressed in the song "The Heart of Worship" by Matt Redman.[6]

(continued)

101

HOW WE BELIEVE	Oral	Print	Broadcast	Digital
	Ancient	Modern	Postmodern	Convergent
Relating to God	**I-Thou dialogue:** We revere, speak, and argue with God on intimate terms.	**I-It monologue:** We see God as a concept to study under the science of theology.	**They-It silence:** Many people see a God who is silent: no center, no dialogue, no reflection, simply the random collective expressions of the crowd. On the other hand, believers experience God in a highly personal, specific, and subjective manner. Both thirst for firm grounding and often find it in the momentum of crowds.[7]	**I-They panalogue:** We see the Internet as a transcendent collective mind. We are in the center and can have a transcendent, omnidirectional dialogue with God. Our relationship to the sacred is like a quest in a four-dimensional chat room, sifting and sorting out the many voices and images claiming to be sacred.
Revelation of God	**Direct encounter:** Revelation comes through a direct encounter with God. Revelation is personal. Abraham's covenant, Samuel's voice in his sleep, Jacob's ladder, and Paul's road to Damascus are just a few examples.	**Scripture:** Revelation comes through reading the Bible. Revelation is conceptual.	**Experience:** Revelation through Scripture, presentation, or events touch our emotions and change our state of mind. Revelation is relational.	**Immersion:** Revelation will come through more intimate encounters with truth and individuals. Digital capabilities for simulation will reclaim the power of oral traditions of initiation. Revelation creates a clear divide between past and future.

Time	**Liturgical time:** We experience past sacred events in the present through faithful adherence to ritual and song. This idea is clearly communicated in the Catholic liturgy and calendar. The words from the hymn "Joy to the world, the Lord *is come*," reflect this present tense.	**Chronological time:** We see past events as history—mile markers that provide a legacy and confirmation for faith. These events offer reassurance through recall and application. We don't participate and recreate Christ's birth or crucifixion as a means of sacred connection; we celebrate the historic event as a historic fact.	**Existential time:** We see past events as catalysts for our own psychological and spiritual journeys. Carl Jung first popularized this notion by comparing many contemporary struggles with ancient mythological themes.	**Virtual time:** We see past events as malleable scenarios for manipulation in a theological lab of what-if questions. Virtual-reality time spans millennia and projects forward into any multitude of settings. We journey as if in both fantasy and reality, with the potential to either catch a brighter glimpse of God's mystery or descend into an abyss of narcissism.

(continued)

THE COMPLETE MILLENNIUM MATRIX *(continued)*

	Oral	Print	Broadcast	Digital
	Whole	Parts	Fragments	System
HOW WE KNOW				
Self-understanding	**Tribe:** We see ourselves in relation or connection to others. Character derives from role models.	**Individual:** We see ourselves as autonomous and in contrast to others. Character derives from principles and the reinforcement of a cause-effect worldview.	**Member:** We see ourselves as both part of and isolated from our affiliations. We are fragments of one another. We might also call this *together/alone*. Character is a collage of events, individuals, passions, and accomplishments. The *together/alone* dynamic provides the drive behind our culture of self-discovery.	**Passport citizens:** We may call a particular community home, but we also have passports allowing us to participate within many other communities. The many hats we wear give us the ability to try on virtual personae in a highly interactive feedback environment.
Sense of time	**Present or presence:** The time is the continual present because we have no recorded history, only our retold stories. The word is sound. Retelling stories and performing rituals preserves the past. In order to remember the stories, we use	**Past or objectification:** Time marches on. Reading successive symbols on paper creates a sensation of progress as the eye proceeds from word to word. A word read is a word in the past, and that past word	**Future or impermanence:** History is dead; the future does not yet exist; the moment is impermanent. The word as sound-image captures the awareness but leaves nothing to connect to. The continual flow of	**Virtual or time travel:** The word is simultaneously seen, heard, felt, and experienced. The future is now.[8] The tense is future perfect.[9]

(continued)

	Local or tribes	National or ideological identity	Global invader	Global microcosm
	common themes and formulas to simplify memory. The retelling experience makes events seem current. "Do not forget" (Deuteronomy 6:12) is not only a solemn warning but is built into the daily rituals of life. Recreating the past maintains a sense of continuity that keeps life in a perpetual state of suspended animation.	stimulates a current thought. This contrast between past words and current thoughts creates a sensation of progress—moving forward from the permanent record. Print creates a sense of passing time because we have the means of comparing past words and descriptions with current thoughts and reality.	broadcast media wipes away past references. The ephemeral quality of broadcast does not quench the senses but leaves a stimulated void that anticipates what's coming next. There is no past, only a fleeting present. What's left is a drive for the future.	
Sense of space	**Local or tribes:** The world is fixed in space. We live in one place and have little exposure to areas that are more than a day's travel. Hence, we have an intimate understanding of our community and a mystical understanding of the world. Even nomads have an intimate understanding of the world they travel through. We are parochial in our boundaries.	**National or ideological identity:** We have mapped the world, defining territories and space. The impetus to find the spaces in the world that are still unknown creates forward movement. We can now travel over distances (whether by improved transportation or by reading books), and this creates continuity between communities. Written language is credited for the establishment of kingdoms and empires.	**Global invader:** Television, radio, and the telephone have eliminated perceptual distances and definitions of boundaries. Our worldview is fluid, and we can receive a diversity of influences.	**Global microcosm:** The digital world removes barriers of geography, ideology, and even matter. We redefine space in terms of mind, world, and networks through an architecture of intelligence.[10] We live in a world that is both vast and intimate.

THE COMPLETE MILLENNIUM MATRIX *(continued)*

	Oral	Print	Broadcast	Digital
	Whole	Parts	Fragments	System
HOW WE KNOW				
Sensory bias	**Ear:** The ear creates a sense of inclusion and immediacy. Hearing accepts beautiful sounds and noise equally. It is sensitive to volume, pitch, pacing, and inflection.	**Eye:** The eye creates a sense of exclusion and distance. Sight objectifies the word and is inherently discriminating. It can view only objects that pass in front of it. The eye is silent and distant from emotions.	**Nervous system:** The engagement of the ear and the detachment of the eye create passivity. The brain generates beta waves while watching television. The same waves generated while asleep. Television's continuous flow of stimulation shuts down the analytical side of the brain, bypassing cognition.[11]	**Touch-mind:** The ultimate instruments of manipulation are the mind (interiors) and one's fingers (exteriors). As we endlessly reconfigure and rearrange, we become active participants in a changing world.[12]
Sense of identity	**Tribal village:** The person is a composite of the community. Interaction is restricted to a small population. Impartation comes from a core of intimate relationships. Tradition and mentoring develop character.	**Independent individual:** Concepts and principles inform character. We come in contact with a wider range of individuals through the thoughts and ideas of teachers and through books from around the world. Input is more formal and abstract.	**Crowded stranger:** Image and impressions inform character in a fluid ephemeral world. We interact with an even wider range of people through television and radio. These unattached and often unselected sources aim at a broad audience. The individual	**Cybersoul or anonymous intimacy:** Individuals design separate identities for different roles and contexts. Identity comes from the multitude of interactions from around the globe. We can be a member of numerous communities and experiment

	with numerous identities. In one sense individuals will be able to create their identities. In another sense they will have the greatest difficulty dealing with their essential human nature.	as spectator participates vicariously. Image and impressions weigh more than character in a fluid ephemeral world.	**Flow logic:**[14] Thought is a process that flows like water, leading to many possible outcomes.[15] Conclusions are not fixed and will change, and the results can take quantum leaps. Post-Newtonian physics postulated a universe that defies the clean and orderly process of logic. Quantum physics deals with the unpredictable microuniverse. Relativity calculates the uncertainty of the macrouniverse. Now the answer to any logical question is, "It depends." *(continued)*	**Systems thinking:**[16] Understanding how the parts of a particular system interrelate and how the system works over time leads to determining probable outcomes. Reality is complex and interconnected. Individual events appear random. Instead of a causal chain, multiple potential outcomes are measured by probability. Once the system is understood, it creates a context for anticipating behavior within the system. This can be applied to previously *(continued)*
Reasoning process	**Dialectic:** Open-ended form of question and answer. Dialectics does not aim for a fixed conclusion but attempts to reach equilibrium between two juxtaposed concepts. Dialectics achieves understanding through open inquiry and through a process of questions. Every answer forms the basis of a question, which then creates another question, and so forth. This method of reasoning, common in preliterate cultures means investigation by dialogue. Socrates used this style of inquiry, as did the *(continued)*	**Logic:** Linear thought arrives at an either-or conclusion. Logic grew out of the sequential characteristics of the alphabet. Writing is a process of assembling letters into words and words into sentences. Writing allows one to develop a thought one step at a time. It is easier, for example, to write in sequential thoughts of conversation. Logic (and writing) reaches its destination with greater efficiency than open-ended conversation, and logic offers closure.		

THE COMPLETE MILLENNIUM MATRIX *(continued)*

	Oral	Print	Broadcast	Digital
HOW WE KNOW	**Whole**	**Parts**	**Fragments**	**System**
Reasoning process *(continued)*	prophets and Jesus.[13] The Beatitudes is one example of developing a dialectic tension.		Context and bias are now part of the equation. Results often mirror expectations.	unpredictable arenas such as the weather, the stock market, global negotiations, relationships, and so on. Fractals are the computer methodology that extrapolates these conclusions.
Lens of perception	**Revelation:** Understanding comes through revelation, direct experience, and knowledge handed down over generations.	**Law of identity:** Understanding begins by recognizing the objective reality of a thing. Aristotle's law of identity postulates that "All that is, is" (A is A).	**Uncertainty principle:** Understanding reflects the unique and intimate interplay between the observed and the observer and is no longer considered fixed.[17]	**Chaos theory:** Understanding reflects the fact that reality is fluid, highly complex, and interconnected. It behaves as a system rather than as discrete events and is understandable by means of general patterns.[18]
Worldview	**Theocentric:** Circles of life, centering on God. The world operates as an interconnected whole, as extension of heaven.	**Newtonian:** Cause and effect. The world operates by discernable universal laws.	**Einsteinian:** Matter and time are interrelated. Matter transforms into pure energy, and time slows as matter and energy achieve the speed of light. The world is not objectively discernable.	**Bohmian:** The subatomic world is not subject to indeterminism and chance. There is an objective reality that can be calculated but not witnessed.[19]

	Process-centered	Content-centered	Experience-centered	Context-centered
Learning	Learning is a preparatory process, and the skills of learning and inquiry are often the focus of the teacher and his or her student(s). The search for truth and understanding comes by sitting at the feet of a master or guru. Jesus said, "I am the way and the truth and the life" John 14:6 (NIV).	The orientation is toward standardized learning. Students are batched according to age or learning level. The material is taught consistently to all, and students work to achieve tangible milestones. Exceptional students or students with special needs are batched according to their category of need. The primary goal is consistency and continuity. Learning shifts toward texts and learning abstract principles and concepts. Teachers focus on the structure and discipline of learning.	The focus is on individual students and their unique needs. This creates a proliferation of curriculum and services to address those needs. Text learning is supplemented with movies and videos. Group presentations, participation, and life experience are often factored in.	Teachers create a collaborative learning community. The collective experience takes priority over individual and private needs. The learning collective community works hard to meet individual needs.

(continued)

	Oral	Print	Broadcast	Digital
	Whole	**Parts**	**Fragments**	**System**
HOW WE KNOW				
Collective memory	**Bard:** Play, recitation, family, elders, and genealogy provide continuity with the past.	**Book:** History, indexing, encyclopedias, dictionaries, catalogs, museums, schools, and organizations help preserve the past.	**Documentary:** Excerpts from newspapers, magazines, television programs, news, audiotape, and videotape help viewers research and relive the past.	**Database:** Networking, user groups, FAQs (frequently asked questions) search engines, and databases help to examine the past and model it toward the future.
	Tribe	**Nation**	**Region**	**Planet**
HOW WE LIVE TOGETHER				
Authority or leadership	**Divine or power:** The leader's authority stems from an outside source, the power of the original source of delegation or control—divine, delegated, hereditary, or raw force. The leader's focus is twofold: to maintain control and to govern.	**Credibility or control:** The leader's authority stems from personal capabilities, experience, or past performance. The leader's focus is on achieving the goals of the organization and execute its operations efficiently.	**Relevancy or influence:** The leader's authority stems from the ability to meaningfully connect to the constituency. The leader's focus is on harnessing the potential of the organization by rallying constituents around central principles, a mission or a theme, and creating an identity distinct from its competition (branding).	**Resonancy or catalyst:** The leader's authority stems from the ability to create a context for meaning, purposeful work, and community. The leader can provide a clear understanding of current conditions, opportunities, and challenges and facilitate a collaborative response.

Influence	**Positional:** A person's position in the divine order of things establishes his or her influence.	**Credentials:** A person's training and social, political, and education credentials establishes that person's influence.	**Impression:** A person's rapport with others, in combination with achievements, establishes that person's influence.	**Connection:** A person's resource and relational network establishes that person's influence.
Commitment or contract	**Covenant:** Sacred, vested with blessings and curses. A union of two individuals. The connection between speech and being is reflected by people giving and relying on one another's word as the basis for commitments. One's word is one's bond.	**Vows:** Solemn, vested with duties and obligations. A partnership of two individuals. The disconnection of the content from the messenger brings a shift to written contracts as the basis of commitment.	**Promises:** Serious, vested with promised intentions, benefits, and role definition. An experiment between two or more individuals. Litigation becomes the necessary remedy to resolve the inherent discrepancies between written contracts and actual circumstances. Conflict and change replace order and stability, reflecting the continued disconnection between the content and the messengers.	**Agreement:** Pragmatic, tailored, and defined to meet specific mutually agreed-to goals and interests. May or may not define a time duration. The bond of attachment revolves around a tight inner circle of trusted relationships. Those so bound form a microcommunity and private think tank. This creates a virtuous cycle reinforcing trusted bonds. Once trust is broken, the microcommunity dissolves without a trail or a trace.

(continued)

	Oral	Print	Broadcast	Digital
	Tribe	**Nation**	**Region**	**Planet**
HOW WE LIVE TOGETHER				
Social dynamic	**Cohesive:** Reinforcing the whole.	**Progressive:** Moving forward toward a collective destination or goal.	**Centrifugal:** Moving away from the center and searching for the fringes.	**Centripetal:** Searching for a center or multiple centers and reconnecting those centers.
Ethics	**Moral view:** The mystical laws of reciprocity.	**Ethical view:** The logic and universal laws of relational imperatives.	**Practical view:** The path that benefits the most and harms the least.	**Reciprocal view:** What goes around comes around—with lightning speed and through multiple sources.
What we value	**The good:** Plato and Paul: all things in moderation. Morality is the harmony of the whole.	**The right:** Aristotle and natural law. We act and behave out the inherent laws of what is right.	**The useful:** Hume's pragmatic ethics. The good is a calculus of what benefits the greater population. The value chain of self-help to self-fulfillment to narcissism is tightly linked.	**The significant:** The brave new reality of competing micro-worlds and values will create a search for intimate connection and lasting value.
Community connections	**Tradition:** Elders, tradition, and genealogy provide continuity to the past. The blood connection to society and lack of mobility act as social anchors.	**Creeds:** Creeds, doctrines, constitutions, and law form the anchors that hold society together. These call forth allegiance to a set of ideals that are worth banding together for.	**Issues and interests:** Issues, problems, and events are the center, holding people together in debate. The term *special interest group* is a metaphor for the current anchor.	**Questions:** Searching draws people together into new configurations. Fluid networks of mutual interest take the place of rigid and polarized special interest groups.

HOW WE SEE BEAUTY

	Wholeness	Proportion	Deconstruction	Innovation
Sacred architecture	**Ornate:** A physical expression of the heavenly realm. Designed to evoke awe and reestablish one's place in the universe. The building is part of the story.	**Rational:** Designed with a conscious attempt to focus on the function of preaching the word. Only primary symbols like the cross are used as a remembrance. The building is not the focus. The building form follows its function.	**Promotional:** Designed as theater. It creates an audience-performer relationship. The building is the drawing card. Building design does not follow any unified criteria except to reflect the personality of the congregation.	**Experimental or eclectic:** A variety of designs to fit the community. Common features include modular flexibility, multiuse capability, smart facilities,[20] low overhead.
Art	**Symbolic:** Art is a means of interpreting the meaning of life and the sacred. The mystical union between heaven and earth can only be portrayed symbolically. Intricate and disciplined symbolic language is developed to reveal the multidimensional reality behind the stories and characters of faith and lore.	**Perspective:** Art seeks to become visually true or accurate. Focus is on how the person fits into the landscape. Art is also expressed from the artist's perspective. The artist takes center stage, whereas the symbolic language of early art removed the vantage point in order to portray the mystical reality of the story.	**Conceptual or process:** The artist moves away from a focus on content to a focus on process, approach, and medium. Deconstruction of familiar expressions (as seen in cubism) and exploration of irrational patterns of chance (as in Jackson Pollock's work) and the subconscious (as in surrealism) are another focus.	**Interactive-participative:** The observer's intimacy with the message is of key importance to the artist. The observer must be drawn into the experience and own the artist's perspective through the participation. Participation drives the medium more than content or emotion. The line between artist and observer blurs.

(continued)

	Oral	Print	Broadcast	Digital
	Wholeness	**Proportion**	**Deconstruction**	**Innovation**
HOW WE SEE BEAUTY				
Art *(continued)*				Art within a digital medium is completely malleable. The artist might become more of a facilitator of real-time experiments in altered perspectives stimulated by the content and the observer's unique response.[21]
Sacred music	**Chant:** Single melodic line (monophonic). Simple songs originally built around Scripture singing, creating a mystical quality. The practice of chant has a psychologically integrating quality and a collectively unifying dynamic. Instruments were viewed as distractions.	**Hymn:** Complex melodies and harmonies (polyphonic) aided by a printed system of writing music. Hymns communicated complex truths of the faith and were aided by large choirs and musical instruments. Many hymns tell grand stories of cosmic or personal struggle that is overcome by Christ's victory.	**Song:** Simplified melodies and harmonies with more complex rhythms. Amplification and numerous electronic instruments aid and shape this style of music. Songs express more relational than doctrinal subject material. This music is often presented in a contemporary concert style and allows audience participation.	**Contextual composition:** Music prompted by the occasion instead of prior programming, with many different styles fused together. Audience-prompted worship, jam sessions, praise concerts; formal hymns are brought together and aided by technology. Polyphonic rhythms

characterize some of the new influences in more mystical worship.

The ability to select and remix different styles of music during the actual service allows congregations to use established meaningful music and tailor it for the worship moment.

The multisensory capabilities allow altered-state worship, shifting the emotional context to enhance or stay consistent with a theme.

Interactive: A divergent path of exploration with convergent means of compressing the content into an interactive. multisensory result.

Approach	**Holistic:** Views the depiction as an interconnected whole.	**Framed:** Views the depiction as an observer with a framed point of reference.	**Existential:** Portrays the depiction through an internal and subjective interpretation.

(continued)

115

	Oral	Print	Broadcast	Digital
	Essentials	**Goods**	**Services**	**Experiences**
HOW WE WORK AND TRADE				
Manager	**Steward:** *Oikos*—economics—managing the household. A steward acts as a caretaker for the entire household. These goods are an extension of the owner both to those who work in the household and to the community.	**Manager:** Command and control, division of labor, vertical integration (owning all of the resources and means of production instead of outsourcing), economies of scale and hierarchical. Theory X (the management premise that people need to be structured and tightly supervised in order to be effective) describes a management approach that characterizes the impersonal application of management techniques, viewing the organization as a living machine.	**Leader:** Mission, empowerment, profit centers, outsourcing, Theory Y (the management premise that people want to do a good job and need positive motivation) is developed as an evolutionary step that recognizes the effects of a more educated workforce and the beginning shifts toward an information-driven economy. The focus is on how to release the potential of individual workers as opposed to how best to control them.	**Interweaver:** Grass roots, roving leadership, networks, virtual teams, and virtual corporations. Theory Z (the management premise that people work best in teams with shared input and responsibilities), introduced in the 1980s, recognizes the complex nature of information, work, and the power of working collectively in teams. Management takes on a less definable structure and behaves more like a web of collaboration.

Mechanism of wealth	**Land:** Acquiring land and developing its use is the common foundation for wealth.	**Capital and manufacturing:** The focus on wealth acquisition centers on the use of capital to supply goods and services through	**Distribution and debt:** These are the tools for accelerating growth. The shifting tastes of a culture shaped by broadcast create opportunities for companies that can quickly respond to those tastes. This shifts the focus toward more efficient means of distribution. Speed to market also creates the need to leverage resources through debt.	**Creativity and community:** The intellectual tools of the digital medium allow individuals to create solutions that once took vast corporate resources. The intellectual content of products is now more valuable than the material itself. This creates volatile markets. Building a loyal and interactive following is the key to building long-term wealth.
Metaphor of work	**Farm:** Focus is the land. The goal is to grow the crop. The farmer needs consistency and the ability to deal with circumstances as they come. The outcome cannot be controlled. Harvest is the reward.	**Factory:** To reduce things and labor to their simplest components along with a logical process of assembly. More output with lower costs is the goal. Productivity is the reward.	**Service:** Use information about consumers to make products they want or create demand. This shifts the focus to collecting and using information in the design, production, and delivery of goods and services.	**Federation:** Work is organized around federations of common interests. In this structure the consumer and producer collaborate on the production and delivery of goods.

(continued)

THE COMPLETE MILLENNIUM MATRIX *(continued)*

	Oral	Print	Broadcast	Digital
	Essentials	Goods	Services	Experiences
HOW WE WORK AND TRADE				
Value	**Reliability:** There is value in what is tried and true.	**Productivity:** Input over output equals productivity. Break work down into its smallest tasks and focus effort to accomplish each task as quickly as possible.	**Quality:** The process and the whole are important. Lower cost and improved performance are not contradictory.	**Creativity:** Interactive relationship between the consumer and producer.
Production	**Meet need:** People take what they get.	**Improve condition:** People take what they need.	**Create want:** People take what they want.	**Create fulfillment:** People design what they want.
Medium of exchange	**Barter and trade:** Relationship, the ethic of reciprocity, and one-on-one valuations.	**Currency:** A rational means of standardizing valuation and providing a flexible, efficient means of exchange.	**Credit:** Accelerates the cycle of transactions. Allows for local and global transactions to occur with equal ease	**Techno-barter:** Different mediums of exchange—forums like eBay, standardization of the euro, frequent-user currency, affinity programs, a rise in local and traveling farmer and craft markets.

CHAPTER 5

The Church in Transition

Navigating Changing Worldviews

> We are, at this very moment, passing through a change of age.
> Beneath a change of age lies a change of thought.
> —Pierre Teilhard de Chardin, *The Phenomenon of Man*

A few years ago, I sat next to an executive from a leading ad agency on a flight from Minneapolis to Seattle. Wearing beat-up jeans, fashionably shaggy hair, an earring, and slinging a backpack, he plopped down next to me. I didn't think I would have much in common with this kid, but we ended up having a fascinating conversation about global realignments. He was on his way to meet with Nike, his client, about a worldwide campaign. Its studies showed that a teenager in Beijing would soon have more in common with a teenager in Los Angeles than with her own parents. Nike recognized this as a major cultural realignment and synthesis of youth culture.

By their very nature, digital communications ignore the old boundaries of time, space, distance, age, nations, ethnicity, organization, and belief—the retaining walls of previous eras. A Web site created in Manhattan is as easily accessible to a Sherpa sitting in the Internet café fifteen thousand feet up the slopes of Mt. Everest as it is to anyone with Internet access—a student in a Berkeley classroom, a factory worker in Warsaw, a salaried employee in Tokyo, or to you in your home and me in mine.

Old boundaries also represent the paradigms of our understanding and the institutions we erected to project those understandings. Liturgical, Reformation, and celebration institutions represent separations based on ideas, forms, and eras. These separations no longer fit. They cannot hold what digital communications represents: the ability to permeate and penetrate all of the old boundaries, linking what was formerly separate.[1]

We Are Strangers in a Strange World

> The emergence of a new theory is generated by the persistent failure of the puzzles of normal science to be solved. . . . Failure of existing rules is the prelude to a search for new ones. These failures can be brought about by observed discrepancies between theory and fact or changes in social/cultural climates.
>
> —Thomas Kuhn, *The Structure of Scientific Revolutions*

Digital interactive communications represent the revolutionizing force reshaping our lives and worldview. The speed and interconnected nature of digital communications corrects the direction of drift of our old paradigms. For example, the suburban template, which came into being after World War II, reflects the broadcast culture: bedroom communities provide cookie-cutter homes in which families can disappear from their neighbors to enjoy their fenced-in privacy, watch television, and eat frozen dinners. The ubiquitous and impersonal one-size-fits-all big-box stores, malls, and health maintenance organizations developed to serve this faceless population. New sensibilities are rising. The connected nature of digital communications has already created a shift back to community: to more open and connected neighborhoods, town centers, and urban revitalization, as well as the smaller, more human-sized services that go along with them.

A similar phenomenon has happened in the church: to get the most church to the most people, we have created what we might call a spiritual delivery system (not unlike other institutionalized delivery systems such as education, health care, our judicial system and government) so that our congregations can grow faster and deliver care more efficiently. For example, Willow Creek Community Church became one of the first churches to provide a spiritual experience familiar to a broadcast generation and consequently one of the model mega-churches in the United States. It began as a youth church meeting at the shuttered Willow Creek movie theater in Palatine, Illinois. Willow Creek's success has provided a blueprint for countless churches adopting a main-event format within a veritable spiritual mall of activity and services. Willow Creek has ministries for those with trade skills, for singles, for those who have a postmodern interest, for creative arts, and for groundskeeping, as well as recreation, a call center just to help people find out who to contact, counseling, and several pages of special interests.[2]

Although some segments of the church try to model the mega-mall approach to church growth, many are finding a need to quickly develop new strategies. Rapid member turnover and staff burnout within many such churches keeps them forever having to replenish their congregations and leadership core. We are beginning to realize that much of our churches' emphasis on growth has produced the spiritual cousin of suburban tract homes, strip mining, and fast-food franchising. Unfortunately, many hungry churches are still buying into the fast-growth premise and promise without fully understanding the side effects.

When the dust settles, we may find that instead of extending the adoption of Christ, we've created in many cases a clumsy spiritual foster-care system. Instead of finding vital and lasting relationships they journey through a series of classes and casual acquaintances. The successful growth of this model for society and the church have come with a price: a lack of relational cohesion. That in turn has left us with a social and spiritual generation of broken families and missing parents. These costs are the hidden flip side to broadcast currencies of communication. The first step toward restoring wholeness and moving forward is to understand that each medium offers two sides. Unless we counterbalance the expansive nature within any medium, it too will create a toxic backwash.

Once We Were Blind

Why do we hold on to ideas and beliefs that aren't so? Call these blind spots, paradigms, mind-sets, or anchors—they all represent deeply rooted human nature. Even Jesus' inner circle didn't see who Jesus was and what he was really doing because they held on to old ideas about the Messiah. They show us that we can live with the potent incarnation of reality and completely miss what is going on.

One solution to our myopia is to recognize our attachments and repent. If we can, and then reenter our previous domain as outsiders looking in, we will be able to see the temporal paradigms of rational rigidness and the spiritual narcissism we gave ourselves to and that hold others. The first step is to achieve a renewed mind to see the unchallenged effect of our dominant media.

The second is to rediscover original thinking. If we are going to transcend our current condition or address our many crises, it will not be with the same approaches and thinking that brought these about. That is one reason this book does not offer trend analysis, how-to recipes, or seven easy steps to freedom. We need to look at our communication media the way artists look at their raw materials.

An artist, for example, knows that oils on canvas create a different experience than watercolors on paper, even if the subject of both paintings is the same. Master artists select the medium that best conveys the message and impression they want to create: a sculpture allows the viewer to see a subject from many angles; a performance piece brings the viewer into the work of art.

Art is always a collaboration between the artist and the medium. Some artists become captives to the medium. Some can achieve only a proficient level of imitation. The masters, however, are able to transcend the medium and bring truth to life before our eyes. Like master artists, we need to understand how the new medium behaves so that we can use it with purpose and precision, empowered to communicate the word of God, penetrating through the techniques to touch a transcendent essence.

The church has periodically collaborated with God's paintbrush to transcend the current context and bring an essential truth to life before the world's eyes. The church has the ability to provide a fresh, creative, and original expression of what community, society, and culture can be like. First, however, it must free itself from captivity to historical, doctrinal, sectarian, and cultural biases. If we can achieve that release, then we can explore the dimensions of original thinking and culture. That original thinking will certainly include experimenting with past mediums of expression and finding new expressions that are more than a simple patchwork of old and current.

As Matthew tells us (13:53, NIV), "He said to them, 'Therefore every teacher of the law who has been instructed about the kingdom of heaven is like the owner of a house who brings out of his storeroom new treasures as well as old." As the digital era dawns, the church will begin to master the new medium. We will develop new skills that enable us to think in multiple media, work collaboratively, organize as distributed networks, affiliate with diverse individuals of common interest, think with both sides of the brain, and define our communities more loosely but also more deliberately as intentional communities.

Emerging Skills of the Digital Age

At the beginning of any new enterprise, we tend to see the potential for good, and this book is making a case for the positive nature of the revolutionary changes the reign of digital communications will bring. As with just about anything in life, I have faith that the downside of digital will emerge in time—to be replaced by another revolutionary and evolutionary worldview. For now, however, here are just some of the skills I see coming into play, skills we can use to build and inform the new church we are already in the process of creating.

Individual Trends

Increasingly, we will learn to use the power of both left-brain and right-brain thinking. Whether this is an outgrowth of new learning contexts in more flexible institutions or an influence on those new institutions, this new kind of multipowered thinking will free us from a one-size-fits-all universe.

As a result of this mind shift, we will move from mastering content—names, dates, equations—to mastering context. Just as the calculator freed us from calculating endless math problems by hand, technology will provide the tools of analysis that allow individuals to bypass the drudgery of technical details and develop the skills for recontextual-izing information, concepts, and things into new forms.

As the new rules of integration and interaction become com-monplace, we will naturally reintegrate our personal lives with our community and business lives. We are going to have more tools and opportunities to work outside the office, to get in contact with the peo-ple we need anywhere and anytime, to structure the way we work or learn around our needs and schedules, to better merge our interests into vocations, and to reduce nomadic mandates in order to climb the cor-porate ladder. (We will look more deeply at community in Chapter Seven.)

Leadership Trends

Leaders too will benefit from the new sense of community, becoming more accessible and connected to their flock. They will become more significant to fewer people instead of a peripheral influence to many. They will become more involved with the congregation's culture, not just its mission and programs.

Leaders will also become more influential by becoming less vis-ible. Smaller, more intimate networks provide the new structure within a digital environment. Cohesive networks take on a life of their own and can grow in dramatic fashion. Growth becomes the natural by-product, not the desired end.

An "impartational" style of leadership based on mutual trust will replace today's top-down, hierarchical leadership styles. This is such an important trend—one we can see happening right now—that it is the subject of the next chapter.

Church Trends

Large and rigid organizations (some denominations and overgrown congregations) will break down. Information and change are moving too fast and are too complex for such organizations to keep up with. They will have to spend a disproportionate amount of resources on repair and maintenance instead of health and maturity. At the same time, walls and barriers between neighboring churches will dissolve as theological differences between churches continue to decrease. Hopefully, as they discover what they have in common, practical differences will become the bridges to future collaboration.

Church traditions, styles, structures, and community will undergo a major convergence. The Communion of Evangelical Episcopal Churches, for example, combines a liturgical ceremony with Reformed theology and contemporary worship.[3] Organizations like Vision New England create an umbrella for more than eighteen denominations and close to four hundred churches to interact and share resources.[4] Interaction is the first step toward collaboration, and collaboration leads to integration. These are simply forerunners of more to come.

Franchise models for growth will give way to a looser network or federation structure. Networks reflect a key organizational model for the future. They allow groups to better integrate into their local context and to align with other groups with similar interests.

Spiritual orphans will find adoption. As we have seen, churches have become very efficient on the acquisition or growth side of the equation.[5] The shift to tighter relationships in a smaller circle will allow the extended-family ethic to reemerge. In the same vein, we will also see a shift from organizations using people to fulfill their mission for mutual benefit to people using organizations to fulfill their missions for mutual benefit.

As a natural outgrowth of community, our overbuilt mega-organizations will evolve into community centers. Enlightened organizations will recognize the greater impact they can have by opening their doors to the neighboring community, including other churches. Once they have overcome parochial obstacles, these organizations can become the center of community life, strengthening outlying churches with training, resources, and facilities.

Many churches will shed their buildings in order to reinhabit their neighborhoods, turning to grassroots strategies to reach an emerging population that feels that smaller-scale gatherings are more authentic. As a result, the "invisible Christians" in your neighborhood will become visible and vital to your life and mission.

The recontextualizing nature of digital sensibilities will provide the great benefit of reintroducing some of our significant traditions and practices back into our worship lives. Ancient sensibilities once expressed in ritual will find new power for strongly integrated faith communities. The digital world of interconnectedness provides a new context for using the calendar and the clock to create a new sense of synchronicity with one another. Our digital calendar reminders will aid us in pausing, remembering, and connecting to others. For example, instead of simply having good intentions to rediscover and celebrate Advent, we can be prompted by our digital calendars, which can provide instant access to the background we need to understand the celebration. Our experience and questions can then be linked to others forming a virtual communal celebration of faith. These reminders, aids, and shared dialogue provide a new opportunity for reclaiming our spiritual past. Digital tools to simulate past and future create unlimited prospects for reinterpreting our faith traditions, teachings, and expressions.

We will see a convergence of church, community, commerce, and charity. Greater ecclesiastical integration will extend toward more integration with the community and then further into commerce, providing the latticework for grassroots governance.[6] Reverend Lee Earl offers an example of the positive convergence of church, community, commerce, and charity. A Harvard study credited 12th Street Baptist Church in Detroit with reducing neighborhood crime more than 37 percent over three years. Jammin Java, a unique Christian coffee house and entertainment venue, offers another example of bringing churches together through a business serving the local community. There are certainly others, and we are just seeing the beginning of this development.[7]

"We are at that very point in time when a 400-year-old age is dying and another is struggling to be born—a shifting of culture, science, society, and institutions enormously greater than the world has ever experienced."

We will see a renewed understanding of morality, the by-product of connected relationships, and communities of purpose. I need to emphasize the words *renewed understanding*. My reference to morality is not code language for revisiting a 1950s caricature. It has to do with a new awareness of our interconnected dependency and the reciprocity that grows from this kind of awareness. We will rediscover the Golden Rule, as if for the first time.

Spiritual Hungers

> We are at that very point in time when a 400-year-old age is dying and another is struggling to be born—a shifting of culture, science, society, and institutions enormously greater than the world has ever experienced. Ahead, the possibility of the regeneration of individuality, liberty, community, and ethics such as the world has never known, and a harmony with nature, with one another, and with the divine intelligence such as the world has never dreamed.
>
> —Dee Hock, *The Trillion-Dollar Vision of Dee Hock*

It all sounds great, doesn't it? But that doesn't change the landscape we are walking through right now. Recently, I heard an audio recording by New Age author Jean Houston, in which she described an encounter with a Japanese businessman. The man told her that his country conducted the largest poll in its history, asking what the population thought Japan's biggest challenge is. The response of one million citizens was that Japan is threatened by "spiritual aridity," spiritual dryness.[8] The shallow pursuit of material success, the erosion of extended family and community, and the hard and rapid pace of life have left the cultural and psychic landscape as dry and inhospitable as the desert.

The parallels between Japan's emerging crisis and our own crisis in the United States should grab our attention. One difference between that nation's awareness and ours is that the Japanese clearly see the despair of their condition, whereas we have erected a kind of Disney World facade to distract us from our own desert.[9] Still, our spiritual hungers are rising in response to the diminishing capacities of our current worldview and the promise of a land flowing with the milk and honey of deep relational connection and the kind of spiritual community that develops from these relationships.

What spiritual hungers propel us to strike out through the wilderness in search of spiritual sustenance?

The Hunger for Homegrown Prophets

The 1960s provided us with an incredible era of prophets both secular and religious. Bob Dylan ranks among the top social prophets of that era. Rachel Carson's book *Silent Spring*, among the first to warn the general public about environmental destruction, fundamentally changed the world debate on environmentalism.[10] Francis Schaeffer woke the sleeping church to deal positively with the cultural shift instead of retreating and retrenching.[11] Many prophetic voices cut across the conventional thinking of the church, business, psychology, education, health care, media, and society. All of these voices helped us to see.

The tool of the prophet-poet is the power of the metaphor. That power comes from tapping into the deeper archetypes for our times. Pastors and teachers offer analysis and application, but the prophet can cut through entrenched thinking like a two-edged sword. We are hungry for poets who are able to find metaphors that unite deep, unvarnished earthly realities with timely and timeless wisdom that frees our minds to wonder.

In order to make the transition to the new era successfully, we need new prophets. There are new voices, equally penetrating for the current time, products of our broadcast generation, pointing outward and beyond: U2's Bono, Anne Lamott, George Gilder, and Christopher Locke[12] represent just a few of the voices challenging our current assumptions with new ideas and examples of how we might live. But the finest prophets are often anonymous, serving people. I suspect some of them may already be right here, hiding in plain sight just inside the conventionally unconventional uniforms of contemporary worship leaders.

The Hunger to Make a Real Difference

People who work in large, anonymous organizations often express frustration about wasted effort and dollars—the comic strip *Dilbert* is based on this unfortunate truth. We want our jobs to help us support ourselves and our families, but we also want to feel that we are effective—that we make a difference.

We join causes, trumpet urgent issues, spend energy, and empty our pockets to bring about positive social change; but we still feel impotent to fill a black hole of needs and problems. In frustration, on talk shows, and in the streets, we have joined the stone-throwing mobs of the past, expressing our religious indignation at schools, the government, feminists, liberals, secular humanists, Hollywood, media bias, and every new offense that confronts our religious sensibilities. But when we get caught up in a "holy" mob hysteria, we neglect to look at our own condition. The better choice is to battle against the rigid mind-sets, fears, and hatreds in our own backyards. We must first look to ourselves.

How can we make a difference at home, to ourselves, our families, our neighbors? The first step is to cease trying to protect and expand our material, social, and political positions. When we focus on things like our tax status and school vouchers, we are not giving those who are sincerely looking for answers a real reason to take us seriously. In the convergent church, we must hope that our prophets will look much more like Bono or Mother Teresa than political lobbyists.

The Hunger for Authenticity

Recently, I had dinner with a true Gen-Xer named Brandon. At twenty-eight he is passionate, skeptical, and amazingly unencumbered by any overt agenda. Brandon told me that he and his friends have a finely tuned ear for authenticity—otherwise known as a "B.S. meter." He said he can tell in the first few moments whether a pastor or the congregation is "plastic" or not. Brandon has a not-so-delicate way of seeing through the image and the words. As we talked, I had an image of this generation like bloodhounds sniffing out the trail of reality.

He and I had a lively, intense three-hour discussion, at the end of which my new friend commented that my credibility had risen a few points. I was, of course, curious as to why. He said he appreciated the way I shared about God's work in my life, marriage, and with our adopted children. He appreciated that I listened and found some genuine connections. He said he was comfortable because I did not "hype" him by portraying an image of having my act together. He appreciated that I did not open the Bible in order to leverage my perspective. We talked friendship, not formulas, and we did not end with any agenda accomplished. He found the encounter unusual for "someone [my] age," concluding that he could sense "the scar of life" that my wife and I embraced.

Brandon also made a similar comment about our senior pastor. After telling me why our church is "lame" in some areas, he said the reason he can connect with the pastor is because he is "real" and has "paid some dues." In other words, there is some intangible characteristic that "the scar of life" creates; and the authenticity meter measures how much you rely on that scar in order to maintain a sense of perspective.

Authenticity derives its power out of a clear sense of identity. In his seminars Michael Vance, former dean of Disney University, author, and speaker on creative cultures, quotes a nun he once knew who said, "The more you are like yourself, the less you are like anyone else, which makes you unique."[13] Authentic cultures combine the qualities of reality (seeing things as they are) and authenticity (being who you really are) in order to connect with those unique qualities that define their identity. Once they grasp those qualities and harness them, these cultures quickly become beacon lights that attract others. When the church reclaims this wisdom, the world will come to its doors.

The Hunger for Mystery

For more than four hundred years, the world assumed certainty. The current era has been described as an age of uncertainty.[14] It's no wonder that we have a rising hunger for mystery, which wraps the unpredictable and inexplicable within an envelope of certainty.

Dee Hock, founder of Visa International, has coined the word *Chaordic* to describe the new reality of chaos working with order.[15] In the synthesizing spirit of the digital world, this concept fuses the underlying assumptions from print and broadcast eras.

Our culture's skills for describing and dealing with mystery are fairly rusty. The mystery for many will begin once we launch out from our safe, familiar, predictable surroundings and venture into the wilderness. Those individuals who are currently breaking out to search for the mystery of significance play a key role. As more transformed individuals return to tell their stories and give us a taste of what might be, the church can make the transition from success to significance.

The Hunger for Depth

Interactive technology creates an absorbing connection between medium and user. My children, who can sit in front of the television in a mesmerized stupor, have intense and often highly animated exchanges with our computer. Adults who spend any time at all surfing the Web sooner or later find something that compels them to search deeper and deeper. Digital media is reconditioning all of us to dig for bedrock, fundamental understandings, especially our youth.

Every day that someone finds a long-lost relative over the Internet, discovers a new business opportunity, completes a homework assignment, finds comfort chatting with a sympathetic soul, saves money on a transaction, discovers answers for a confounding medical condition, receives advice before a decision, listens to a long-forgotten archived soundtrack, views his or her neighborhood from a . . . satellite, the appetite for depth gets stimulated. I can see the new hunger for deeper understanding and experiences rising in my children and among my peers. In fact, all the hungers I have described so far point to an overriding hunger for depth.

Restoring depth is about reversing the fast pace not only of our outer lives but of our inner lives, which creates that drive for efficiency and all of its trappings. The relentless drive for efficiency has created our spiritual aridity.

A number of years ago, I heard a speaker use the phrase "the speed of going slow."[16] It sounds like a paradox, but it's not necessarily a new paradox. Jesus invited Martha to abide (Luke 10:41). The tortoise beat the hare. Will the drive to be first result in finishing last? Is the desire to lead less productive than the desire to serve? Will influential new leaders graduate with honors from prestigious MBA programs and seminaries, or will they arise from some other source? The answer to these questions lies in going deeper: in considering these issues with friends, neighbors, companies, congregations, elected officials, and beyond.

The Hunger for Deep Support

In the fragmented reality of most of our lives, we bounce between unconnected worlds—work, school, kids, activities, church, charity, community, neighborhood, home, and more. Each of these worlds has its own center of gravity, and each has the potential of taking on a life of its own. We are hungry for help in connecting these dots in a way that brings integration and synergy; for relationships that can guide us through the confusing maze of choices, obstacles, and specialties that come our way. I see this as a hunger for deep support.

In their book *The Support Economy*, Shoshana Zuboff and James Maxmin suggest that federations of support will become the new vehicle for people to reconnect the dots of their lives. They describe a job for individuals who will provide "deep support," connecting people to the help they need and remaining involved until the product, service, or support is completed. Instead of dealing with countless anonymous disconnected people through the course of a day, a person deals with one or a few advocates that he or she knows intimately, who work through a common federation to provide support.[17] This is a strikingly digital way of doing business and living our lives that may feed at least some of our hunger.

Building to Stay Afloat

These hungers clearly raise a multitude of implications for our current structure, practice, and thinking within the church. If you identify with any of these hungers or hear them expressed within your church, you are not alone. The need for new wineskins has never been greater. How can we create a new vessel for the Spirit in the coming digital age?

Perhaps the most fundamental lesson of the digital era is that we do not have to throw out everything we know and start again. The power of the digital era is in its ability to take the old and make it new again, to allow us to experience a variety of perspectives and ways of being. We can revisit and reintegrate the best of oral, print, and broadcast sensibilities so that they do not get pushed aside, as has happened during previous transitions. In fact, our survival and growth depend on learning skills that recontextualize all of these languages of perception.

In this time of crisis and confusion and uncertainty, when the forces of vertigo have knocked us off our feet, a historic opportunity is unfolding. We can let the dike burst, and surrender as the water rushes over us, or we can embrace the new paradigm along with the best of the old and actively participate in changing the world.

> The power of the digital era is in its ability to take the old and make it new again, to allow us to experience a variety of perspectives and ways of being.

The church rose to a similar challenge during the Reformation, and the results salted the cultural atmosphere for more than four hundred years.[18] Right now we have an opportunity to recapture the high ground and reframe the rules of engagement for the coming era. The power of the church does not lie in understanding the place and use of technology and media. And that's OK, because the key to changing the new era lies not in the technology but in the power of the relational metaphor of connection, one of the powers behind digital culture.

Remember my story about building oil tankers for the North Atlantic? That harsh and turbulent environment requires ships that can stand up to the forces of nature. If the church is to stay afloat in the seas of the digital culture, it will need to refit itself with at least eight criteria in mind.

- *Agility:* The church will need to be responsive to ever-changing conditions. That will require a light and loose infrastructure, tight relationships; decentralized decision making, and a nonhierarchical structure, such as a network or federation.
- *Transparency and authenticity:* Just as nothing can stay secret for long, given the speed and reach of information on the Internet, the church must clean out its dark corners and let its light shine inside and

out. The convergent church will encourage and allow congregants to be active participants in shaping the organization.

• *Cohesion and balance:* Our current organizations, often fragmented with programs and activities and torn by competing interests, cannot stay afloat for long. The emerging church will need to provide a means for individuals to combine commerce, community, charity, and church in ways that reinforce one another.

• *Resiliency and forgiveness:* When the church begins to focus on long-term implications rather than on short-term results, resources will not be overburdened. This will allow organizations to build up a margin of reserve that can weather turbulence and the inevitable contingencies of life.[19] Stewardship, in its root context, can then reemerge as a primary function of leadership.

• *Sustainability:* When growth is seen as a natural by-product of building "internal integrity" on an individual level and expanding outward to external integration,[20] the church will become sustainable. Our current model for growth, which attempts to work backward from disconnection to integration, is an unsustainable strategy in a culture of rapid and complex change. Information flow and extrapolation is another key source of sustainability; and networks and federations gain exponential value by their size, diversity, and commitment. The distributed power structure of networks[21] along with tightly aligned common interests provide resources, insight, involvement, and cohesion to accomplish ends that no single leader, committee, team, or board could achieve.

• *Open-endedness, embracing the possibility of change:* The church will need to remain open-ended in purpose, structure, facilities, and strategies, always embracing the possibility of change. Every dedicated resource or fixed concept represents an impediment to change. Although the church is unlikely to become completely free of impediments to change, most organizations are now so heavily invested in their current infrastructure, approaches, and ideas that they cannot afford even to consider major and sometimes minor changes in direction.

• *Accessibility:* People should be able to connect quickly and easily with what they need, when they need it—this goes for information as well as people. This level of accessibility will stem from the distributed power that members have. Providing member advocates to ensure that individuals find what they need and get the support they want is one way to facilitate this. These organizations will also provide an accessible asylum for spiritual orphans, those seeking refuge, or those who simply need help with a life issue.

• *Collaboration:* Finally, the church will need to be a collaboration of aligned interests. The collaborative structure provides the ethic for digital cultures. Right now most churches are not collaborative because of the inherent power structures. They can have collaborative moments and even collaborative projects; but without distributed power, there is no collaborative DNA. Collaboration is more than an interactive idea session or team-based initiative; it is a mind-set and a posture toward others. In Philippians 2:2–4 Paul sets a useful benchmark for developing a collaborative culture.

Seeing the Iceberg

> The church's leaders have Alzheimer's disease. We still love them. We remember and pass on their stories. But they're living in another world. They're totally clueless about the world that is actually out there. The problem is that they are captaining the ship.
>
> —Leonard Sweet, *Post-Modern Pilgrims*

Still, as the fixed gaze of the broadcast era begins to give way to the engaged and collaborative energy of digital convergence, many institutions find it difficult to adapt. Institutions that are locked into sequential motion (bureaucratic), reinforced by mass (big and slow), divided by function (fragmented), and leveraged with debt have no way to respond to fast-paced, complex, fluid, and unpredictable threats and conditions. As we move from one era to another, some of us may not make it.

Our institutions and churches seem to be like the Titanic:[22] heading blindly for the iceberg of the digital worldview, certain they can withstand the blow. So instead of thinking deeply about what kind of changes will help them move forward, many churches stay busily engaged in treating symptoms of low commitment, declining membership, or high churn—adding cutting-edge sound systems, revising their mission statements, getting politically active—without dealing with the deeper realities of a changing cultural terrain.

A similar lack of understanding is reflected in our nation's struggles to defend against new threats of terror. If you look through the frame of the Millennium Matrix, you will see the inertia of gigantic bureaucracies—entities rooted in linear thinking—compared to the agility of a loosely structured but highly aligned terrorist network empowered by digital communications. Not long ago I had a conversation with a division manager for a large defense contractor. His division specifically deals with this new form of war—called asymmetrical threats, of which the 9-11 attacks are a perfect example. Such acts, he said, have an impact far greater than the amount of effort required to carry them out. The men who hijacked the planes used to destroy the World Trade Center buildings used fairly unsophisticated means that resulted in tremendous physical, mental, and emotional damage; a restructuring of our federal government; a war in the Middle East; and a seemingly unending ripple effect of change.

Any organization confronted by similar asymmetrical challenges must face the great challenge of unlearning, dismantling, divesting, relearning, and moving forward. It's a difficult demand, especially for those who are locked into the prison of their own worldview and have grown to love it. Moving from captivity to freedom can be a confusing and disorienting road to travel, but the time has come to begin the journey.

The View Through the Millennium Matrix

The world and institutions we thought would stand forever are crashing down like the Berlin Wall. At the same time, a tremendous convergence of thought, desires, disciplines, organizations, and people is rushing toward us. This is the new digital paradigm, and it's not going away. Herein lies the challenge: we need a framework to guide us through the numerous trends and changes. As the water rushes over the dam, taking with it our past and current sources of stability, we are caught in a current with tremendous speed but no visible shoreline. We have more experience and more information than any previous generation in history but no context in which to channel it.

Any tool of communication— be it speech, writing, print, photographs, movies, telegraph, telephone, radio, television, or computer—also functions as a metaphor. The power of metaphor is one key to understanding how communication tools express and shape our reality. Once you expand and extend the inherent natures of oral, print, broadcast, and digital media, you begin to see how they created the worldviews that governed and will govern their time.

> The world and institutions we thought would stand forever are crashing down. At the same time, a tremendous convergence of thought, desires, disciplines, organizations, and people is rushing toward us.

When a new means of storing and distributing information gains dominance, it creates new paths for our minds to travel. Remember when we used to sit back and passively listen to the songs on an album in the order in which they were recorded? Today we take it for granted that we can change the order of songs on a CD to suit our taste. Further, we can take songs gathered from many sources—records, tapes, MP3 files grabbed from the Internet—and create the perfect mix CD that exists for no one but us and our friends to enjoy. This is a product of a new mind-set.

Communication Tools Become Worldviews

Each tool of communication favors some forms of expression over others. Conversations are intimate. Books promote structured thought and reflections. Television encourages action and story compression. Computers allow simulation, simultaneity, and interaction. Each medium has a built-in and unavoidable bias. And as tool-using children of the culture we were born into, we reflect that medium's bias. Understanding the shift from print and broadcast to digital requires understanding these tools as tools.

FOUR IMPORTANT POINTS ABOUT COMMUNICATIONS TOOLS

I meet many people who are afraid of the new technology and fear that it will control them. They typically don't see that their fear comes from their own dependence on an earlier era of technology. Technology is simply a tool and theoretically under our control. But technology is also like raising a tiger for a pet. It serves our interest while a cub but our attachments can cause us to forget its nature and power when it's grown. If we don't forget we can still manage the tiger. Here are four important points to remember about tools:

Tools gain their value and power by their specialization. Specialization is a subset of a broader principle of efficiency. Hammers pound nails; they don't drive screws.

Specialization works by strengthening and narrowing some capacities over others. Brain surgeons don't perform kidney operations.

When we use a tool, we narrow the universe of solutions. If all you have is a hammer, then every problem looks like a nail. Or as Einstein said, "No problem was ever solved by the same mind that created it."[23]

Tools begin as an aid, grow to provide an advantage, rise to compete with and defeat those with inferior means; if left unchecked, they take on a life of their own, eventually growing beyond our control. The story of Frankenstein's monster is the warning built into every tool.

When we rely on specific tools, we inevitably narrow the universe of solutions we address or even see. We have only recently discovered the world of right-brain thinking and begun to address the educational issues that conflict with a linear, structured curriculum oriented to the left brain. The same blind spots interfere with our vision when we attempt to apply our tools of Western democracy to other parts of the world.

What capacities have we traded off in moving from an oral to a print culture? What capacities have we traded off in moving from print to broadcast? What capacities are we likely to lose or gain as we move into a computer-based interactive culture? These questions take on a much greater meaning when society is in its present turbulent, undefined zone of transition.

A new medium always reveals the limitations of the previous medium—when people began watching television in the 1950s, the radio programs they used to enjoy listening to began to seem pretty one-dimensional. Soon an entire industry based on live radio broadcasts virtually disappeared. As we get used to playing interactive video on the computer, sitting back and watching whatever is offered on television seems similarly limited.

We are not yet fully integrated into an interactive culture—perhaps some of us never will be. We read books; we watch television; and not all of us are comfortable with computers, personal digital assistants, and cell phones that also allow the user to send text messages and snapshots and surf the Web. We are still self-conscious about using these technologies, and that self-consciousness is the antidote to their alluring power. Soon an entire generation will take these interactive technologies for granted. They will look at television in the same way that baby boomers looked at radio—as outmoded and old-fashioned. By the time digital media become fully integrated and ubiquitous in our lives, they will dictate the governing worldview.

Institutions will shift, decline, or be created to align with the new realities. Mergers in the financial industry provide a clear illustration of how once-separate fields are converging onto common platforms. Credit card issuers, insurance companies, mortgage brokers, security investment firms, commercial banks, and investment bankers deal with the same bits and bytes. That capability has removed the former walls of separation. The JP Morgans and the Citigroups of the world represent prototypes of future and even more radical convergence.

The new means of using our senses, along with new ways of ordering the world, effectively rewires our brains. We are becoming psychologically different from our predecessors. If you doubt me, ask yourself: How often to do you find yourself asking your child or grandchild to help you program the VCR or get your printer to work? And how easily do they perform these tasks?

Let's take it to a deeper level: the act of communicating reflects an extension not only of our being but of God's essence. So when we explore the tools of communication, we touch the core elements of our nature and God's.

We know the power and potential of communication—God set the standard when he spoke creation into existence. The hologram of God's nature is in his very breath, reflected in creation and within each human interaction. Co-union is the by-product of communication at its highest level.

But what happens when the character of that experience changes? What is the impact when Spirit, which was first mediated through voice, expresses itself through print, electromagnetic images, or a silicon-based binary code?

The changing technology of communication has also inevitably and fundamentally altered the character of the church. If you will take a brief detour with me through the Millennium Matrix, you will begin to see that the secret to the power of each tradition lies within the context of the communication era that gave it birth.

Right now jump over to the abridged matrix chart on page 225. Beginning with the row labeled Worship, work your way across the columns. Here's what you should see:

- The secret to the power of the liturgical tradition lies within the unified worldview of oral cultures.

- The secret to the power of the Reformed tradition lies within the rational worldview of print cultures.

- The secret to the power of the celebration tradition lies within the experiential worldview of broadcast culture.

- The secret to discovering the power of the emerging convergent church lies within connected interactive worldview of the digital medium.

Now work your way down the rows to find "Sense of identity," and read across the columns. You can see immediately that people who live in a particular communication epoch see themselves and their world very, very differently:

If you live in an oral culture, person-to-person contact is what counts and what is real. You identify with your community: you are one people, without question.

If you live in a print culture, you are what you read, and this may mean embodying different ideas at different times. You are free to wander through the thoughts of others. You see yourself as an individual, at once part of your community and apart from it.

If you live in a broadcast culture, the world streams through your living room, but you have the option of turning it off. You live in your own space and may identify not with your community but, for example, with a sports team, a generation, or your religious denomination.

If you live in a digital culture, you can be everywhere at once. You see yourself as part of the global village, a far-reaching network of humanity, connected to people you may not yet know.

Using the Millennium Matrix, we can—at least for a few moments—make time stand still so that we can take a good look at it. As a new paradigm rises to replace the previous one, old and once-important ways of thinking take on a marginal role in the vital decisions of our lives and the culture. Using the context that the Millennium Matrix provides, you can understand the inner workings of digital culture and how it will reshape our perceptions, identity, relationships, community, and society. You can also stroll through the matrix like a museum and see attributes that once reigned during their era but have either become endangered or receded beyond our current awareness.

PART 2

New Visions for a
New Millennium

> Nor do people put new wine into old wineskins, or else the wineskins break, the wine is spilled, and the wineskins are ruined. But they put the new wine into new wineskins, and both are preserved.
>
> —Matthew 9:17 (NIV)

Over the last few years, we have witnessed the first signs of the new wine's search for suitable new wineskins. It may be too early to tell precisely what form the newly emerging convergence church will fill with Spirit. For now, however, we can imagine a new structure that embraces the connected intimacy and simultaneity of the digital culture.

How will we change in the coming years? As we have seen, the digital paradigm—interactivity, connection, transparency—gives us some clues.

The final chapters in this book take a closer look at three fundamental aspects of the church in transition: a new kind of leadership, a vibrant and growing sense of community, and the revitalized organization and culture of the emerging convergence church that has the potential to restore the moral ecosystem of society. Ultimately, I hope the ideas in these chapters will help you begin to build a conceptual and practical bridge from your current worldview to the emerging interactive worldview.

CHAPTER 6

Trust Connections

Impartational Leadership

> And when he putteth forth his own sheep, he goeth before them, and the sheep follow him: for they know his voice.
>
> —John 10:4 (KJV)

One of my favorite companies has been Herman Miller, Inc., especially when Max DePree ran it. The company—whose designers created everything from the office cubicle to the ergonomic chair—revolutionized the workplace and achieved the highest levels of success. Much of this was due to the philosophy of Max DePree.[1] DePree is a great example of a leader who trusts. Even though his books were written more than a decade ago, and Herman Miller is a secular company, they provide a positive image of the kind of interactive and connected leadership philosophy to guide the church into a digital era.

In the 1950s the Herman Miller Corporation was one of the first to initiate employee participation, one of the first "green" companies, and one of the first companies to recognize the need to make the workplace fit the worker rather than the other way around. It invented ergonomic work seating, and in the mid-1970s the company introduced the first ergonomic chair. In the early 1990s it created what has become the most popular office chair in history, as well as one of the most recognized icons of status and success: the Aeron chair. More? The company's buildings harmonize with the semirural settings of Zeeland, Michigan, and the surrounding areas.[2] The company initiated the first professional facility management program at the University of Michigan, a program that eventually led to a degreed profession for facility managers and an international trade association.

Herman Miller offers a case study of what can happen when a culture tied to an inspired philosophy takes precedence over the bottom line. This was not a mission-driven company. It did not set out to accomplish any of the achievements it has been recognized for. Herman Miller has been a culture-driven company centered on relationships, community, and serving the needs of the marketplace. It is no coincidence that this kind of company emerged from the small Dutch Reformed farming towns of central Michigan, and it is a good model for any church.

Herman Miller did not manufacture its values or get them from a prestigious MBA program. The values that guided DePree and translated into the corporate culture came from his life and his inclusion of great minds and collaborators. This secular company actually uses the word *covenant* to describe the mutual level of commitment between employees and the company, and especially between the company and its designers. In this way it has been able to transform not only the industry it serves but also the way every corporation in the United States operates.

As DePree says in *Leadership Is an Art*: "The leader is the 'servant' of his followers in that he removes the obstacles that prevent them from doing their jobs. In short the true leader enables his or her followers to realize their full potential."[3] This seems like a pretty good goal for church leaders as well.

Leadership in the church today is suffering under the stress of shifting paradigms. The how-to books on church leadership, high levels of burnout, high rates of divorce, and a low assessment of personal fulfillment are symptoms of models that are hopelessly out of sync not only with the times but with the church's servant roots.

Many church leaders must live in the fishbowl of public observation and the competitive world of their peers. They are burdened with unprecedented financial pressures and frenetic and physically taxing schedules. They bring this internalized pressure home to their families and somehow try to transform themselves into normal human beings. Our current leadership models leave our leaders stuck at the top of the mountain without anyone to turn to and with only one way down—a long fall. It's no wonder so many pastoral families live on the ragged edge.

If this is a common condition for church leadership, what is it producing? What is behind the facade of most congregations? Many look and sound in far better condition than their hidden infrastructure belies. The growth and prosperity of the 1990s is one factor that blinds us. Staff and member turnover is another factor that delays dealing with an ever-weakening foundation. We feel safe because we know how to achieve the narrow results of greater member growth, more professional presentations, and programs to meet expanding demand. We are beginning to see the natural consequences of weak foundations, but these consequences will be more dramatic as the paradigm shifts to favor less massive, more connected and decentralized organizations.

What Kind of Leaders Do We Need?

> The presence of a gargantuan personal ego contributes significantly to the failure of companies. Charismatic leaders succeed admirably in achieving their personal ambitions, but they fall short when it comes to building and sustaining great companies.
>
> —Jim Collins, *From Good to Great*

During the 1960s and 1970s, business books like Peter Drucker's *Preparing Tomorrow's Business Leaders Today* began to make a distinction between management and leadership, revealing the new broadcast bias. Management was relegated to the domain of "doing things right," whereas leadership was elevated to the status of "doing the right things." Broadcast also heralded the age of empowerment, which meant greater autonomy and entrepreneurship (risk).[4] While print-based organizations became characterized by analysis paralysis, broadcast companies took action. These distinctions and many more like them became the major debate and revolution for business during the late 1970s through the

1990s. This is essentially the same debate that has ripped through the church and catapulted the growth of nondenominational churches and the seeker (or customer) movement.

Today we are abandoning the broadcast paradigm of leadership and looking for leaders who express connection rather than division. The partners in Graft, a young architectural firm in Los Angeles that exemplifies this new ethos, use the gardening metaphor of grafting to describe its working style. An article in *Forbes* explained: "Since 1998, [Graft] has combined materials, styles and even cultures that conventionally aren't thought to go together.

"'We aren't looking for a signature style,' says 35-year-old Thomas Willemeit, one of the firm's three partners. 'Our philosophy is to bring together as many interesting, different approaches and ideas as possible, then see what comes out of it.'"[5]

This ability to graft different relationships, backgrounds, and resources onto a strong core is what will also distinguish leaders from all disciplines. Control and celebrity are the fading banners of leadership. The new signs include a different group of C words: connect, coalesce, converge, collaborate, and commune.

The speed and complexity of the digital environment require depth and richness as a counterbalance. Print and broadcast dominance is waning because of the spiritual and relational aridity they've created and the attraction and power of the digital experience. The efficiency of our means has drained the inefficient reservoirs of relational complexity and community. It is further evidence that we are at a crossroads.

We have a rising hunger not only for leaders we trust but for leaders who lead by trust rather than by fear or coercion. Jim Collins, author of *Good to Great*, recently completed extensive research into the characteristics of leadership that produces lasting results, and his conclusions challenge our popular models of the iron-fisted leader (think General Patton) or the highly charismatic leader (like Bill Clinton). Abraham Lincoln embodies a third style of leader. Neither domineering nor endearing, he lost more than he won; but the traits he exhibited are similar to current business leaders who have led their companies to sustained preeminence—what Collins calls "Level 5" leaders: "Level 5 leaders are a study in duality; modest and willful, humble and fearless. To quickly grasp this concept, think of the United States President Abraham Lincoln . . . who never let his ego get in the way of his primary ambition for the larger cause of an enduring great nation."[6]

So why have the high-profile leaders so dominated our attention? Maybe because by nature we are attracted to people who make a big first impression. It might also have to do with the fact that these two distinct styles of leadership (the iron fist and the charismatic figure) also fit well within the paradigms of their respective media eras. There is no doubt that the print era favored commanding and forceful leaders who defined right from wrong and could show us the world in black and white: the Allied leaders of World War II, Churchill, and Franklin Delano Roosevelt all fit this model. The broadcast era favors leaders who can finesse and charm, like Clinton, and his predecessor John F. Kennedy.

> We have a rising hunger not only for leaders we trust but for leaders who lead by trust rather than by fear or coercion.

Print cultures, beginning with Reformation churches, shift away from the influence of the leader as a holy man and source of community life and to the leader as a provider of reliable rational methods and expertise. Print-based organizations naturally divide into functional units because print creates categorical and hierarchical thinking and organizations that reflect this mind-set.

With the rise of broadcast culture, the bias shifted to leaders with strong communication skills. These leaders rely on delivering motivating communication rather than directives. Broadcast-based organizations organize around a top leader—the center. Mission drives the corporate structure.

During the 1980s, in both corporations or churches, the mission became the customer—that is, the congregant. The customer had supposedly always been right, but this is very different from having the customer actually be the mission. Most of the religious books focusing on church growth and the need for change address exactly this gulf between the print and broadcast worldviews.[7]

The digital era is already shifting the emphasis against old uni-lateral approaches of print and broadcast's spin masters. Most of our cur-rent public leaders reflect the biases of the era they grew up in—some in print and a growing number shaped by broadcast. But new leaders will of necessity begin to reflect digital qualities such as connection, complexity, and a more dispersed idea of authority.

Web Sites Reveal Worldviews

> The first printed books imitated handwritten manuscripts. The first photographs were portraits. Many early motion pictures captured theatrical plays on screen. So it's not surprising that in the later 1990s companies tried hard to re-create their familiar business environments.
>
> —David Siegel, *Futurize Your Enterprise*

The difference between these worldviews is quite visible when you browse through church Web sites. As you can see in Figure 6.1, the Vati-can Web site is comprehensive and rich in depth. It provides a complete guide to the liturgical calendar, historical developments for the celebra-tions, and on-line devotion complete with audio of the appropriate hymns. Graphically, the Vatican page is circular and layered with ancient paintings and scenes. Catholic Online offers another very interesting Web site rich in content. It carries its oral roots of community into a well-developed virtual community.[8]

The Reformation sites, such as the Presbyterian, Methodist, Lutheran, and Baptist, are stark by comparison.[9] They get straight to the point—no frills (Figure 6.2). These sites focus on content: beliefs, church locations, daily devotionals, ministries, resources, events. Not surprisingly for a print-based tradition, there's a lot of text to read.

Celebration churches like the Fellowship Church, Willow Creek Community Church, Saddleback, and McLean Bible Church sites imme-diately reflect their broadcast nature.[10] These sites are all about events, promotions, activities, and celebrities—indicating their broadcast roots. Visually appealing, they are easy to navigate and offer layers of content to browse through. They offer mission statements, not creeds. Their pro-

Figure 6.1. The Vatican's Web site, reflecting oral tradition, has a rich collection of ancient images.

Figure 6.2. George Barna lists the Southern Baptist as the only mainline Protestant tradition that has maintained growth since 1950.

grams and activities are branded with names like "The Big Idea," "Frontline," "Purpose Driven," "The New Thing Network," and "Promiseland." They have the pop, upbeat feel of a *USA Today*—no surprise. And even though it is a print medium, *USA Today* is consciously designed to provide the look and feel of a television experience and offers a familiar point of reference. Only one of them offered a virtual community, and that was for the church's singles group.

Figure 6.3. The Fellowship Church Web Site.

Now we get to the emerging digital culture churches. And here we begin to see something quite different. If you visit Web sites of The Ooze, Kaleo Fellowship, Emergent Village, or Mars Hill Church, you will see the difference immediately (Figures 6.3, 6.4, and 6.5).[11] These sites use colors and graphics that are more subtle and complex than most of the broadcast-oriented church sites. They use icons for navigation, like the broadcast sites, but the icons are more than a brand—they are more symbolic. On The Ooze, for example, under the category of "Faith," the icon is an intriguing high-quality photograph of a double door slightly ajar.

The Mars Hill site shows a small banner above its video clip that says "Meaning, Beauty, Truth, and Community." The site also makes access to audio on-line sermons, discussions, and music a priority over downloading print. It allows viewers to dive in and participate right away. Issues and topics are intimately linked with culture and subjects about meaning. The site contains fewer how-to topics and more social awareness topics. Many of these sites offer virtual communities.

Where does your church fall on this continuum?

Figure 6.4. The Ooze's digital-age Web site uses conceptual navigation icons and content that is intentionally thought-provoking.

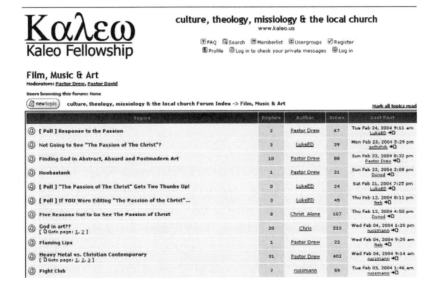

Figure 6.5. The Kaleo Fellowship Web site, reflecting its digital foundation, offers several on-line communities.

The Leadership Riddle

Current leadership models taught in seminaries and business schools emphasize that leaders should lead to serve. Those who lead to serve, however, often bring with them the baggage of being a loner, a need for achievement and recognition, the instincts for competition, a tendency toward political maneuvering, the quest for power or control, the fear of losing that control, and the insecurity of not being able to live up to their advertising. Today's leaders have a tiger by the tail, and many dare not let go.

For institutions with roots in oral culture, the mind-set of leading to serve emphasizes holding fast to the traditions and rituals of faith and protecting the sanctity of the office bearers, regardless of how distorted these become. The tragedy of this kind of leadership has even made front-page news in recent years. The Catholic Church, for example, finds itself in the worst kind of dilemma. The sexual scandals of many priests have ripped apart even the best efforts to restore the once sacred unity of the office with the officeholder. Some sectors of the Catholic Church have retreated to protecting their interests and responding to their victims as adversaries.

The lead-to-serve mind-set for organizations and institutions with a print orientation emphasizes intellectual expertise. Leaders are tied to accomplishing goals, maintaining predictability, achieving control through stability, climbing the ladder of success, analyzing, following a chain of command, preserving tried and true methods, building a hierarchy, and so forth. This has built organizations and institutions with layers of insulated management, and it has led to cultures in which budgets and power politics occupy considerable time and resources.

The lead-to-serve mind-set for organizations with a broadcast orientation rewards skills like persuasion, a high-profile image, innovation, risk taking, ability to keep up with the times, novelty, leaps up the success ladder, interpersonal skills, the ability to think on one's feet, and so forth. But some of these churches have had their own scandals, when reality can't quite live up to the projected image. High-profile scandals of several televangelists have captured our attention, but even more alarming are the statistics about the general condition of church leadership.[12]

Today many leaders of these organizations are getting tired of playing the game, but they don't know how to get off the treadmill. Congregants in the emerging digital culture are hungry for leaders who are approachable, touchable, accessible, transparent, and real. They want to connect with someone who is unscripted, unrehearsed, and not "on." They want a real person who walks among them, not someone who periodically comes down from the mountain to deliver a prescription for life or platitudes of hype.

As we move more deeply into a digital frame of reference, the old paradigms will not give up easily: they will likely become more extreme themselves. Print will push toward greater functionalism and control, whereas broadcast will push the extremes of personal experience and hyped events.

Most church leaders typically spend up to 50 percent of their time preparing for Sunday, approximately 25 percent of their time in various staff and leadership meetings, and the remaining 25 percent putting out fires and dealing with dysfunctional members. Leaders have to meet with people by appointment, cover their agendas, take care of their checklists, and touch all of the bases. Relationships become a functional way to complete objectives. And if they can accomplish more than one thing at a time, then all the better. Leaders, stretched for time, have honed the art of small talk—making just enough contact in order to move on to the next person or thing on the agenda.

But real contact and connection are what will allow today's leaders to step off the treadmill and start breathing the air of the emerging culture. Larry Crabb, noted psychologist and author, says in his book *Connection*, that most of the therapy and counseling people seek would be unnecessary if they had vital and intimate relationships.[13] David Schwartz, author and journalist, draws similar conclusions from his research into the condition of senior care.[14] John Naisbitt, best-selling business and future trends author, coined the phrase "high-tech/high-touch" to describe the need to offset lives of ever-increasing efficiency with more human and relationally oriented practices.[15] Where is it all heading?

Impartational Leadership: Leading in Real Time

We are now moving away from the intellectual leader valued by print and the motivational leader beloved by broadcast. We are moving at light speed toward what I call the impartational leader of the digital culture.

An impartational leader teaches not by exhortation but by example. In a way this harks back to an oral apprenticeship model: the student or follower absorbs character and identity from a vital relationship over time. Interaction and connection place a new premium on understanding and building vital relationships. Without leaders who value, practice, and model relational leadership, these growing desires will become distorted. In a deeper way, this model reflects family relationships between parents and children.

Leading to Serve

Leaders who trust integrate themselves into the lives of those they work with. Leaders who do not trust rely on filters to insulate them from the people and problems on the front lines. I met with the chief operating officer (COO) for one of the largest mega-churches in the country. I was with a friend who held a similar position at another church and wanted to learn from the COO how to handle rapid growth. My friend and I gained several valuable insights, but four observations framed my experience.

The first observation came when we walked into the building and saw the cleaning and setup crew. They were all minorities and were not members of the church; many did not speak English. The people doing the work had no ties to the congregation, and the staff in charge obviously viewed these tasks in similarly detached and functional terms. Second, about thirty minutes into our interview, the executive assistant interrupted to let the pastor know it was time for his next appointment. This kind of third party filter is part of the insulation that prevents leaders from dealing with people on an individual, unscripted, and personal level. We actually met for another forty-five minutes and had a wonderful time of fellowship. Third, the COO stated that the church had a staff of more than five hundred people, about half of whom were part-time employees. He said that part-time employees work about as much as the full-time employees, and the church did not have to pay benefits. Fourth, when asked about regrets over the growth, he talked about how his workload prevented him from getting to know those who work directly for him. This was a godly man, a sincere individual who felt called to the work he was performing, but he seemed to be trapped by his paradigms. The compartmentalized and insulated leadership structure that so many large organizations have evolved keeps leadership out of touch. In its place we compensate by creating a mirage.

Serving to Lead

Dr. Ron Anderson, CEO and president of Parkland Hospital in Dallas, Texas, since 1982, is what Jim Collins would call a "Level 5" leader. He also exhibits many of the qualities emerging in the digital shift. Parkland is one of the leading hospitals in the country, serving close to nine hundred thousand patients a year. What makes the hospital special is its commitment to serving the underserved community: Parkland turns no one away.

I had the good fortune to hear Dr. Anderson speak at a Dallas Real Estate Ministries luncheon in 2002. After that luncheon I wanted to learn and read more about him, curious about his leadership philosophy and approach. About eight months later, I called his assistant to ask for an appointment. To my surprise Dr. Anderson called me himself and accepted my request. As I waited for him in his office, I noticed that it was simple and worn—not what I expected from the head of an organization with more than six thousand employees. He entered the office wearing his white medical jacket (he still sees patients), and we sat together at a small circular conference table. Three things struck me about that encounter. The first was his demeanor: I felt as though I had him all to myself. There were no interruptions, no watching the clock— in fact, after ninety minutes I was the one squirming and feeling I had taken too much of Dr. Anderson's time.

Second, he spoke intimately about several of the employees, but one in particular stood out. This woman had come to the hospital three decades earlier. She ran the laundry service, a difficult job. He spoke proudly about her leadership skills and the many times she was offered a promotion. She turned each one down because she saw the laundry room as her call, a place where she felt she could do the most good. Because it is one of the lowest entry positions in the hospital, she found it an ideal place to recruit people who needed a chance in life. She worked with and developed them until they could get a promotion and a foothold on an upward ladder—an incredible and improbable dream for most of them. It was a moving story but more so because I was hearing it from the man who planted this garden of care at Parkland. When Dr. Anderson attended her funeral, the fruit of this woman's life was obvious by the large number of people who came and shared how she had changed their lives. It is one thing to recognize talent or give a person a break in life; that's what good leaders do. Extraordinary leaders, however, are secure and humble enough to place others at the center, are able to see a person's greater call, and then give that call a garden in which to grow.

The third thing that stood out in our conversation was Parkland Hospital's mission: to serve the underserved population of Dallas County. More than that, however, was how integrated and internalized this mission was with Dr. Anderson's own call and passion. He describes his mission in terms of the good Samaritan and the biblical reference to entertaining angels without knowing it (Hebrews 13:2). Parkland Hospital is where the homeless go, where AIDS patients without insurance go, where most of the weekend violence and tragedy ends up. From Dr. Anderson's perspective, this is his garden, where "you never know who God may ask you to serve."[16]

As I reflected on our talk later, I could plainly see how all of these images merge together into one: his interest in our conversation, his love for his employees, and his compassion for the underserved work in harmony. I am sure there are separate compartments in his life; however, unlike most leaders I've met, Dr. Anderson's effectiveness seemed to emanate from the convergences in his life—the integration.

A New Premium for Making Disciples: Family Style

I had a chance to engage in a lively discussion about impartational leadership with my friend Rich, who was describing how a new "discipling" curriculum works in his church. *Almost,* I thought, *but not quite what I had in mind.*

I asked Rich to compare this program with how he trained his own children. "Do you gather your kids in a small group and then launch into the character trait of the week? Do you show up once a week and offer a well-researched and motivating family sermon? Do you set appointments to further address these with your kids?"

As we sparred, we were able to deconstruct the church program down to the fundamental assumption behind this brand of discipleship. In the end the purpose is not in the content or even good intentions but in passing along the character of Christ.

How do you adequately pass along Christ's identity? We have to reexamine our means, especially if we understand the truth behind McLuhan's phrase "the medium is the message." Truly effective discipleship has to be tied to the practice of family. If our current religious approaches won't work within our natural families, why should we expect them to work within our spiritual family? Perhaps part of the answer is that we see the church as an organization rather than a family.

Rich and I continued to talk about the life-changing moments for our families. Without exception they occurred outside of preplanned family improvement sessions. They happen during the unpredictable situations and crises of normal, everyday life. Rich shared about how one of his sons radically turned toward Christ after a period of rebellion and how the lesson of God's faithfulness and mercy penetrated the entire family beyond any minisermon.

Discipleship is not a small group or classroom topic. It is a lab project, a choreographed dance, an art taught under the eye of a master. It is apprehended first through demonstration, not intellectually.

Show Us How *You* Do It

Print created a focus on the universal principles of life. Broadcast shifted from the abstract to images of lifestyle and life's events. Interactive communication is creating a very interesting shift that integrates both print and broadcast. The interactive medium of digital communications, along with the connection between thought, dialogue, and the keyboard create a hands-on immersion experience. People will want, more and more, to see how life works in real time as opposed to the abbreviated seminar version.

Here is a business-world example of the power of this kind of reality training. While conducting a telemarketing seminar, I provided a very good print-based session with background, principles, and techniques. If we had been in a more print-based company, and these had been older people, I would have simply had to say, "Here's the phone, here's your script. If you follow it, you will get the results we expect. Besides, it's your job." But I knew I would have to overcome some of the built-in resistance that these young salespeople had to doing telemarketing, so I also offered an entertaining broadcast approach with stories, anecdotes, and visual aids. I made telemarketing sound wonderful, effective, and motivating—which it can be, given the right frame of mind and preparation. But these young people wanted a more interactive mind-set and hands-on experience.

As I finished my great presentation, someone asked, "Could you show us how *you* do it?" I was prepared for this, but that still did not prevent a brief moment of apprehension and nervousness. Why? Because this would be the real thing, and I would lose my nicely controlled, artificial environment.

I took a list of names from one of the salespeople and began dialing the phone. In thirty minutes I hit several voice mails, found a few alternate names for contact people (who were not in), and had one solid conversation that ended abruptly with "Thanks but no thanks." The pace of this live demonstration felt slow (life is slow), and I kept thinking, *They have got to be bored with this.* However, those calls were the one portion of the training that all of the salespeople enjoyed most—and remembered. No one commented on the charts I had prepared; no one commented on my twenty-three years of insights and stories. But they could not get enough of my less-than-stellar real-life phone demonstration! My live and up-close demonstration broke the primary barrier to telemarketing that neither reason nor persuasion could accomplish. It took away the fear of being rejected over the phone by showing my own rejection several times.

Life is not a performance or an abstract exercise of intellect: it is a kinetic experience. We often say that time is our most precious commodity, yet we offer so little of it to the critical relationships we are preparing for life. Here is the paradigm riddle for leaders: Over the long run, do you affect more people and build a healthier community by investing your time in study for Sunday's platform or through building vital relationships that can then go and build other vital relationships?

The first challenge for the leader is to figure out how to provide a sufficient amount of "natural" time to those who are interested and who accept the reciprocal responsibilities of vital relationships. When you allow someone to share a meal with your family, help you with a task, relax watching a television show together, or share other elements of your normal life, that constitutes "natural" time.[17] A life apprentice has to reciprocate; otherwise, the mentor becomes spent. Reciprocity comes in the form of service. The second challenge is for the congregation to understand how to serve those who shift their time to invest in others. We have habits acquired from our spiritual fast-food diet. We are used to eat-and-run relationships.

A focus on discipleship or impartational leadership can overcome the bottlenecks inherent in our current forms of leadership. The demand for a leader's time far outstrips their time or capacity. Under the current model, the primary way to expand that limited time is by focusing on the weekend's main events. Others expand that exposure using television, radio, or books.

The leverage for relational leaders, however, is not with their content or delivery. It is in the relationships they form and the time they have to invest in those relationships. This changes the rules of the game. It suddenly opens the doors to hundreds of second- and third-string players who watch the game from their pews every weekend. If the vitality of the congregation comes primarily from relationships, then that creates opportunity for greater involvement, energy, and health throughout the church.[18] To repeat my earlier comment, the church has built a complex and cumbersome spiritual foster-care system when the world is looking for adoption.

New Leadership for a Digital World

New leaders are emerging out of their digital cocoons. Their behavior and roles differ from current and past leadership models. Digital leaders are building agile networks of intensely aligned interests that are highly transparent, easily accessible, and collaborative. Digital leaders are mentors and

> Digital leaders are building agile networks of intensely aligned interests that are highly transparent, easily accessible, and collaborative.

actively part of a narrow circle of relationships. You have probably already read about many of the qualities and skills I will list. Although you may understand them and be attracted to some, they may feel a bit foreign to you—as some do to me. But these are the attributes for successful leaders in a digital world.

Advocates

The Support Economy puts it this way: "Deep support provides ongoing relationship based on advocacy, mutual respect, trust and the acute alignment of interests."[19] Leaders are becoming less like prime movers and more like advocates and facilitators. They have an ability to see and cultivate collective potential. They are less driven by their urge to recruit people to serve their vision. Their sensibilities are different. They find fulfillment by helping individuals connect and develop a unique familial expression and then watching it grow.

The implications behind this shift are huge. The older leadership paradigm requires large nets and infrastructure to attract individuals who will join the cause. The new model can achieve similar results without large facilities but instead within current neighborhoods and communities. Reaping the harvest does not require creating a vast campus or staging marquee events. Life and community—not the building or the program—provide the new context, the new stage.

The old assumption was, "If you build it, they will come." The new assumption realizes we cannot change the cultural climate of our communities inside our church buildings. My generation of leaders has been saying this for years, but it has continued to build resource-consuming infrastructures that create an inwardly focused culture. The emerging generation is forgoing buildings and getting beyond the slogans like "the harvest is outside the barn" and "we are fishers of men, not keepers of the aquarium" and acting missional. Leaders have to stop preaching about being missional and start facilitating it.

Creators of Continuity and Context

The driving reality of change requires the ability to adapt quickly. Adaptation requires that leaders continually scan the horizon; adjust to the ever-changing landscape; and reframe structure, mission, and resources to current realities. Past leaders have had a well-defined field of play, clear goals, and a means of keeping score against the competition. The current condition of relentless change is more similar to navigating through the North Atlantic than driving down the highway.

Public schools offer a good example of the kind of relentless need and change the church is facing and how it is falling ever behind. Schools are fighting with an unending fragmentation of needs and confronting a bureaucratic environment full of confusing and conflicting programs and procedures. New educational needs surface daily, requiring a modified curriculum. Implementing the new curriculum reveals new problems and on and on . . . Responding to these realities is a bureaucratic structure, process, and mind-set with filters, archaic budgeting, and fragmentation adding years to implementing change. By the time change reaches the students, the material and processes are several years out of date. At the end of the cycle, the solution little resembles the original need.

Students who require individual attention, good or bad, either struggle within their class or are batched together and sent to a more suitable program. We've blamed teachers, parents, politics, money, violence, loss of authority, bureaucracy, and other factors for the continuing decline.

Every now and then we hear of a teacher who rises above all of the systemic dysfunctions and lack of resources to create a powerful enclave of learning—a small community—that elevates and transforms kids. These teachers understand the power of creating continuity and context—a place for a moment in time where collaboration around a need becomes transformed into an inspiring goal that leads to collective achievement and personal transformation. The continuity is almost universally the relational connection the teacher has to the students' individuality. How do we make this kind of experience commonplace? We need to understand how print and broadcast media have shaped the current systems as well as understand how digital media are already shaping and enabling alternatives.

Print culture provides continuity, and broadcast focuses on individuality. Within the current realities of complex and changing needs, print fails at offering individualized support, whereas broadcast fails at providing a relational context for meaning. New leadership skills, shaped by interactive media, will first provide relational connection and then break down bureaucratic barriers by creating loosely structured federations aligned by acute interests and able to respond to both complex and changing needs. Teachers will shift from being grade and subject specialists to learning specialists.

Perhaps this shift is because new and younger leaders also appear far more accessible. They seem less driven by the clock, more curious and conversational. They like to "hang" with people. They make extensive use of digital technology. This offers more freedom to conduct business wherever and whenever they need to. The accessible mind-set is the opposite of the current highly scheduled, screened and filtered, running-behind reality of many leaders.

Collaboration

New leaders are growing beyond their monthly prayer breakfasts and luncheons to develop cooperative arrangements. They are less possessive and fearful. That cooperation is one of the effects of an Internet-nurtured mind-set. Kids are growing up playing with interactive games, downloading one another's shortcuts and tricks. They download shared music and pass along their comments or changes. They send instant messages to one another and chat on-line in real time. They cut and paste material from multiple sites, creating a new and tailored work. This cooperation, however, is getting ready to jump to a new and revolutionary level.

It has always struck me as curious that some churches seem to be very good at attracting membership but lousy at developing leaders or running a smooth operation. Others seem excellent at providing pastoral care and developing leaders but have trouble attracting new members.[20]

Although individual churches seem committed to being all things to all people, most businesses learned years ago that such a strategy eventually leads to disaster. Business has articulated this concept in several ways, but one way to sum it up is with the idea of core competencies. *Core competencies* are the unique and superior skills that define an organization. Companies that focus on their core competencies or strengths achieve higher returns and better results than those that spread their resources by trying to cover all of the bases. Companies then outsource (or farm out) other types of work to those who specialize in these functions. Using this strategy brings trade-offs; but as technology continues to open doors to resources located anywhere, organizations will be more able to focus on what they do best.

At the turn of the nineteenth century Vilfredo Pareto, an Italian economist, recognized that a minority of the Italian population owned the vast majority of the land.[21] This general observation also applied in other areas and eventually became known as the Pareto or 80/20 principle. It is based on a more general recognition that some efforts produce exponentially higher results than others. There are even structural reasons why organizations excel at some things and not others. Fred Wiersema and Michael Treacy's book *The Discipline of Market Leaders* provides the best explanation, in my opinion, for why churches need to focus on the few areas in which they do well and partner with other churches who can complement their efforts.

Outsourcing is a broadcast concept in that organizations excel by focusing on what they do best—their brand, so to speak.[22] Most churches, even broadcast churches, have not begun to approach the concept of outsourcing even though many have embraced the idea of core competencies and branding. These, however, are giving way to the revolutionary digital reality of open-source and federation networks.

Open-source and federation networks supersede our ideas and efforts at cooperation. They challenge the essence of our ideas of collaboration. It is the virtual digital expression of having all things in common. Whoa! This is a paradigm-busting, don't-want-to-deal-with-it idea. Except for the fact that it is happening on the business front and smart people are laying the conceptual foundation to extend this model further. Visa International provides an early successful business example but a valid one nonetheless. Visa International's founder, Dee Hock, envisioned a means of exchanging value electronically through an association of members. He saw that the value of this structure would grow as the number of users grew. A single company could not reach enough people by itself to entice vendors to join or enough individuals to use credit cards. Visa's mission, therefore, became the creation and expansion of associated banks. Visa gave the governing power to its members. The powerful secret behind Dee Hock's vision surfaces when you consider how little you actually know about such a powerful force. For example, you probably don't know where Visa is headquartered, or that they only have about two thousand employees. You probably do not know who runs Visa or how the company does what it does. This network model illustrates the potential effectiveness of distributed authority and federations of common interest. Zuboff and Maxmin create a conceptual example with two fictitious federations, Sweetsupport and Goldenapple, that could provide a complete infrastructure of support for families and small businesses. Churches that want to move to collaborative federations that offer "deep support" will require "infrastructure convergence": "Infrastructure convergence not only eliminates redundant activity across entire federations; it also creates an environment of complete transparency and shared data, allowing everyone in the federation to see the same reality."[23]

Churches can share their technology, their facilities, their support staffs, their experts, and their counselors. They can offer to others what they do well and import from others where they lack. I can hear the arguments for why this won't work, why your organization is unique or why it is too risky. There are obstacles, large obstacles, including trust, technology, cost, control (politics), and so on. The economics and technology are quickly developing. The politics loses some of its interference in the design of a decentralized federation. A good example is the Chaordic Commons. This is a nonprofit organization founded by Dee Hock. Its mission is the following: "The Chaordic Commons is a global network of individuals and organizations in every sector committed to pioneering new ways to organize, based on the discovery and expression of deep common purposes and essential principles of right relationship."[24] Trust, however, is probably the largest obstacle and will require a new ethic.

I'm using the word *covenetwork* (pronounced similarly to *covenant*) to express this new ethic. Covenant relationships communicate a level of trust and commitment that leaders do not usually share. It will provide not only a positive level of cooperation but also a degree of security that protects one church from attracting members from another. Covenant relationships open the door for developing a network of capabilities that far exceed what they can do on their own. Covenetworks allow churches to funnel their resources into the areas in which they are most competent and protect them from venturing into higher-risk areas that they may not have the skills or resources to enter.

Open-Source Leadership

> You can never change things by resisting the existing reality. To change something, build a new model that makes the old model obsolete.
> —Buckminster Fuller[25]

For many years most software companies created proprietary source code for their software. They controlled everything about the code, and no one could alter it even if they had better applications. The proprietary, vertically integrated (owning and controlling all of the means of making something) approach describes the organizational logic of the past. In a complex, interactive, and virtual environment such a system requires large dedicated resources to maintain and is inflexible to rapid changes in circumstances.

Today we see a growing movement toward an open-source approach: the source code is available to anyone and everyone to add to or alter. You might think that this process is chaotic and subject to errors and flaws, but interactive technologies have fostered new mind-sets that create just the opposite. Linux software is probably the most notable example of open-source programming. Its creation provided one of the first credible examples of the potential of collaborative leadership empowered by the new technologies. In fact, Linux offers a credible alternative to Microsoft's Windows operating system, and it illustrates a new kind of competitor to companies like Microsoft. Microsoft cannot use its muscle against Linux because there is no central entity to go after.

The metaphor of open source has grown beyond the software industry. Interactive media are changing our bias away from closed and protected domains to open and transparent domains. An article in *Fast Company* provides an example: "Rob McEwen owned an underperforming gold mine in northwestern Ontario, and he needed new ideas about where to dig. So he broke new ground—and made data on the mine available online to anyone who wanted to help. Eureka! The Internet gold rush was on." The article goes to describe the company's open-source approach and how a three-person firm in Australia solved the problem.[26] What if our government implemented an open-source strategy in its fight against terrorism?

More to the point, what might open-source Christianity look like? Churches within the same community can easily begin sharing technical resources such as information technology, facility management, finance, audiovisual equipment, and so on. Churches can begin to share event calendars to reduce competing activities and at the same time open these events to their church neighbors. Outreach and charity efforts can and should become community collaborations. Home groups might consider forming around those who live within a radius of a few blocks rather than importing members from our own churches who have to drive twenty to forty minutes to participate. Community churches can work together developing a common Web site facilitating many of these suggestions. An interactive Web forum could expand efforts to help one another and create communities of common interest that cross traditional boundaries and cross-pollinate the constellation of congregations involved.

Interactive and Hands-On Leadership

As they develop their congregations, new leaders will act more like gardeners than field generals or motivational speakers. New leaders are far more perceptive to the power of interactive dynamics. They also understand the complex nature of initiatives and are sensitive to the unintended negative consequences of hasty or unilateral actions.

Organizations that are coming out of both print and broadcast feel awkward in truly interactive cultures. They've lost their sense of touch. They are also less cohesive and more relationally volatile. Bureaucratic organizations rely on their structure and inertia to maintain cohesion. Broadcast organizations rely on psychological stimulation and sense of mission to maintain their cohesion. The digital environment moves too quickly and unpredictably for either of these paradigms. Digital environments totally disrupt the continuity and cohesion that hold these organizations together. Digitally oriented environments rely on relationships along with collaboration to provide a means of not only cohesion but also strength.

Gospel Narrators

New leaders are developing new skills for conveying the gospel. Print audiences relate to a logical presentation of the message. Broadcast audiences connect through anecdote, dramatization, and concise slogans. The more people experience the complexity of digital reality, the more it creates a demand for thematic structure and the ability to diverge within these themes. Narrative and story, the ancient art of storytelling, is growing. These are not the anecdotes pastors commonly use to illustrate a point. The stories stand alone and convey transcendent and epic themes. Garrison Keillor, host of public radio's *A Prairie Home Companion*, is one of my favorite contemporary storytellers.[27]

The logical apologetic case for faith with its absolute conclusions breaks down under the complexity of contemporary life. Real-life characters are not simply good or bad. Outcomes are not always predictable. The end of the chapter, or presentation, does not mean the end of the story. Meaning is not obvious, nor is the response. In fact, there is probably not one single meaning to walk away with. Anecdotes, skits, and seven-step formulas become increasingly shallow when contrasted to society's growing thirst for depth. The new generation is demanding more.

New leaders will rediscover and reenergize classic stories and songs that carry with them eternal themes, challenges, and conflicts. They will move away from the neatly wrapped stories that point onward and upward or provide black-and-white outcomes. The new storytellers will be comfortable detouring down a path, just like someone following a trail of hyperlinks on the Internet. The new storytellers will be able to build a story around the interaction with a current audience.

Look Around You

These new ideas have radical and disruptive implications. I've encountered a full spectrum of reactions, from panic and anger to true delight and excitement. If you are intrigued but without a clue about how to get started learning more, it's important to realize that the answers and resources for this journey are all around you. Simply recognizing the host of those already searching, digging, questioning, experimenting, and creating the new way is the first step. Many may be inside your own organization! As Elisha pointed out to Gehezai, we are surrounded by a great (virtual) army (2 Kings 6:15–17, NASB).

It's also important to realize that no system is perfect. The emerging digital models, which seem to hold so much promise when compared with models that have virtually ceased to work, will eventually become entrenched in their own ways. The Millennium Matrix provides tools to anticipate the stronghold tendencies that will eventually take root once digital media reach a tipping point (threshold) of dominance.

CHAPTER 7

Growing Vital Relationships

Reclaiming Community

And who is my neighbor?
—Luke 10:29 (NIV)

Have you ever spent a nostalgic afternoon on Main Street at Disneyland or Disney World? This is a visit back in time to a picture-book setting built by print culture, one that is hard to find any longer in the real world. Almost overnight, at the height of broadcast's power, anonymous and generic shopping malls replaced the mom-and-pop stores of the town square and shifted our sense of community. This is the world we live in today.

> What will happen when digital culture says, as it will, "We don't need or want your colossal buildings"?

But the onrushing digital culture, with its notions of connectivity and immediacy, is already raising questions about our current notions of community. The period of "if you build it, they will come," a hallmark of the broadcast mentality, is coming to an end. Many churches have confused providing a giant one-stop spiritual convenience mart with providing real community. They have responded well to broadcast's consumer orientation, and it worked—for a while. But what will happen when digital culture says, as it will, "We don't need or want your colossal buildings"? We will have to make major adjustments if we want to reach the next wave.

Broadcast Brings You . . . the Mall!

> [Mega-churches] are tapping into the bigger is better,
> mall-like mentality of America. And they are not going
> away anytime soon.
>
> —Betty Liu, "Bigger Suburban Churches are Attracting the
> Masses," *Financial Times*

Television exposed us to a world beyond our local surroundings, exposed us to the latest goods and information, and made us want more things than we ever thought possible. This exposure, combined with our increased mobility, created a culture that values choice and convenience over loyalty and community. Town squares, on the other hand, offered the necessities; you found a Bob's Market with a real Bob who knew most of his clientele (Figure 7.1). The shopping experience was also an interactive human experience.

Ironically, as we watched and reveled in television shows about small towns, like Mayberry RFD, broadcast shifted our attitudes toward our wants and away from Bob. Why buy from the limited stock Bob offers when you can go someplace that offers what you really want or choices you never even considered? You may have to shop among strangers, but that's the trade-off. You won't find a Bob at the mall. After a while you don't want to find Bob: Bob takes too long, and he knows too much about you. You just want to find your meat and hit the road.

The destruction of the old town square has resulted in a new irony: the town square–urban feel mall, in which an entire town square or shopping street is created to look like a real street but is filled by brand-name shops you'd find in a mall![1] These shopping experiences attempt to recapture that feeling of shopping in a small town or urban street. Remember Bob? You won't find Bob at the town center, but you will find Kind of Like Bob's, a franchise designed to feel like a home-town business and sell "real" food. I still miss Bob.

Malls, including the spiritual kind, were built to facilitate taking care of business and moving people in and out efficiently. We have little attachment to a mall, commercial or spiritual, because it is designed to facilitate efficient transactions, not relationships.

Figure 7.1. Bob's Market.

The End of the Main Event

The mall mentality was reflected in the concert format for entertainment, where the main event replaced spiritual and community rituals and shifted us in another way. In those giant arenas or enormous cathedrals, we can't really see the performers or pastors. But enormous screens and great acoustics make us think we share in the real thing. The concert format provides a powerful mirage of connection.

Concerts have created a powerful collective experience. Crowd dynamics allow people to lower their inhibitions and experience the exhilaration of releasing otherwise restrained emotions. The celebration church has understood this attraction and power. Such churches spend a lot of money buying the equipment and assembling the talent to scratch this itch. However, a trap of diminishing returns leads to an escalation built into the nature of the broadcast medium. Once we taste that vicarious thrill, we want it again—only the next time we need it pushed a little further or stimulated by a new novelty in order to feel something close to that original experience. A repeat diet in a broadcast medium quickly becomes boring. That is one reason why most concerts move from town to town and a particularly dynamic speaker travels from church to church.

Broadcast spawned the celebration church, which got people up and out of their pews and got them to loosen up and openly express their worship. The digital culture still looks for collective rituals; but it wants smaller venues that are more interactive, intense, and tailored. Children of the digital culture will want to be able to see, touch, and dialogue with one another as they explore new avenues for personalized ministry.

During the print era, as described earlier, the orchestral model symbolized church experience. During the broadcast era, the pop concert model has symbolized church experience. Today we are moving into a more eclectic jazz model. Leaders are learning skills that enable them to conduct a collective dialogue weaving worship, story, ministry, and celebration around a theme. This requires a new kind of rehearsal. Pastors can't be off preparing alone; the worship team can't rehearse alone; and the drama squad can't do its thing alone. The power of jazz comes from the interaction and times of spontaneous creativity. The jazz experience also requires a much smaller scale and more intimate venue than orchestra and band formats.

What does this shift mean for the future of celebration churches that have attracted broadcast audiences raised on the vicarious buzz of the main event? Those audiences are aging. What is going to happen to the First Church of the Main Event? Some will remain; some will grow as a result of consolidation; but most will either reinvent themselves or suffer a painful decline.

The End of Branding

The ubiquitous brands—GAP, Nike, and the rest—each project their own version of hipness or coolness, and they symbolize our quest to be part of something significant. What will happen when digital culture rejects self-conscious efforts to produce authenticity? Broadcast culture has sent us on a journey to build a vicarious world to compensate for our lack of original encounters. A world where we can imagine what the real thing might have been like—or, even better, a world offering the romance of the real thing without any of the drawbacks, like the scripted and televised world of *The Truman Show*.

Church branding is drawn from the same inspiration. We drink the same water and exhibit all of the same behaviors. We have our seeker brand, charismatic brand, messianic brand, postmodern brand, Hosanna brand, Maranatha brand, Willow Creek brand, and so on. Each began as an original inspiration, grew, and then became wildly popular. The broadcast culture almost automatically turns a popular concept into a brand and then begins to package, promote, and franchise the living daylights out of it.

These methods do not work within a digital culture, a medium of tailored personal experiences, whose users view promotion as spam and see brand franchises as the sign of an artificial production.[2]

The End of Fast Growth

What will happen when digital cultures reject fast growth as a virtue? No matter where you go, the church is absorbed with programs and questions about growth and expansion. Fortunately, any church that seriously wants to grow need only follow one of at least a dozen success formulas. There are seeker models, cell-based models, youth-oriented models, purpose-driven models, and others. Books list the seven or eight or however many essential elements for a healthy "organic" church. They all work.

This premeditated growth formula is what environmentalists would call unsustainable. Everything may grow and expand, but nothing integrates with anything else. There is little or no natural infrastructure to nurture and sustain new growth. This kind of growth requires continual outside resources to keep the church alive because it consumes more than it produces.

Here is what you will likely find in growth-focused churches: getting any one-on-one time with the pastoral staff (at least more than once) is next to impossible. The crowds continue to grow along with the programs, and of course buildings continue to expand. When the main event is over, what do you have? You have pockets of believers but no overall community, consumers of the faith, a huge overhead cost, an overworked leadership core, and high turnover in membership.[3]

When a business, community, or organization is in a growth and especially a hyper-growth mode (more than 15 percent a year), the growth hides the true cost required. As long as growth continues, that 15 percent margin stays ahead of consumption and everything looks fine—in fact, it looks great. Costs, however, lag behind new growth. That lag represents the time required to add the infrastructure and staff to support new growth. When that growth slows or even declines, the lagging costs of infrastructure catch up with frightening speed. Suddenly, the true cost or consumption of the organization raises its ugly head. When growth stagnates or declines, it leaves a scary monster behind. We have recently witnessed several corporate failures that bring home that fragile balance. An organization can drop from the heights of admired achievement to absolute meltdown overnight.

A second side effect of these kinds of churches is what might be called the Wal-Mart effect. These churches drain the talent from surrounding community churches, weakening the local spiritual ecosystem. Mega-churches attract once vitally connected members from other churches who want a broader spiritual experience outside. It sends these small churches into a vicious death spiral of diminishing strength.

I debated this point with one pastor during a seminar. He made a very good point that if these smaller community churches had met the needs of their congregations, then members never would have left. My response was and is the following: opting for consumer choice over community still destroys community, regardless of how it is portrayed. The church is not a capitalist organization in competition for spiritual market share. Yet there is little distinction between the marketing approaches that many churches and businesses use. Such churches seem just as happy to have Bill and Mary from the church next door as anyone else, and they show little awareness or interest on this impact on other neighboring churches.

The Beginning of Lasting Growth

Let me offer a slight adjustment to this current conflict between mega-churches and local churches by providing a more sustainable and connected model. Mega-churches provide something that many traditional or community churches can't. That's a fact. The leaders of adversely affected churches are still brothers in Christ, however, and we are still one body—at least in theory. These small churches, on the other hand, provide something that the mega-church doesn't have—community and proximity to its constituents.

We have to reconcile the conflict between a more effective evangelism and a more effective community. A broad program selection, talented and professional staff, and large-scale venues provide a more effective draw; but depth and relationship provide more effective communities and are more vital for sustainable growth over the long run.

Mega-churches are realizing their weakness regarding community, and they are shifting their strategies toward smaller groups, some which meet in homes providing a more casual and intimate setting. They are also launching satellite franchise churches, reducing the scale in order to provide support closer to their constituencies.[4] The problem with this franchise strategy is that the leadership talent and infrastructure that excels at staging events and drawing crowds is not the same as the talent and infrastructure for care and intimacy.[5]

For this reason most mega-churches are destined to provide mediocre community and pastoral care. These churches can fight their way upstream and think that establishing franchise churches will solve their dilemma. These smaller churches are simply going to produce the same effect as the mother church—only in a new location. They may start out with that community feel simply because of their smaller size. When they reach five hundred members or so, however, that feeling will disappear quickly.

The Federation Model

If mega-churches used a federation model with their neighbors, then both could potentially fulfill needs that neither can do alone. Mega-churches would have an outlet for developing new talent. Community churches can continue to focus on their backyard and provide the ongoing in-depth pastoral care that mega-churches can't. Mega-churches won't have to siphon resources to build additional redundant facilities.

Mega-churches also have the potential of becoming Christian community centers that feed and develop the broader Christian community. Sustainable growth does not mean static, slow, or limited growth. Other promising models are already emerging that combine elements of celebration gatherings with a network of community congregations. This shift can begin as soon as communities are viewed in terms of spiritual ecosystems and neighboring churches are viewed as brothers and sisters.

The digital generation is extremely sensitive and attracted to ideas for sustainable growth. They understand the scale and limits of meaningful connections. They hate treadmills. They despise becoming fodder for futile ambitions. They prefer off-brands to marquee churches. They prefer flying under the radar. And there are fewer in this generation than in the baby boom generation. The demographics that have fueled the growth of celebration churches are quickly diminishing.

New Role Models

What will happen when the next generation of youth (the next-geners)[6] say they can't relate to the role models we parade onstage? If you go inside most celebration churches, you find what I call the beautiful people. Most of the staff, at least those allowed onstage, look like they come out of magazines or the television studio. They all project happy, positive, sincere, and peppy attitudes. What does the congregation think about all this?

What may have worked for the broadcast babies isn't working for the digital kids. This new generation is composed of thinkers. They have been exposed to a digital world far more raw (less filtered or produced) than most of my generation is used to. They know better than to think that life is happy, positive, sincere, and peppy or that it is meant to be. That does not mean they are looking to be discontented and negative. On the contrary, they want something that reflects life more directly. They don't want to be patronized or given simple formulas that promise to solve complex questions. Our current leaders often represent to next-geners what Ward and June Cleaver or Ozzie and Harriet Nelson represented to my generation—a chuckle.

Who will the new role models be? U2's Bono, a current rock-and-roll celebrity and icon, is the consensus favorite prototypical next-generation leader, according to my conversations with about a dozen culturally minded people in their mid- to late twenties. When I asked why, I got the following responses:

- He has sustained success while staying true to his message.

- He has a purpose (Africa) beyond his success.

- He has remained down-to-earth and approachable.

- His life is "blended" and simple; he has not crafted a particular persona made for public consumption.

- He has maintained integrity in what he represents and has stayed free from scandal.

Bono represents a coalescing point both in his music and his African mission mobilizing the world community to deal with poverty and AIDs. He has found a way to fully engage worldly affairs as a Christian without compromise and without creating polarization.

After we discussed Bono, there was a long pause. The next-geners I spoke with had to think hard to come up with other names, none of which received a wholehearted endorsement. This would make sense because next-geners really don't look for public figures as role models. They are more inner-directed and gravitate toward intimate, personally validated influences.

I will offer one more public figure who I hope stretches your perceptions about the neatly packaged public face of our spiritual heroes and heroines: writer Anne Lamott. A best-selling author and outspoken promoter of the faith, she is becoming a familiar face within the Christian world, particularly among the postmoderns and ecumenicals. Lamott is a compelling antidote to the peppy role models available in some churches. She is not one of the beautiful people we might naturally gravitate to—by her own admission. She does not try to come off happy, peppy, or positive. She is a former alcoholic, drug addict, current single mom, gay rights activist—someone who is a bit geeky and admittedly neurotic. Yet she touches hundreds and perhaps thousands for Christ by simply being transparent and consistent in her faith. She is the woman that Christ pointed out who "loved much" because she was forgiven much (Luke 7:47, NIV). Lamott's particular appeal is that her love is much stronger than her baggage; she focuses a lot more on the source of her love than on trying to unload all of her baggage.

Human-Scaled Communities

What is a human-scaled community? There is a desperate cry to counterbalance society's pace and fragmentation with oases of cohesion. These oases, however, cannot become Christian islands and ghettos; part of the counterbalance is the ability to fit within the natural communities of their constituents, serving those communities.

We are at a time in history when civil society is at a low point and declining. Part of that is a consequence of a weak Christian community. We have pulled all of the salt and light out of our neighborhoods and brought them into our safe, hermetically sealed churches. Nextgeners instinctively want to be on the front lines. They want to be where the action is. The church has been working at the margins of society for over a generation and getting marginal results. We have a new generation equipped with new tools that have the potential to completely alter our rules of social engagement. Only the church has the wherewithal to create connected communities of cohesion, if we will simply step outside our doors and focus on rebuilding society with intentional communities—one neighbor at a time. We can't do this unless we adopt a new cooperative and socially engaged wineskin for the local church.

Restoring the Moral Ecosystem

For fragmentation is now very widespread, not only throughout society, but also in each individual. . . . The notion that all these fragments are separately existent is

evidently an illusion, and this illusion cannot do other
than lead to endless conflict and confusion.

—David Bohm, quoted in M. J. Wheatley,
Leadership and the New Science

We are moving out of the age of manufactured culture, just as we are
moving away from a manufactured economy. We are moving toward a
designer culture, and we have the potential to take a fresh look and fresh
approach toward moral and civil society. But before we go forward, we
must first look at what we currently have. We cannot turn the tide and
recover a moral society until we first change our worldviews.

The roots of morality, and its natural environment, are in oral
cultures. Ethics, on the other hand, is primarily a by-product of print.
Morality governs relationships. Ethics governs behavior. The former cal-
culates the mystical relational law of reciprocity; the latter provides principles that apply individually and universally. The former is situational,
whereas the latter is universal. Morality requires free choice; ethics
defines obligation. So we might put forward that vital and connected
relationships are a prerequisite for moral society.

In order to recover moral society, we have to look back to oral
culture. Jesus set a benchmark for morality: "Love your neighbor as
yourself" (Mark 12:33, NIV). Paul uses the same line of thought when
instructing the Corinthians not to use their freedom in any way that
causes younger Christians to take offense (1 Corinthians 8:9). Jesus provides both the context and measure for morality. Questioned by one of
the legal experts attempting to pin him down regarding the law governing salvation, Jesus asked the lawyer, "What does the law say?" He
answered, "Love the Lord your God . . . and love your neighbor as yourself." The legal expert confirmed the ethical standard but went on to ask,
"Who is my neighbor?" Jesus then told the famous story about the good
Samaritan (Luke 10:25–37, NIV). The good Samaritan is far more than a
parable: it contains the DNA for restoring moral society. Many of our
criticisms on the condition of current society are like criticisms of a harvest whose seeds were planted in a field with no topsoil. It is worth considering, then, how the more interactive environment and mind-set of

digital media can help us restore a moral environment. Without this DNA our ability to recover the mystical power of morality and our culture will continue to erode.

Remove the Disconnects

> When no firm and lasting ties any longer unite men, it is impossible to obtain the cooperation of any great number of them unless you can persuade every man whose help is required that he serves his private interests by voluntarily uniting his efforts to those of all the others.
>
> —Alexis de Tocqueville, *Democracy in America*

We must begin by examining the disconnects within the church. If we continue to serve our private interests alone, without expanding and uniting our efforts with those of all our spiritual kin, then how long can we legitimately stand, let alone act as the moral conscience of society? If what we offer is a weekly experience or presentation that does not raise the urge or provide the opportunity for connection resulting in community, then we might as well take down our label as church and proclaim our facility a house of religious entertainment.

The Disconnect Between Self-Sufficiency and Community

The first disconnect for me is watching the way many churches handle their growth. It bothers me that so many churches can pick up and leave their communities at will. They feel this way because they are disconnected from their immediate community and feel self-sufficient. Like sports franchises, they are no longer part of their constituents and work only to serve narrow self-interests, all in the name of serving the greater good.

When churches expand or enter another community, their intrusion stirs the same kind of debate we see over Super Wal-Marts coming to town. Most communities are unprepared for something so out of proportion to everything else. Wal-Mart at least pays taxes and provides jobs. Churches that are internally focused and self-contained lose sight of the broader implications. If the neighbors object to the intrusion, then churches can and have taken communities to court to assert their rights.[7]

A church that is connected to its neighborhood and sees itself as an integral part of the community behaves differently. It dialogues (before making up its mind) with local leaders to find a way to accommodate growth and at the same time better serve and integrate into the community. What many consider dialogue is little more than providing a sales presentation and afterward offering perfunctory sessions for community comments. Part of a moral or civil society is finding ways to live together for one another's benefit. It's hard to do that if there is no moral attachment or investment in the community.[8]

The Disconnect Between Knowing and Acting

The church has long been accused of talking the talk but not walking the walk. The hypocrisy they perceive in churches is among the top reasons nonbelievers and the unchurched stay home. The Internet is creating a bias toward the unvarnished and developing ways to uncover pretense. There is little room to hide. If you want to remain part of an Internet community, you have to be real and relatively transparent, because if you are found to be a phony, everyone will soon know about it, a conditioning that is carrying over into face-to-face relationships.[9]

Most churches deliver the majority of their payload on Sundays. It's a once-a-week gig, for the most part. That creates part of that disconnect between knowing and acting. Moral behavior is a kinetic experience. It's easy to learn the principles, but you have to practice them and be coached in order to develop them. Otherwise, they never take root.

For several years, during college and shortly after, I taught tennis. Some of my students took lessons but never played during the week, so at every lesson they would be back reviewing the same things over and over again. Tennis lessons typically have more tangible effect than most Sunday sermons because students at least try out the skills and techniques taught during the lesson. Students often told me, "Gee, I thought I had it down pretty well during the lesson, but when I tried to play over the week, I couldn't figure anything out. In fact, I played worse." The students who took lessons and played in the instructional leagues improved, often dramatically.

One of the biggest disconnects the church has in attempting to influence society is its own gap between what it thinks it understands and its actual behavior. If improvement in playing a sport takes consistent practice and coaching, how much more do we need practice and coaching to instill spiritual discernment along with moral skills and sensibilities? To provide practice fields for morality, churches must provide areas for members to serve under the oversight of mentors.

The Disconnect Between Acting and Being

What does it mean today to serve Christ, following his instruction to show our love by laying down our lives for one another? Does this mean teaching or attending Bible studies and small groups, attending youth camp, ushering, or participating on the worship team? As important as all of these efforts and others are, I'm afraid they contribute little toward building the moral sensibilities, topsoil, the church and society desperately need. Why? They focus on the activity, the event, or the content— not the relationships.

Most task givers don't view tasks as a mentor would, as a means to uncover and attend to motive and character, but simply as things to get done. Consequently, when we are asked to perform an act of service, we don't do so as an apprentice would. We instead focus on completing the task and not relating with the giver of the task. This is so commonplace that you may wonder why I'm turning a seemingly subtle distinction into such a big deal.

If you read the book *Tuesdays with Morrie*, you glimpsed the big deal. The author, Mitch Albom, tells the story of a chance reunion with his old journalism professor, now dying of cancer.[10] That reunion led to fourteen consecutive Tuesdays and a transformed life. It was a two-way mystical bridge uniting a master of life with his eager apprentice. This is the kind of context that bridges and unites knowing and acting.

Stories like this remind us that these kinds of relationships are still possible. If we neglect building relationships of this quality in our churches, they won't filter into our families; and we will fall back on more programs and events to try to make up the difference. *Tuesdays with Morrie* touches a deep chord—enough to have become a major best-seller. The tragedy of a book like *Tuesdays with Morrie* is that we let that deep chord vibrate for only a moment before we are off to the next item on our busy schedules.[11]

Churches can go beyond simply strumming similar chords for an hour each Sunday. They can do this by finding the tested masters of life hidden within their own congregations. They can then create a context (not a program) to connect with those who are seeking apprenticeship. As long as our church models center on the contributions of a small circle of individuals each Sunday, the congregation will likely never know these masters exist. Consider the number of members there are to your core leadership team. If there are one hundred members to every on-staff leader (in many cases it is more) there are probably ten people per hundred that have enough life experience and spiritual maturity to make a significant contribution.

The Disconnect Between Cause and Effect

There is a terrible disconnect between our actions and their subsequent effects. We are in an age where unintended negative consequences are rising to crisis proportions. Our nation has a long legacy of providing well-intentioned relief programs to inner cities and impoverished nations; instead of creating greater self-sufficiency, these create a more dependent subculture. Each new effort to fix one problem regardless of where we find it seems to sow seeds for a variety of new problems. Like using our fingers to plug the leaks in a dam about to burst, by the time we plug one hole five more have sprung open beyond our reach. Our current models make us blind to the downstream ripple effects of our choices. Until we see ourselves, our groups, and our behaviors as part of a larger social ecosystem, each decision to serve narrowly defined needs will continue to conflict and reverberate against all of the other self-serving decisions around us. The key to bridging the gap between cause and effect is to focus less on specific outcomes and individual agendas and more on context.

The Disconnect Between Thinking Big and Seeing the Small Stuff

One example of the power of context comes from the story behind the dramatic drop in crime in New York City beginning with the transit system in the 1980s and then throughout the city in the 1990s. It centered on the broken-windows theory that James Q. Wilson and George Kelling developed. They posited that broken windows that go unrepaired are symbols to a neighborhood that "no one cares and no one is in charge."[12] It creates the context for disorder, which leads to crime. The revelation is that in complex systems the leverage comes from a fanatical focus on small things like fixing the windows and removing graffiti—not constructing a grand plan and bold campaigns.

In his book *From Good to Great,* Jim Collins refers to the same idea, using the analogy of a flywheel. After researching numerous companies, he came to this conclusion: "There was no miracle moment. Although it may have looked like a single-stroke breakthrough to those peering in from the outside, it was anything but that to people experiencing the transformation from within." Collins summarizes by saying, "The confusion of end outcomes (dramatic results) with process (organic and cumulative) skews our perception of what really works over the long haul."[13]

These two examples indicate just how out of sync we are with most of our planning and programs. Focusing on the small stuff leads us back to some of the biblical parables regarding stewardship. The seemingly dramatic breakthroughs are actually the result of the compounding effect of simple but relevant efforts. Jesus said in Luke 16:10 (NASB) that "He who is faithful in a very little thing is faithful also in much. . . ." Wendell Berry, a noted social and environmental writer, exposes the hidden dark side of the same coin: "The environmental crisis should make it dramatically clear, as perhaps it has not always been before, that there is no public crisis that is not also private."[14] In other words, we are individually culpable and cannot hide simply because we are no longer able to trace through the complexity of public problems back to our own front doors.

Our culture has a bias toward the big, the important, and the novel. We neglect and disdain the mundane and routine. We're an overweight, sickly, indebted society stretched beyond our limits. We know this and yet refuse to alter our path. This is a huge disconnect and gets to the root of why next-geners distrust our leadership.

We seem locked into a vicious cycle of diminishing returns. The way out is not to establish more programs or charities. These compound our troubles with additional narrowly focused efforts and agendas in what Collins calls "Doom Loops."[15] The way out is first to gain a more systemic understanding of our unintentionally destructive actions.

The Disconnect Between the Parts and the Whole

Again, we turn back to oral cultures and their inherently holistic view of life. They were connected. And that connection developed an inner understanding of how to live in harmony. Each person provided a living tuning fork for the other. The wisdom writings gleaned from oral cultures consolidated the peculiar insights of harmony.

> Just as each of us has one body with many members, and these members do not all have the same function, so in Christ we who are many form one body, and each member belongs to all the others. [Romans 12:4–5, NIV]

We've lost the vital connection to that harmony. It is broken and fragmented. We've spent centuries developing an inner understanding of how to impose our wills over our environment. The unintended by-product is destroying the rain forests and plundering the earth for fuel and gold, polluting our rivers and oceans in the narrow name of economic progress. Now we are experiencing the cumulative backlash for that approach, as are many areas around the world—both ecologically and culturally.

So where are the church's broken windows and the flywheel of transformation? Repairing the broken windows begins with restoring integrity—internal integrity. In other words, we ultimately produce what we are—individually and collectively—not what we intend. We make the mistake of measuring our intentions and our causes when instead we should be measuring whether we are bringing more or less wholeness into the broader context.[16] Restoring integrity results in harmony, which in turn closes the gap between cause and effect. "The Kingdom of God is . . . righteousness, peace and joy" (Romans 14:17, NIV).

Ingredients for Community

> Churches are rarely communities. More often they are social machines that run smoothly for a while, break down, then are fixed so they run smoothly again or noisily chug along as best they can.
>
> —Larry Crabb, *The Safest Place on Earth*

We have a huge challenge ahead of us. We have no reservoir of wisdom, no natural connection to our environments or one another. We still have the habits of rational planning and program implementation. To make matters worse, the pace of deterioration is accelerating, and we are in crisis.

On the other hand, we have digital tools that allow us to see the complex implications of our actions; we have the tools that allow us to restore some of our ancient understandings of wisdom; we've been chastened by our condition, and a shift to digital technology provides an opportunity for society to disengage from its current path and make fundamental change.

This brings us back once again to the church's primary mission: redeem lost souls, place the solitary in families, disciple diverse peoples, build a local unified body (community), and become salt and light to society. When we become vital to one another, we become vital to our larger community. Let's review the ingredients for real community that we can begin to incorporate back into the mission of the church.

Covenant and Security

Churches must be safe places to come to. Right now, by and large, they're not.[17]

Reclaiming the concept of covenant is key for a digital era because we are losing many of the structures that print created, which developed and maintained what we've come to know as civil society. We are also losing the print mind-set that provided external filters with either-or precepts and cause-and-effect implications for behavior. Broadcast created new filters, internal filters that have blurred well-defined (and rigid) print borders with a subjective frame of reference. The interactive nature of digital media and the new mind-set will draw us back to oral sensibility where goodwill, open intentions, and reciprocity govern the dynamic of social interaction. Covenant becomes a vital tool once again not only as an ethical boundary of commitment but as a moral choice in establishing relationships and building community.

Covenant is not a principle we can discuss in an audience of a thousand or broadcast to millions, coming away as covenant brothers and sisters. Covenant is relationally specific, jointly crafted, and derived from and established in faith. People today experience covenant, though this is not common. Once they have been "salted by fire" (Mark 9:49), they possess an internalized cohesion, a saltiness that allows them to live among others who similarly understand covenant.

As digital media continue to break down existing physical and conceptual boundaries, the church has an incredible opportunity and need to rediscover covenant in terms of building integrated and cohesive individuals, families, neighborhoods, communities, and congregations.

The covenant cohesion of an assembly reestablishes the moral salt that Christ said could preserve society (Mark 9:50). We can again look at oral cultures to learn how to rediscover and recover covenant for our families, our spiritual assembly, and ourselves. I can't provide a seven-step how-to approach for covenant any more than I could provide a formula for courtship and marriage. Print substituted an external ethic of social bonds for the internal reality and practice of covenant. Once broadcast culture removed the external walls, society has struggled with maintaining cohesion. It is clear too that the church has also followed the dominant mind-sets of print and broadcast and is not currently in a position to offer a sufficient degree of cohesion to bind our families and churches together, let alone the world around us.

Promise Keepers, a national phenomenon through the 1990s, is one attempt to reverse this loss[18] (Figure 7.2). In a generation that has grown up with a 50 percent divorce rate (including within the church) and lives immersed in a medium of ever-changing reality, we can't take for granted that we tangibly understand covenant love. As digital media continue to break down existing physical and conceptual boundaries, the church has an incredible opportunity and need to rediscover covenant in terms of building integrated and cohesive individuals, families, neighborhoods, communities, and congregations—in that order.

Fellowship and Time

Fellowship provides the context in which we can explore and find covenant. We can't just fix a deficit or seminar our way to covenant— even with a national tour. We have to shift our focus away from meetings and agenda-driven activity in order to enjoy each other and regain the ability to see Christ in our brothers and sisters. "How good and satisfying it is for brothers [and sisters] to live in harmony . . . it's like fragrant oil that covers our bodies and like the abundant morning dew that waters our souls" (Psalm 133:1–3).[19] Grab hold of this word picture and bring it with you the next time you go to church or attend a church gathering.

In this regard I would like to reapply John Naisbitt's counterbalancing concept of high-tech/high-touch for the church and make it high-agenda/high-fellowship. Naisbitt introduced this concept in his first best-selling book, Megatrends. He recognized that technology had reached a tipping point and could easily impose its drive for efficiency on to every facet of our lives. Naisbitt argued the need to consciously restore the balance with human-centered, high-touch considerations. For example, in an office environment a company might counterbalance the Dilbert effect of cubicles by providing high-touch lounge areas and

Figure 7.2. Part of a crowd of an estimated 700,000 Promise Keepers, Washington, D.C., 1997.

access to natural light or allowing individuals to personalize their space. The church might consider counterbalancing the nature of its purpose-driven meetings and programs with less structured family gatherings and more interactive formats.

Reclaiming the Beloved

Mother Teresa provides my earthly benchmark for fellowship because of her ability to see Christ in the most repulsive conditions. I am moved to tears when I consider the power of this woman's compassion and the profound understanding of her source for that compassion. Jeanne Houston, futurist and author, once asked Mother Teresa,

> "How does it happen that you're able to do these things that most international development organizations can do only with immense trouble?" And she said, "My dear, it's because I'm so deeply in love." I said, "You are in love, Mother? Would you mind telling me who you are in love with?" She said, "Not at all. I'm in love with Jesus. I'm married to Jesus." I said, "Well, of course, all nuns are." She said, "No,

you don't understand, I really am. I have such a love for Jesus that I feel the presence of Jesus everywhere—in that day-old child that was left at the convent door who needs a life and an education, or that leper who comes to me and wants to be of some use in the world. I see Christ in that child and that leper. I cannot do enough for my beloved. And so my beloved, I feel, cannot do enough for me. That is why I am able to do these things."[20]

The Apostle Paul begins defining love as patient, patient enough to see Christ's image buried beneath the life of another.[21]

When I think about Mother Teresa's words, I can't help remembering Jesus' own words when answering those who asked, "Lord, when did we feed and clothe you?" Jesus said, "When you did these for the least you did it for me" (Matthew 25:31–40, NIV). He didn't say we do these things on his behalf. He said we do them for him! We've also entertained angels and have been unaware of it. Jesus addressed this crowd who were completely unaware of the connection but sensitive to its implications. Today we are aware of the connection but completely desensitized to its implications. We are part of an age that can do more—less significantly. We have the liberty, through Christ, to choose otherwise and become significant to fewer people, which in the end achieves more. None of these qualities can be achieved in a hurry nor scripted on a time line. I've heard this present condition described as spiritual autism, an orientation desensitized to outside realities.[22] We will need time together—a completely different kind of time and fellowship than we currently understand in order to bring back the subtle moral receptors we once possessed. Perhaps the shifting medium can help restore some of our oral sensibilities so that our eyes can see and our ears hear our real and integral connection to one another through Christ.

Relational Accountability

The ceremonial symbol of covenant is salt, as we discussed earlier. We seldom see salt in its original form of chunks mined out of the ground. You may have noticed salt blocks used on farms for animals to lick.

Farmers use salt in this form because it holds up against the elements. Salt's cohesion and ability to stay together through any and all circumstances symbolizes the quality of our commitments. Accountability has become the current buzzword for our substitution of covenant. Covenant goes deeper; finding its power may require that we restore a more ancient understanding of how one's behavior and well-being become intimately tied with another's. David and Jonathan provide a vivid description of the quality and commitment of covenant beginning in 1 Samuel 18. When we overlay the image of this story with our current images of accountability and accountability groups,[23] they really don't intersect. We have new tools of perception that allow us to reframe our paradigms of commitment.

The heart of covenant conveys that our words are reliable and binding. Covenant says that we count the cost and weight of what we say and do. Covenants are explicit and tangible. If we break a covenant, the consequences are dire. Not keeping one's word means more than an inconvenience or a misunderstanding. The consequence erodes the salt. As we explained earlier, the bonds of oral culture access a life force that empowers words. Preserving integrity preserves meaning and preserves the bonds of community. If words don't hold together, then the mystical umbilical cord of life becomes severed between lives.

Fortunately or not, we are so far removed from this level of intimacy that our daily lapses don't bring about imminent destruction. On the other hand, our words carry little value or cohesion. For example, if someone tells us they will do anything they can to help us, we automatically discount the offer. In fact, we unconsciously transpose most of the promises from others with little expectation for fulfillment. Imagine how life might change if we did what we said and could rely on what others said. Setting aside the practical benefits for a moment, what would this mean to the quality of our relationships? This may seem hypothetical, too far removed and impractical to consider. But not if we take the Wendell Berry approach and build integrity first into our private lives. In fact, this is one of those broken windows the church has neglected to repair that has set the tone for the rest of society. If the salt loses its saltiness, then what?

Transparency and Truth

Safe environments, secure relationships, time together, and mutual accountability create an atmosphere that allows transparency and creates the foundation to deal with reality: truth. When Jesus says, "You will know the truth and the truth will set you free" (John 8:32, NIV), one of the meanings of the Greek word for truth is "reality."

If people in a church cannot express what they think or see, or do not feel it is safe to do so, then there is no basis for community. You can have the security, fellowship, and commitment; but without transparency and truth, people submerge their feelings, thoughts, and behaviors into politics. People will go underground with their agendas, create quiet coalitions, resort to competition and conflict, posture, and create confusion—as soon as they understand that speaking openly is risky. The same path applies as soon as people realize that leadership is unwilling to see or acknowledge the actual state of affairs and deal with it. If people perceive that maintaining the party line or protecting certain interests takes priority, then politics prevail and inner and outer circles form. Code language develops, and the seeds and cycles of division grow. If an organization has become political, it can typically be traced to a breakdown in security, fellowship, commitment, or transparency.

Organizations can prevent this or reverse it following the research that Jim Collins lays out in the fourth chapter of *Good to Great*. "The moment a leader allows himself to become the primary reality people worry about, rather than reality being the primary reality, you have a recipe for mediocrity or worse." Here are four elements Collins's research suggests for building an environment of reality:

- Lead with questions, not answers.
- Engage in dialogue and debate, not coercion.
- Conduct autopsies without blame.
- Build red-flag mechanisms (early warning systems).

Confession and Repentance

Confession and repentance are an outgrowth of transparency and reality. When there are breaches in covenant, insensitivities in fellowship, lapses in behavior, or sin, they need to be repaired. If the organization is not vitally connected, then confessing and repenting for the sake of the assembly makes no sense. When relationships are vital and safe, then we recover the corporate healing power through confession and repentance.

These breaches are part of the disconnecting forces that drain away our life from one another, divide us, and remove our salt to society. The world has no idea how to mend itself. The church holds the secrets to that healing power. The more interactive and nonterritorial nature of digital space will help to shift toward restoring harmony and mending the breaches and away from keeping score and hanging the guilty out to dry. James says that confession to one another is essential to maintaining our saltiness (James 5:16). Digital proximity removes some of the layers of formality and abstraction that confession has acquired. It adds an easy escape, however, into virtual confessionals. Reclaiming the ancient practice in the physical presence of those we are intimately tied to provides the restoring and transforming power that Paul describes.

Service as a Servant

Serving is not a function. Serving, from a biblical and oral perspective, is a moral expression of our being. God's love was expressed in his Son, who came to serve and become a ransom for our sins (Matthew 10:28). Jesus said that we can't show any greater love than by laying down our lives for one another (John 15:13). This is the central message for all who would lead the church; at the same time, servant leadership has lost a lot of its original context and clarity.

Serving is far more than volunteering one's time and teaching classes. It has little to do with how much effort or passion we invest. Christ gave up his rights, his agenda, his approach, and even his life in order to serve his Father. Serving is giving up what we hold dear in order to conform to someone else's desires. It is a process whereby we learn to conform to another's image and becoming that person's servant. It is a process of becoming malleable and open-handed.

This attitude is reflected in the rabbinical tradition of discipleship. Christ reflects this attitude when he struggles with his Father in the garden (Matthew 26:39). Paul says, "In Christ Jesus I became your

Father in the Gospel. Therefore, I urge you to imitate me" (1 Corinthians 4:16, NIV). He also describes this posture in his letter to the Philippians (2:5–11) when he exhorts them to take on Christ's submissive attitude toward one another. Why is this so critical to community and moral society? Because it is our only vehicle to unity. Covenant without serving one another eventually loses its attractiveness and value, just as does a marriage that loses its mutual love and affection.

Servant leadership, however, has become overshadowed by academic degrees, professional polish, big business, conflicts of interest, busyness, and a host of other invaders. I remember playing tennis when I was a kid simply because I loved it. Then I played to compete, win, and achieve recognition. Finally, I played to make a living. All of these phases were good for me. However, as I look back, I can see the distinct change in motivation. I played for different reasons. Since I've left the tennis profession, I have found it difficult to get back on the court with any degree of enthusiasm or regularity. Somehow along the way, my initial enthusiasm and love was lost, and I haven't found it yet. I wonder sometimes if some of our leaders would still choose to lead or do similar things without the paycheck, competitive drive to achieve, or the recognition. We all have to ask if we are doing what we do for the love of it.

Firsthand Charity

The Greek word for charity, *charis*, means "gift of grace." Again, the moral connotations make *charis* personal and specific. The power of the gift is the connection to the giver behind the gift. When we directly extend charity, we extend Christ.

It's not about the gift. We have so disconnected *charis* from the giver that we now focus almost exclusively on the gifts. In fact, we've delegated our charity to people with whom we have no connection or relationship. It doesn't matter what images we receive of those our dollars have supposedly helped. Unless we have a relationship to them or those serving them, our dollars are simply dollars. When we give in this way, we place the emphasis on the gift and lose the bonding power of love that represents the real motivation behind the gift.

Should we reject the efforts of all those groups and individuals who are doing everything they can to meet insatiable and unspeakable needs? No, but we could wish they were empowered by the motivated relationships behind the money. Money is a weak substitute for the collective power of love, but it currently provides a remnant to build from and something to which we can connect more personally. I suggest that you become involved with charitable efforts that put you in direct contact with those the charity serves. Habitat for Humanity is just one vehicle that allows you to have a firsthand involvement with those you are helping.

If you give money, don't give it only to organizations; give also to people you know that you can empower. Most of our charitable contributions are like purchasing our produce at the supermarket. We give to an invisible corporation with invisible layers between us and those who might actually receive our gift. View your charity as you grow your own garden. View it not as a transaction at an intersection but a relationship that can grow.

The Next Step

Reclaiming community is not a digital domain but a timeless challenge. The opportunity to restore the moral topsoil comes from the magnitude of our shift from broadcast culture than from any inherent virtues of digital media. We will be better prepared to reclaim lost virtues by better understanding the nature of the new soil of relationships and give up plowing old ground with dull tools.

The soil for community comes from the church's vital relationships, initiated by the example of leadership. As an organization restores the wholeness of its members, working outward to create a cohesive congregation, it will see the unfolding revelation of the bigger picture as an ever-expanding expression of a harmonious body of Christ. As long as the church remains fragmented, hurried, pressed, and driven, it will never be able to see much beyond ever-pressing urgencies. If, however, we restore the priority of relationships and community over projects, agendas, budgets, and mission statements, then not only will we survive the transition into a digital world order but the new environment will provide a potent soil for growth and an expression of the body of Christ.

CHAPTER 8

Convergence

The Living Church

> "I am the Vine, you are the branches. When you're joined with me
> and I with you, the relation intimate and organic, the harvest is sure
> to be abundant."
> —John 15:5 (MSG)

At the beginning of this book, we looked at seven emerging realities that will drive society in the very near future: interconnection, complexity, acceleration, intangibility, convergence, immediacy, and unpredictability. Every person, organization, and institution—including the church—is confronting these conditions right now. In this final chapter, we'll address how the church will need to adapt in order to survive and thrive in the new world ahead.

In Chapter Five we looked at how the new church would need to be designed in order to be a strong vessel capable of advancing the righteousness, peace, and joy of God's kingdom. Boiled down to its essence, this church will need to be both flexible and permeable, able to bend and stretch with the fast-changing times and able to take in what is good from the new culture and filter out what is harmful. This is more than a reorganization; it is the positive outgrowth of convergence and a new metaphor for Christ's body—a living church for the new millennium.[1]

The image of a living church embodies the interactive, highly networked, deeply aligned, and distributed community of the digital era. It embraces new concepts like collective intelligence, self-organizing structures, systems archetypes, and continuous learning (evolution) and living. This is a wholly other wineskin than most of us are familiar with, but those who have experienced even a taste of the wine inside agree: it's potent and liberating.

Living churches will have new characteristics of leadership, worship, community, virtual community, message, growth, and architecture. These seven aspects are so dynamically different that I first called the new framework spiritual environmentalism because of their interwoven nature. However, some of the emerging young leaders I have spoken with have taken issue with this term. They tell me that I am really speaking of a new "vibe." This term, which at first reminded me of the 1960s, also fits another, perhaps more intriguing image: tuning into a new, higher vibration in this digital culture, which is calling to us to listen with new ears. The specific new vibes I want to address here are the seven I feel are most important: leadership, worship, community, virtual community, message, growth, and architecture.

> The image of a living church embodies the interactive, highly networked, deeply aligned, and distributed community of the digital era.

The Leadership Vibe

> Don't become so well-adjusted to your culture that you fit into it without even thinking. Instead, fix your attention on God. You'll be changed from the inside out.
>
> —Romans 12:2 (MSG)

Shepherds knows their sheep, and sheep know their shepherd: that deep sense of identification is a trademark of leadership in any era. As we have seen, the future will require impartational leaders: men and women who are truly accessible and connected to their constituents in a way we rarely see today. Instead of looking for leaders who are the best and the brightest, we will see a renewed premium on the life and integrity of the leader. The digital culture requires that leaders first and foremost love what they do and offer themselves as living models.

The old schools of leadership—in our case, the seminaries—are turning out professional experts who may or may not be leaders. Look at a picture of this year's graduating class from whatever seminary you choose, and lay it side by side with another showing Jesus' leadership team: fishermen, tax collectors, lawyers, and prostitutes. The contrast is startling. Do we so underestimate God's capabilities and the objects of God's affection? We are at a tipping point for a new framework, one moving from professionalism to its opposite, amateurism: people who do what they do for sheer love of God and God's children. These leaders will look at the world not through the eyes of overworked administrators who are running as fast as they can to keep the church afloat for one more week, but with what Zen master Shunryu Suzuki calls *beginner's mind*, "an ability to look at the world with fresh eyes and an open spirit."[2]

The Worship Vibe

This is the air I breathe, your Holy presence
living in . . . me.
—Marie Bennett, "Breathe"

Worship leaders bring the current worship vibe to the church service—the Sunday main event. But in the future they will help protect the vibe and nurture its growth every day through every aspect of their organization's structure, facility, programs, and culture. This means that the living church will be very different from previous churches.

The old liturgical model provides the most comprehensive example of an all-encompassing worship vibe, but it does not meet the future criteria for flexibility and accessibility. The Reformation model provides deep worship content, but it is hierarchical and certainly not interactive. The broadcast or postmodern model creates a worship ambience that connects with worshipers but lacks true interaction or content depth. Like the Reformation model, it is not integrated into the congregational culture.

Reformation pastors have focused on oratory. Worship developed a separate identity as one of the secondary leadership responsibilities. Broadcast elevated worship as a key leadership role and also an industry. Today's worship leaders, charged with producing a Sunday event, are typically musicians. Our current paradigm views worship as a musical activity, and music is certainly a central element of worship expression. Oral cultures, however, viewed worship in a more culturally integrated fashion, and digital culture will return to this kind of integration—and then keep going.

Back in oral times, the priest was not a worship specialist but rather a director of the ritual, which provided one expression of worship. Worship was actually the underlying subtext for experiencing the different sacraments, celebrations, and seasons—expressed through ritual. This brings us back to the metaphor of grafting, which challenges our current emphasis on the pastor's role and the preeminence of preaching and teaching. In some churches, pastors or preachers can be said to run the show, bringing in the worship specialist later to provide the worship portion. In other churches the worship specialist sets the atmosphere and then turns the service over to the pastor. In either scenario this is set up as a top-down experience: the leader spoon-feeds and directs the crowd. But as churchgoers begin demanding more and interactive involvement with the service, we will begin to see how things that once seemed innovative and exciting—platforms, theater-style seating, microphones, wires, and all the rest—actually keep us from real involvement.

The organization side of a living church requires the continual counterbalancing of functionalism and politics. These are the weeds that erode the worship vibe. The worship vibe exists in a culture of openness and freedom: openness to seeing the reality of the current condition and freedom to express what one sees without fear of reprisal or reprimand. Without these conditions a living church becomes a political church with insiders and outsiders, factions and agendas, and a need to shape or spin the way it presents reality to its supposedly uninformed public. This is one of the traps print and broadcast churches fall into. When power is centralized within a small core, it is easy and tempting to present an image of being better than ever. The distributed nature of digital organizations changes the dynamics of power, allowing the congregation not only to see the inner workings but to have input. In business we call this keeping everyone honest.

The online retailer Amazon.com offers a great example. I recently purchased a used book from one of their affiliates for four dollars. I received a follow-up e-mail with a survey asking how I would rate my experience. I wasn't completely happy: the site had presented the book as being in excellent condition, but I found that the pages were yellowed and the book had a black line across the bottom. So I rated my experience as a three out of five, hit the Send button, and off it went to somewhere in cyberspace. But that wasn't the end of the story. Within twenty-four hours I received a very distressed and heartfelt e-mail from the person I bought the book from. In the e-mail she explained the pride she takes in her business and the impact that my rating will have for her future business. She asked me to please contact her directly in the future if I'm dissatisfied, to give her an opportunity to rectify any problem.

Wow! That one e-mail changed my whole perspective. This was no longer a nameless, faceless transaction. My life and this person's life were engaged in a very personal exchange establishing rules for future transactions, rules that I had never really thought about because my exchanges on the Web had never come back to bite me like this. She was protecting her "transaction vibe," and unknowingly so was I. This small story illustrates how valuable a transparent and interactive environment are to feelings of interpersonal connection, to future growth, and to keeping everyone honest—which protects the worship vibe.

Millions of interactions like this occur every day. Dialogue and similar exchanges are the key to changing attitudes and changing behavior. I agree with Christopher Locke's assertion that igniting these is the role of leadership.[3] Unmediated dialogue actually brings about change more rapidly and fundamentally than current top-down vision proclamations and change programs. Imagine your congregation providing similar feedback for each church experience. Were you able to meet somebody new? How did today's sermon affect your thoughts and your behavior? Are you currently satisfied with your experience in our church? The point is not to wear everyone out with evaluation questionnaires but to ask meaningful questions, really listen to the answers, and spark dialogue. If someone responds to such a survey with the statement "I'm not satisfied because I feel like a spectator and I don't know anyone," someone would call this person the very next day and say, "Let's sit down and see how we can change that experience next time."

This worship vibe helps fine-tune all aspects of a church through direct involvement, open dialogue, and a transparent culture. The worship leader of the future will have more to do with maintaining this dynamic than developing the song list for a Sunday service and conducting rehearsals.[4]

The Community Vibe

If you have participated in a large family wedding or family reunion, you know the kind of unique atmosphere that permeates this sort of gathering. Getting together and fellowship (and food) take priority, and family business takes place under this umbrella. This is the community vibe we will see in the living church.

Community has become a popular buzzword. Unfortunately, many new initiatives approaching community are typically efforts to solve a problem in the church or simply to jump on to a popular bandwagon. For example, a church that suffers from high turnover adopts a home-group strategy in order to help people get more connected. In this example community is a means to an end, and manufactured community is an oxymoron. It is without purpose because purpose means original intent. The original intent in this example was to fix the turnover problem, and a community strategy looked like the right tool at this time. Without original intent, however, so-called community-oriented programs get dropped for the next tool to fix turnover, get dropped if they become too difficult, or get dropped out of boredom. Here's the bottom line: true community is a by-product of connected lives; it is not a method to create something that is not already present.

The community vibe contrasts with what we so often see today—church gatherings that are agenda-driven and fellowship that happens in passing as we rush from one meeting to another. Gen-Xers and younger are more interested in "hanging" together first and then taking care of business. Gathering, fellowship, and communion is the end; business is the by-product. This trend reflects the interactive medium.

This brings us back to recontextualizing our image of the church as a body and a family. It also supports the shift away from event-driven Sundays to considering how to better come together in ways that help us remain connected to one another in our daily lives.

When you look at Harley-Davidson gatherings, folk-arts festivals, Grateful Dead revival concerts, the International Worship Institute, ethnic weddings, large family reunions, Macworld, Bill Gaither concerts, and even Mary Kay or Amway conventions, you find an intoxicating mix of fellowship, celebration, and—at least in the nonfamily events—enterprise. Each of these examples has consistently grown over the past fifteen years. They have been unusually effective—not because of an efficient agenda but rather out of the synergy of interaction and fellowship. In fact, many of these examples appear inefficient and chaotic. The lens of efficiency, however, cannot calculate the effects of intimate and complex interaction around common interest.

In the future many emerging congregations will begin to look like extended spiritual families. This kind of ethos will extend into neighborhoods, with Christians favoring the common bond of proximity over church affiliation as a basis for home groups. In some ways we are moving to a modernized parish model.

The Virtual Community Vibe

As individuals seek communion with like minds online, boundaries between real world and online community become blurred forcing us to consider new definitions of what it means to be in community in the 21st century. This is especially true for Generation Xers who are more likely to see their support network coming from a linking of relationships in different context than those located in their common geography.

—Heidi Campbell, "Community.dot.com:
A Look at Networked Community and Generation X"

Some people think that the Internet is simply a more efficient communications tool. But that's like calling Disney World an amusement park or Starbucks a coffee shop. As one commentator on on-line communities puts it, "The net is a planet-spanning virtual ecosystem, a cognitive rain forest teeming with new concepts and connections, issues and inquiries, studies and speculations, proposals, predictions and unlimited potential."[5]

Where is the church inside this universe? Barely to be seen, at least for now. For the most part, it has simply moved old media onto a Web format. Church Web sites primarily offer basic information, brochures, audio sermon downloads, some resource links, and perhaps a little e-commerce. The real power and attraction in Web sites, however, lies in creating virtual communities.[6]

David Siegel says that today's Web sites reflect their organization but tomorrow's organization will reflect its Web site.[7] There is no clearer sign that churches are unprepared for the emerging era than their Web sites. It's easy to fix a clumsy Web site: you can hire someone to upgrade the graphics and update the content. But the really important—I'd even say crucial—job is to begin to understand the inherent power of a church Web site and its future role in creating a living church. To that end I'd like to offer a brief primer.

First, a Web site is not primarily about creating electronic brochures or posting mission statements, event calendars, and staff photos. It is much more than an efficient way to make the latest sermon available or handle event registration. The Internet is fundamentally about connecting with people of common interest, facilitating person-to-person conversations, collaboration, assistance, and collective learning. The Internet inverts the power curve away from centralized control and content to distributed power and member-generated content. The Internet is about the exponential value of networks (Metcalfe's Law),[8] the power of conversation, and liberation from past obstacles of time, location, gender, age, ethnicity, disability, and tradition.

The Internet journey begins with connection, leads to conversation, generates content, builds context, raises consciousness, and produces compounded growth. The virtual community vibe focuses on

KNITWORKS: RECONNECTING
THE DOTS TO COMMUNITY

I've reapplied a term I heard from a local pastor—*Knit-works*—to define the intimate neighborhood gatherings that seem on the rise. I came upon the idea of Knitworks as I have so many other life-changing ideas—as a result of banging my head against the wall.

Several years ago, when our two children were around the ages of three and four, my wife, Lisa, and I were leaders in a growing multiethnic church. We loved it. We lived in Reston, Virginia, and I worked on the other side of Washington's infamous beltway near Landover, Maryland—exactly forty-two miles from home or ninety minutes if the Wilson Bridge and the beltway weren't clogged.

Part of our leadership responsibility included participating in one of the home groups. The home group we were part of was at the home of one of the associate pastors, thirty minutes from our house. On many occasions I would rush home from work and bark, "Let's get to the car, now—let's go, let's go, let's go!" After I wound everyone tight with stress, we arrived at the home group and met with people we saw only once a week. The meeting ended by 8:30, but it was usually 9:30 or later by the time we left. The kids always fell asleep on the way home, and we had to wake them up to get them into the house and up for bed. By the time this ritual ended, it was about 10:30 or 11 at night. The next morning both my wife and I were tired and the kids were cranky. Without questioning the sanity of this ritual, we repeated it each week for several months.

The blinders finally fell off when Lisa and I made plans for a cruise. My parents were scheduled to take care of the children while we were out of town; but a week before their trip my mother fell and broke her arm, and they could not come. We went to our church for help. And as hard as they tried to find people who could help, there were really no families who lived close enough to take care of our kids and get them back and forth to school. Fortunately, our neighbors jumped in to help and did so gladly.

After this experience I began an internal dialogue over the Scripture verse "Love your neighbor as yourself" (Matthew 22:39, NIV). How could I do this? With my work and church commitments, I was seldom home, and we had almost no chance to invite neighbors over because of all of our activities. That is when I started to shift my priorities to favor community over activity.

I asked my senior pastor if we could opt out of our home group and begin inviting our Christian neighbors over for fellowship. He thought it was a great idea. It offered the added benefit of simplifying our lives, developing closer connections to our neighbors, and becoming aware of the needs on the block. We never developed formal meetings, but we enjoyed many occasions of front-step and mailbox fellowship, backyard cookouts, spontaneous visits, holiday gatherings. Kids freely went back and forth between homes; parents kept an eye out for the kids, who played together at the little park at the end of the block, and so on. This may sound like normal neighbor-type stuff, but for our family and others I have met it only happened when we began to shift the reason behind our involvements.

Knitworks, or neighborhood-centered small groups, offer the potential of providing a far more effective means of outreach and community service. Churches that begin to develop a community vibe and teach their members how to take that vibe with them into their neighborhoods and businesses are going to find themselves far more effective with less stress and strain.

leveraging the connections, content, and collaboration of the constituents by creating a Web community.[9]

We have an exciting opportunity before us—to affect the new
cultural landscape in ways parallel to the first century and the Reformation. But truly understanding and being able to use the virtual community vibe will require a profound shift in thought for today's leaders.[10]
We will have to reapproach the Web with a far deeper understanding, as
if we were planning to move to a new country—permanently. We can't
get by with learning just enough of the new language to order off a
menu. We have to continually expose ourselves to those on the frontier
until we can think fluently inside this new continuum of ideas, conversations, and relationships—no longer strangers in a strange land but
vital residents of a new world.

The Message Vibe

> People are more concerned with presenting their mes-
> sages within the constraints of the medium than assuring
> the recipient actually understands the message. . . . We
> use technology to share an experience rather than create
> a shared experience.
>
> —Michael Schrage, *No More Teams*

If, as Marshall McLuhan told us some years ago, "the medium is the
message,"[11] then when we're talking about the message vibe, we're talking about the digital medium. Leaders who understand the new message vibe will empower their message with the virtues of interaction
and relationally linked information,[12] and these connections will result
in better retention.

Connections are not a new concept! One of the best explana-
tions and demonstrations of connection is found in James Burke's
book *The Knowledge Web*. With breathtaking ingenuity, Burke shows how
seemingly unconnected ideas, events, and people are actually "inter-
locking threads of knowledge running through Western history. . . .
how seemingly unrelated ideas and innovations bounce off one

another, spinning a vast, interactive web on which everything is connected to everything else: Carmen leads to the theory of relativity, champagne bottling links to wallpaper design, Joan of Arc connects through vaudeville to Buffalo Bill."[13]

This perfectly describes the Internet experience, with its hyperlinks offering instantaneous leaps through cyberspace that replace linear thinking with something more three- (or four-) dimensional. Those who intuitively understand this kind of thinking, or grew up with the Internet as an everyday tool, feel constrained when they have to sit through a linear presentation with seven alliterated points. The Internet experience typically provides a dashboard summary of vital points and a portal to further explore, through interaction, layers of significance and seeming insignificance. Few presenters have the breadth of knowledge to perform such a feat alone, as James Burke does. But many will be able to launch into a topic and draw from a combination of the audience and technical assistants (linked on-line) in a real-time multimedia format offering a thoroughly engrossing and life-impacting experience.

Regrettably, most seminaries still train pastors to develop the seven-point message—straight out of the print era—but it no longer impresses a broadcast audience already overloaded with slogans and clichés. So contemporary seminaries that focus on relevance make sure pastors connect with the audience by telling a joke or an anecdote tied to the bottom line of the message—straight out of the broadcast era. Many of the stories used to illustrate sermons have been recycled so often that they have long lost their original power. Instead of crafting anecdotes from personal experience, too many pastors fall back on tried-and-true stories they can easily find bound and categorized for any occasion.

You'll find some other emerging models in places you might not suspect.

Blue's Clues, a television show for young children, provides one promising model. If you haven't already, I recommend that you watch a few episodes. The show uses a simple format that follows a single theme—a puzzle for the audience to solve. The theme is reinforced throughout the show using obvious but clever illustrations. The most unusual aspect of the show is that the same episode airs five days in a row. Educators have found that children retain far more information from *Blue's Clues* than from *Sesame Street*. Why?

Part of the reason is the simpler format. The broadcast-based *Sesame Street* is very fragmented, with a variety of vignettes. The humor is often subtle, and it is easy to get distracted by the characters' antics. *Blue's Clues*, on the other hand, maintains continuity through the episode, and dramatic moments always connect to the theme. Educators also found that when children watch an episode for the first time, they are stimulated more by the novelty and their brains develop a general orientation to what is going on. Children start connecting with the story line or the theme as they watch the repeat episode through the week. They build layers of familiarity, grasping subtleties they might never otherwise understand.

The implications for our broadcast-conditioned congregations are huge! First, we have to back up and question our objectives. If the purpose is for the congregation to walk away thinking about the content of the service, asking deeper questions, then our services should look more like *Blue's Clues* and less like *Sesame Street*. Instead of a catchy seven-point message, we need to deliver a one-point message with seven ways to reinforce the point.[14] Using logic, telling an anecdote, or using movie clips can certainly be part of those tools. These all help, but they still maintain the separation between the messenger and the audience.

With digital media shaping our sensibilities, we can bridge the divide by introducing more interactive elements. One example worth considering is improvisational theater, in which audience members participate in creating the show. Some of the "unplugged" concerts also provide a smaller venue with interaction. Bill Gaither struck a chord several years ago when he and several of his musician friends stood around a piano and sang whatever songs came to mind and shared memories together. The response to that ad-lib session was so great that it has become a successful national tour.

A new element in the message vibe is narrative. Narrative is more than anecdotes that punctuate a point. The new storytellers are capturing transcendent and current themes and weaving them into stories of local interest. One of the best examples of these is Garrison Keillor and his *Prairie Home Companion* radio show on National Public Radio.

Keillor has created a context that provides a mix of Norwegian Lutheran Midwestern values along with traditional (print) virtues and small-town quirkiness. The stories he tells from his imaginary hometown of Lake Wobegon, Minnesota, reveal transcending themes and drama through the mundane details of the lives of ordinary people. No matter how old you are or what part of the country you live in, Keillor's stories ring true with a humor and sadness that hit a deeper chord than simply capturing life's ups and downs. Whether you are liberal or conservative, you feel your moral compass reorienting in search of a higher guide.

On the frontier of our current digital world is the multiuser dimension (MUD), an interactive story and role-playing activity within a digital environment. This is one of the further outposts of story creating and storytelling, and an exciting one. In a MUD environment (which exists only in cyberspace), participants—kids, adults, and software engineers—create and build their own on-line characters and worlds. They can even leave their creations behind to become part of the world after they leave.[15]

MUDs reflect the shift toward interactive storytelling, exploration, and ritual. When we look at some of the interactive on-line games available, we can see a definite shift away from linear story lines and toward open-ended interactive games and reenactments. These games and stories set general themes and then develop numerous subplots that trail off and reenter into the larger context. A real-life example you might be more familiar with is the phenomenon of Civil War reenactments, where Civil War buffs dress in period costume, travel to actual battlefields, and reenact the battles.

Developing a message vibe requires change on numerous fronts. Each of these examples touches an element. Collectively, they provide a realignment of thinking. The most profound realignment comes from where we find the power and passion of our message.

The Growth Vibe

As with other elements of current church life, growth has shifted from being a by-product of strong community to becoming a means to achieve strong community; now it has finally become an end in itself.

Most organizations certainly don't think of themselves as growth-driven and certainly don't recognize the symptoms. But the fact remains that many of them are. New-paradigm organizations run rings around traditional ones and force them to spend themselves into oblivion—restructuring, adding people, and increasing the use of technology in an attempt to keep up. Size and rigidity eventually break down in an environment of speed and complexity. It's as simple as that.

We can take a lesson from the original concepts that led to the design of the Internet. Some years ago the U.S. Department of Defense recognized that an enemy that could take out a few central telephone offices (where the switches are housed) could easily destroy our entire communications system. That would leave the whole nation vulnerable. To counter this threat, a small group of engineers working within the Defense Advanced Research Projects Agency (the independent research branch of the U.S. Department of Defense) created the World Wide Web: a networked system of communication. It was built around a completely decentralized structure of servers connected in a weblike manner. If any one server crashed or was destroyed, communication was automatically rerouted along another path. The great success of today's Internet is this survivability.

The visionary thinking that led engineers to redesign our primary means of communication, however, has not translated into similar redesign of society's institutions. Our Internet communication technology can survive attack from multiple fronts, but our institutions and organizations remain vulnerable to the attack of changing paradigms. Many churches are extremely vulnerable because of their size and rigidity, their dependency on a few leaders at the top, their lack of connection to their members, and their lack of connection to other churches.

Many large churches are recognizing their vulnerability, and a number of them have implemented strategies to create smaller-scale venues for involvement. My concern is that the drive behind many of these efforts is similar to attempts to manufacture community, an attempt to recapture paradise lost and not a first-cause or foundational strategy. These are attempts to rectify a single problem instead of working with what is central to the organization's culture and makeup. It's got the wrong vibe for long-term success. If that is the case, these efforts will actually end up competing for resources and the infrastructure will weaken further and remain out of balance.

Some churches are applying the old federalist model. Federalism, the original model for the United States, establishes a network of autonomous organizations or communities that pool resources to accomplish what they cannot accomplish alone. Several large churches are creating satellite churches, but this is not federalism. These are more like franchises; as franchises, they remove the texture of the local community because they focus on the internal success formula that the home office developed.

Our most tangible examples of distributed structures come from business organizations like Visa, Yahoo, and Amazon.com. These are organizations that maintain a relatively small infrastructure compared to the valuations they have achieved and the network of outside resources they employ. Promising elements are growing in various churches, however, that will help paint the emerging picture.

Community Christian Church in Naperville, Illinois, provides an example of a potentially sustainable growth strategy that follows a form of federalism. This church has designed growth around a series of campuses that share common resources. Each campus takes on the size and character of the community it serves. It also extends this model to outside organizations with its New Thing Network. This affords other churches the opportunity to receive training and various levels or tracks of support called apprenticing, coaching, partnering, and fellowship. Although I view future growth models as more organic, less branded, networked, and integrated into the overall local community, models like this federation approach provide a workable structure to accomplish the others.

The Catholic parish model, which focuses on serving the community, is another interesting model. Many Catholic congregations (despite the recent bad press and general criticisms) offer examples of vibrant community life with sustainable growth. The Catholic Church still offers the kinds of relational acceptance and connection, rich liturgical content, narrative, and local autonomy that could easily translate into a digital context and suddenly place the Catholic Church back in the forefront. In order to accomplish this, the church still has to clean out the institutionalized corruption and doctrinal rigidity. A promising and growing movement within the Catholic laity may be the key to achieve these reforms.

These are just a few examples that contain elements of future sustainability. Some additional models bridge our efforts and thinking toward a more distributed and global-local (glocal) culture. Mega-churches can be valuable to their smaller neighbors. Once they build trust and establish structures like covenetworks to protect local congregations from losing members, then doors can open to help with support and training, talent, and the use of facilities. I expect to see many of these mega-churches transforming into local Christian community centers. The Jewish community has maintained its strong identity and values in part because of its many community centers.

These facilities can also offer business clubs similar to the airline clubs for frequent business travelers that provide meeting rooms, copy equipment, computer hookups, lounges, and food. More and more businesspeople work outside an office. I frequently stop at a café to work and make phone calls. I would just as happily stop at a Christian business center. In doing so I would probably meet someone with common interests or find a business contact, as well as further integrate my Christian walk into my secular work. I am convinced that the cross-pollination that would take place in these facilities would create an explosion of positive influence on the local business community—not to mention in the churches. The web metaphor offers a great potential to help tie together the local church community, coordinate resources, and develop a collaborative environment.

Microradio licenses provide broadcast ranges of about five to ten miles, and technology allows small organizations to produce professional results inexpensively. These radio stations provide churches the opportunity to meet very specific and local interests. The stations can provide a forum for members to talk about issues within the church or invite feedback from the community. They can replay sermons, promote events, air music that will be used in future worship service, and develop programming that addresses the unique interests of their congregation.

Such concepts make sense as part of a decentralized and networked world. The first step is to step off our treadmills long enough to really see these new paths and begin to walk them.

The Architecture Vibe

Let's face it: the church offers some of the best and worst examples of architecture. From inspiring, relevant, and integrated to tacky, overblown, and boring, our buildings are all over the map. But a building is not just a roof over the heads of worshipers: it can also embody and sustain the worship vibe in a real and meaningful way. Let's look at some of the key criteria that an organization should consider when building a structure to support its mission.

The role of the architect is to define the nature of social interaction and facilitate human connection (and meaning) through building. The holistic applications of early architecture considered the role each building played with the whole community. This perspective established principles for placement, scale, and relative proportion to one another. Today most architecture focuses on the building, sometimes a campus, as if it were the focal point. In many ways it is an exalted structure intended to draw attention. Interior architecture is often reduced to an exercise in optimizing use and creating a branded image. The vibe of connection and meaning take a back seat.

As we saw in earlier chapters, many of the great cathedrals of the Middle Ages and the Renaissance incorporated religious symbolism into every aspect of the design.[16] Changing paradigms allow us to reconsider architecture as we shift toward relational connection, greater integration with the larger community, and a more interactive and intimate scale. Some of the new design criteria will include fit (within the community), flexibility, accessibility, and inclusion of concepts of virtual space.[17] Here are some questions to consider when you evaluate your current building or think about designing a new one.

• Does it fit the community? It's a shame to see any organization build a structure that dramatically clashes with its surroundings. This reflects a narrow self-interest and sends that vibe to the community. You may think that a large, visible edifice attracts new members, and for some churches it might. But that does not counteract the visual offense it creates and the not-so-subtle message of self-promotion. Plenty of organizations have large structures and have done them well. One of my favorites is Willow Creek in Barrington, Illinois (Figures 8.1 and 8.2). This large structure fits proportionately on the property and is

Figure 8.1. Willow Creek Church fits into the landscape.

landscaped in such a way as to make it seem an integral part of the land. I also appreciate organizations that restore old structures and maintain their primary aesthetic while revamping them for new uses.

• Is our facility flexible to change? Monsanto developed the concept of office areas as stage sets. Using movable partitions, for example, one area may support marketing. When that "drama" is over, the stage can be reset to support product development or customer service. Environmentalists of change require easily adaptable and flexible backdrops. Congregations will have main events but will also be adding interactive venues, embracing more diverse microcommunities, working more with their city, participating in commerce—which all leads to the need for highly adaptable facilities.

Environmentalists of change require easily adaptable and flexible backdrops.

• Is our facility accessible? Do people use it throughout the week or only on weekends? Buildings are the largest financial assets for most churches. Inflexible single-use facilities are dinosaurs in a digital age that will offer congregants virtual gatherings and on-line connection

Figure 8.2. Willow Creek walk and fountain.

with whomever and whenever they want. If a church building's primary function is to hold a lot of people on Sunday, then this creates an opportunity to ask the fundamental questions about what the building is for and how it supports and reflects the life of the congregation and its neighbors.

Some are pushing beyond strictly physical definitions of architecture into virtual domains of intellectual and emotional space. As one thinker says, "The architecture of intelligence is the architecture that brings together the three main spatial environments that we live in and with today: mind, world and networks. Just like 'solid' architecture facilitates and guides the coming and going of bodies in space, the architecture of intelligence, by the combined use of software and hardware, facilitates the free coming together and parting of minds in collaboration for whatever purpose."[18]

This is heady stuff to consider. How can the church contribute to a deeper understanding of constructing domains for mind, emotion, and spirit to connect? Creating these new domains will inevitably originate from the design of our communities and culture.

The Living Church

The living church is as different from the celebration church as the celebration church is from the Reformation church and the Reformation church is from the liturgical church. They each come from different worlds with different perspectives, sensibilities, and languages. But the multimedia-multisensory nature of digital media encourages what I call the convergence church: it provides a platform that allows each tradition to begin moving forward using what we might call its native language, to bridge to the other traditions, and ultimately to synthesize as a digital-era entity.

How can we prepare for this exciting, still forming new world? The best way to prepare is to dip in a toe—just begin to develop a taste and appreciation for the new worldview. Begin now (if you haven't already) using the Internet not only for work but for conversation and play. And do it with the ideas of the Millennium Matrix chart in mind. I hope you'll find yourself looking at the world and its information with a whole new mind-set.

> The convergent church provides a platform that allows each tradition to begin moving forward using its native language, to bridge to the other traditions, and ultimately to synthesize as a digital-era entity.

Here's what I hope will happen: all of the concepts and ideas shared throughout the Millennium Matrix chart will begin to take root as you become aware how digital media already affect your activities, relationships, and changing perspectives. You will begin to look for interaction. You will find places where you experience the power of your voice to influence an outcome or opinion. You will see the richness and effortlessness of sites with member-generated content. You will become engrossed in following and participating in a role-playing environment. You will see the collective power of collaboration and the effectiveness of open-source efforts with distributed power. You will also see, with painful clarity, why your school, church, or local community can't seem to keep up with the times or why it proposes solutions that just don't work. This time, however, you can offer some insight and effective help.

The Millennium Matrix chart is like a new pair of glasses that allow you to see everything with new clarity. Whether you agree or disagree with my examples and conclusions about the matrix's implications, the fact will remain: the world, your church, and the future will look different. For leaders who are ready to take a tangible next step, let me leave you with the story of a successful practitioner of future change, Monsanto, which implemented a major cultural and business shift—a shift similar to that facing the church right now.

The Parable of Monsanto

Monsanto was a large and lumbering conglomerate in 1996, made up of four companies: chemicals, agribusiness, food supplements, and pharmaceuticals. The St. Louis, Missouri, company was riding the wave of decade-old innovations with products like the pesticide Round-Up, Nutra-Sweet, and a sleeping pill with no side effects. But at the end of the twentieth century, Monsanto found itself ill-prepared to address the speed, complexity, and uncertainty of the future. Incredibly, in 1998— just two years later—Monsanto had reinvented itself and was on a brand-new creative and cultural track.[19]

Bob Shapiro, Monsanto's chairman and CEO, saw the future of the business tied to biotech innovation; but the company's structure and environment held on to the old bureaucratic practices and attitudes. He saw that the two could not coexist, so he began the move to redefine the organization's operational focus. To do so, Monsanto made a bold move, spinning off its hundred-year-old chemical business and converging its three other companies into one life-sciences business to be guided by the company's new planet-friendly motto: "Food, Health and Hope."

Once the company brought the separated groups together, it had to eliminate the physical and organizational walls separating them in order to allow the desired discovery and serendipity between them to work. The change process was swift and global and, above all, led by example.

LESSONS FOR THE CHURCH

If a tired old corporation can reinvent itself into global industry leadership and experience this level of vibrant renewal, what opportunities may lie ahead for a church willing both to let go and reclaim the past? Here are some of the lessons we can learn from Monsanto's experience:

It's all about the people: their talents, skills, connectedness, and motivation are what may make a community vibrant.

You can't mandate change. Everyone must be engaged in the process of discovery.

Leaders must really believe in the holistic benefits of the desired change and have a clear vision of where they want the church to go. Then they must share that vision with everyone and have the courage to let them determine how to get there.

Leaders and community alike must be willing to foster experimentation and innocence, shed past baggage, develop new names, and discover and tell a new story.

There are no shortcuts to the process!

It started at the top, with the disbanding of old command structures and the flattening of hierarchical entitlement walls. Shapiro, for example, no longer worked in a huge corner office with glass walls and a secretary to screen privacy invaders. Instead, he worked in an average-sized cubicle accessible to all in one of the many neighborhoods within the campus. Each neighborhood became a stage set supporting the integrated components of all subbusinesses and the fluid nature of each team. Each was a study of the evolving consequences of integrating urban and organic structures in its composition.

The workplace strategies group assembled a multidisciplinary team to bridge Monsanto's new evergreen vision and resulting fluid culture, which the fixed physical environment needed to support. This wasn't a typical facilities team composed of interior designers, architects, maintenance and engineering specialists, and facility managers. It included those but in addition included the diverse talents and emotional intelligence of poets, historians, artists, and specialists in communications and human behavior.

This integrated approach and the resulting environment produced incredible results. After fourteen months of implementation, Monsanto had twenty-eight new products—more than it had developed in the previous two decades combined. The company attributed this unprecedented success to the convergence achieved through the creative interaction between the diverse disciplines within a benevolent environment specifically designed to support the living needs of human collaboration. More important, the process caringly dismantled the company's previously staid culture and allowed a new vibrant one to emerge, unbound by the controlling chains of Monsanto's history.

> The Millennium Matrix is not a call to leave the past behind but to reclaim it and take its best gifts in reframing the future.

The church and society are at a grand intersection. There is no blueprint for moving forward, but we can begin to draw one.

We can systematically begin to address our fears by collecting stories like those of Monsanto and others.

We can allow our congregations to begin to speak the truth regarding the disconnects we all try to ignore.

We can listen more to the younger generation in order to grasp their unique worldview—the worldview of the future.

We can learn the lessons of history and not fight change.

We can approach the future open-handedly.

We are quickly moving into an interactive era powered by mobile digital communications. This is changing not only our sense of time and space but our sense of reality and knowledge, our politics, our meeting and organizational methods, and the institutions that support our communities. It is making us rethink our sense of what is in good taste and what kinds of behavior are acceptable. It is making the world smaller and our own world larger.

In short, it is changing our worldview.

We cannot move forward by destroying or forgetting our heritage. In fact, the only way we can truly move forward is to honor openly those who served God during their time in history and within the spectrum of revelation they had. We are called to keep faith with their legacy and hold to the continuity that demonstrates our common origins. The Millennium Matrix chart is not a call to leave the past behind but to reclaim it and take its best gifts in reframing the future.

Anticipating the Next Great Shift

In a civilization which has lost the meaning of life, the most useful thing a Christian can do is to live. . . . this life alone can break the illusions of the modern world by showing everyone the utter powerlessness of a mechanistic view.
—Jacques Ellul, *The Presence of the Kingdom*

I f I have learned anything from my work with the Millennium Matrix, it is this: times change, and we must be prepared to change with them. The first and most difficult step is letting go of and unlearning our current habits.

When will the next historical shift occur? When a new means for storing and distributing information proves significantly superior to the last one. The silicon-based digital era may give way to optics or genetics. Whatever it will be, we can be assured that it will provide a perspective as shockingly new as the world of print was for the oral world bathed in the sound of voices. The Millennium Matrix provides a structure to begin to explore those possibilities when the time arrives.

Each of our religious traditions was born and crafted in a particular medium, time, and expression of God's visitation. Each provides a unique and important revelation into God's unlimited character. Like a prism, these traditions refract the light of God's revelation and character. No matter which facet we look through, we see the same truth at the center.

Regardless of our structures, styles, content, and expression, we truly are one body. Our task in this time of tumultuous transition is to find a way to rise above our numerous dis-integrations and act like one body. The world will never know Jesus until we do that. To survive we must step into the future with confidence, overcome the tyrannies of tradition and inertia, fulfill our commission, manifest transcendent life and community, offer a legitimate prophetic voice, and provide an ethic based on a world of change—and circle back to where we began and where our communion with God began: with God's word.

The Abridged
Millennium Matrix

THE ABRIDGED MILLENNIUM MATRIX

	Oral-Liturgical ?B.C.–1500 A.D. Ancient	Print-Reformation 1500–1950 Modern	Broadcast-Celebration 1950–2010 Postmodern	Digital-Convergence 2010– Convergent
HOW WE BELIEVE				
Worship	Liturgical	Meeting	Event	Gathering
Truth	Relational	Principle	Existential	Contextual
Understanding	Insights	Facts	Selective awareness	Recontextualizing
Faith	Trust	Belief	Conviction	Pragmatism
Gospel	Reenacting	Retelling	Reselling	Recontextualizing
Godhead	Father	Son	Holy Spirit	Body or church
God's location	Up	Out	In	Everywhere
Connection with God	Face of God	Mind of God	Hand of God	Heart of God
Relating to God	I-Thou dialogue	I-It monologue	They-It silence	I-They panalogue
Revelation of God	Direct encounter	Scripture	Scripture and experience	Immerse
Time	Liturgical time: present	Chronological time: past, present, and future	Existential time	Virtual time: future perfect
	Whole	**Parts**	**Fragments**	**System**
HOW WE KNOW				
Self-understanding	Tribe	Individual	Member	Passport citizens
Sense of time	Present or presence	Past or objectification	Future or impermanence	Virtual or time travel
Sense of space	Local or tribes	National or ideological Identity	Global invader	Global microcosm
Sensory bias	Ear	Eye	Nervous system	Touch-mind

Sense of identity	Tribal village	Independent individual	Crowded stranger	Cybersoul or anonymous intimacy
Reasoning process	Dialectic	Logic	Flow logic	Systems thinking
Lens of perception	Revelation	Law of identity	Uncertainty principle	Chaos theory
Worldview	Theocentric	Newtonian	Einsteinian	Bohmian
Learning	Process-centered	Content-centered	Experience-centered	Context-centered
Collective memory	Bard	Book	Documentary	Database

HOW WE LIVE TOGETHER	**Tribe**	**Nation**	**Region**	**Convergent**
Authority or leadership	Divine or power	Credibility or control	Relevancy or influence	Resonancy or catalyst
Influence	Positional	Credentials	Impression	Connection
Commitment or contract	Covenant	Vows	Promises	Agreement
Social dynamic	Cohesive	Progressive	Centrifugal	Centripetal
Ethics	Moral view	Ethical view	Practical view	Reciprocal view
What we value	The good	The right	The useful	The significant
Community connections	Tradition	Creeds	Issues and interests	Questions

(continued)

227

THE ABRIDGED MILLENNIUM MATRIX *(continued)*

	Oral-Liturgical ?B.C.–1500 A.D.	Print-Reformation 1500–1950	Broadcast-Celebration 1950–2010	Digital-Convergence 2010–
HOW WE SEE BEAUTY	**Wholeness**	**Proportion**	**Deconstruction**	**Innovation**
Sacred architecture	Ornate	Rational	Promotional	Experimental or eclectic
Sacred art	Symbolic	Perspective	Conceptual or process	Interactive-participative
Sacred music	Chant	Hymn	Song	Contextual composition
Approach	Holistic	Framed	Existential	Interactive
HOW WE WORK AND TRADE	**Essentials**	**Goods**	**Services**	**Experiences**
Manager	Steward	Manager	Leader	Interweaver
Mechanism of wealth	Land	Capital and manufacturing	Distribution and debt	Creativity and community
Metaphor of work	Farm	Factory	Service	Federation
Value	Reliability	Productivity	Quality	Creativity
Production	Meet need	Improve condition	Create want	Create fulfillment
Medium of exchange	Barter and trade	Currency	Credit	Techno-barter

APPENDIX

Exercises and Field Trips

Sometimes the easiest way to appreciate something is to experience it firsthand. To that end this Appendix provides some resources, examples, and exercises that should help you experience the mind-set of a digital interactive world. Bon voyage!

Exercises

Exercise 1: Paradigm Shifting

The first exercise is a warm-up. We are going to practice shifting paradigms through a process called stereopsis: seeing a two-dimensional plane in three dimensions. Stereograms provide this experience and have become a popular form of art and fun. Beyond living room recreation and curiosity, however, stereograms create a mind-altering experience.

The images that you see in a stereogram are not subtle patterns hidden within a larger pattern. They are constructed inside your brain. Your mind shifts in order to see them—and many people experience a physical sensation when they suddenly see the image pop out in three dimensions.

To experience this phenomenon, visit the Magic Eye Web site at http://www.magiceye.com. You will find several examples and instructions on how to view them.

Exercise 2: The Linear-Sequential vs. the Interactive-Relational Environment

We are all beginning to digest information in a more interactive and relational manner. The term *relational* refers to information that is connected to another piece of information. There are different graphic ways to show these relationships indicating primary, secondary, and tertiary relevance.

The best way for me to describe this is to direct you to three different Web sites: Merriam-Webster (http://www.m-w.com), Dictionary.com (http://www.dictionary.reference.com), and Visual Thesaurus (http://www.visualthesaurus.com/online/index.html). For this exercise I looked up the word *covenant* on each Web site to demonstrate how differently each presents information.

The Merriam-Webster site (Figure A.1) is a straightforward linear site, in the print paradigm. It provides the word and at least one dictionary definition.

Dictionary.com (Figure A.2) is linear but provides relational content by cataloging ninety-nine possible connections to the word *covenant*.

The Visual Thesaurus (Figure A.3) is created in the digital paradigm. Instead of a linear setup of word and definition, it provides interactive relational content. It shows which words are derivatives of *covenant* by listing them below the term. It shows words that *covenant* is derived from by listing those above the term. It shows words used in connection with *covenant* off to one side of the main word. All of the words are shown darker or lighter, larger or smaller, closer or further, connected with bolder lines or lighter lines, depending on their relationship to the core meaning of *covenant*. This snapshot compresses several pages of content from a linear layout, allowing a more holistic understanding of the word within its related universe. It also allows one to drill down through the numerous links.

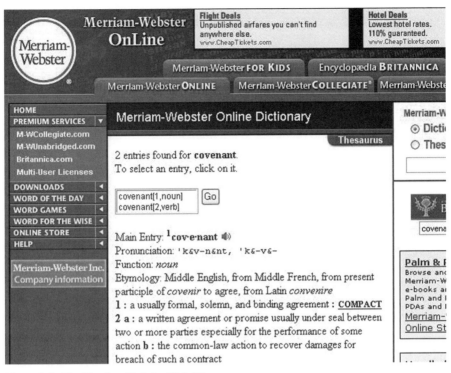

Figure A.1. The Merriam-Webster Web Site.

Figure A.2. The Dictionary.com Web Site.

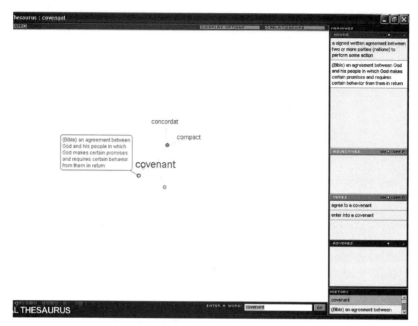

Figure A.3. The Visual Thesaurus Web Site.

Exercise 3: From File Folders to
Relational Links

Once you begin to work with interactive and relationally linked tools, you may want to begin to organize your data in this manner. The mountains of information we are forced to process and the pace necessary to respond require new skills and tools. Finding and storing information is not our challenge. Our challenge is recall, assimilation, and meaningful interpretation.

Robert Probst conducted groundbreaking research in the late 1960s that resulted in a white paper for Herman Miller, Inc., called "A Facility Based on Change." He reached the conclusion that our current information-handling tools limit our capacity for thought and reason, creating a "mind boggle"—and that was more than thirty years ago![1]

The mind requires visual cues for recall, creative connections, and insight. But our obsession with order and neatness have stripped our environments of intellectual stimulation and meaning. Try this: take

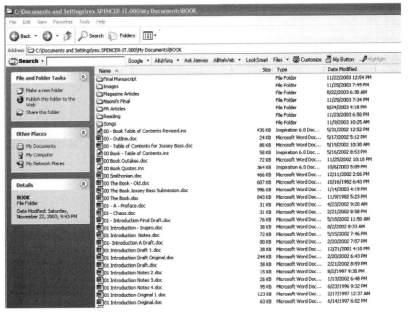

Figure A.4. Standard Computer File Management.

out a deck of cards and look at its structure. Normally, this number of anything would be too large to manage. But cards are so well designed that the combination of structure and visual distinction allow you to quickly recall and remember the content. I have moved to a method of creating my own "deck of cards" for organizing my work. It's called The Brain.

Figure A.4 shows the standard (linear-sequential paradigm) file directory for the manuscript for this book, as my computer files it. You'll see that it shows several file folders on my hard drive and then several documents that are drafts and research. The folders and documents are organized alphabetically. The information from one folder is essentially hidden and discrete from any other information in any other folder.

Figure A.5 shows the same information—actually, more information—as organized with a tool that allows me to make relational connections and display them in a more interactive and visually accessible manner. This tool has allowed me to create my own "deck of cards" for any topic or project I may be working on.

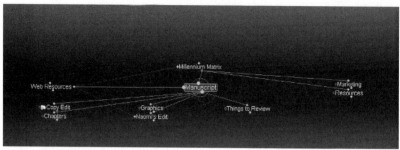

Figure A.5. Relational File Management.

When I click on any of the visible topics, it becomes the center object and all of the related and linked information to that topic surfaces. By clicking on Web Resources, I find dozens of sites that I have referenced and can easily go back to. These sites are also linked to the specific chapters in which I wrote about them. This interactive cross-referencing capability creates an intuitive means of synthesizing information and stimulating fresh insights. This particular program is called The Brain. To see it, visit http://www.thebrain.com.

Field Trips

Field Trip 1: Living Museums

You may not be able to take a trip to Washington, D.C., but you can visit the Smithsonian Institution on-line and have a great experience. Even more important, for our purposes, the Smithsonian Web site provides a great example of print, broadcast, and digital approaches.

If you visit http://www.si.edu and browse, you will find examples of cataloged information with simple texts. You will also see historical events presented with audio and video clips that feel like a documentary. The Smithsonian is beginning to add interactive elements like timelines and maps. A new venture for the Smithsonian is moving more fully into the interactive-relational environment. It is called Smithsonian Without Walls (see Figure A.6). Visit http://www.si.edu/revealingthings and look around.

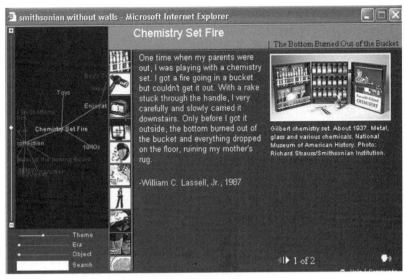

Figure A.6. Smithsonian Without Walls Web Site.

Field Trip 2: Finding Trace Elements of Digital Culture

I strongly recommend building your own list of Web sites and places to visit, with a mind toward experiencing them through the lens of an individually tailored interactive worldview. Following are some of my favorites.

An on-line museum about the history and making of news, the Newseum has a highly interactive Web site: http://www.newseum.org.

The Holocaust Museum in Washington, D.C., provides a multi-sensory immersion experience to people who walk through the exhibit. Visit its Web site at http://www.ushmm.org.

The Blue Man Show provides a powerful example of multi-sensory interactive art onstage. Experiencing this show is a paradigm-shifting experience. Visit the Blue Man Web site (http://www.blueman.com) to find a show you might be able to attend.

The Chicago Children's Museum (http://www.chichildrens museum.org/) provides another favorite expedition. I'm sure there are several like it across the country. It is a learning playground and offers one of the metaphors for learning environments of the future. The Exploratorium in San Francisco (http://www.exploratorium.edu/) offers another interactive learning experience aimed at children but also enjoyable for adults.

Field Trip 3: Finding the Fringe Without Getting Singed

It is worth noting cyberculture's outer boundaries as a leading indicator of trends and attitudes. Many of these will likely fade, but elements will find their way into our daily experience and vocabulary.

The Cyber-punk project (http://project.cyberpunk.ru/) provides a comprehensive chronicle and catalogue of cyberculture.

An Atlas of Cyberspaces (http://www.geog.ucl.ac.uk/casa/martin/atlas/atlas.html) provides an incredible overview of all things cyber. I highly recommend visiting this Web site. Once you do, you will have a much greater understanding of the design, expansiveness, history, and layers of cyberspace.

This is the kick start to your trip into the world of digital culture. For additional resources, please visit my Web site: http://www.millenniummatrix.com.

Notes

Preface

1. This section is adapted from Arie de Guess, *The Living Organization* (Cambridge, Mass.: Harvard Business School Press, 1997), p. 6.
2. High churn rates create a vicious cycle of added leadership responsibility and fewer members receiving needed care and attention. As leaders take on this added responsibility, they have less opportunity to build a broader leadership base. Members with less access to leaders eventually look elsewhere to meet their needs.
3. A. de Guess, *The Living Organization*, p. 2.
4. According to D. Schwartz, *Who Cares? Rediscovering Community* (Boulder, Colo.: Westview Press, 1997).

Chapter Zero, Vertigo

1. Toffler's book (New York: Bantam, 1970) captures the essential qualities of the broadcast era as an environment of unrelenting novelty and change. This chapter updates Toffler's argument, taking into consideration the new dynamics of change in a digital world. The quotation is from p. 2.
2. S. Davis and C. Meyer, *Blur: The Speed of Change in the Connected Economy* (Reading, Mass.: Addison Wesley Longman, 1998).
3. An organizational consultant and freelance writer, Ed Chinn has published in the *Wall Street Journal*, the *Christian Science Monitor*, and

the *Washington Post.* "Vertigo" is a draft for a future article or publication.

4. Complex systems interact in what appears on the surface to be unique, or chaotic, fashion. The science of chaos theory identifies the larger common patterns. Fractals represent a repeated geometric pattern found within the tiniest element of a system emanating outward.

5. *Systems thinking* is the discipline of looking at the world in terms of networks. MIT professor Peter Senge is one its leading practitioners.

6. Derrick de Kerckhove, head of the McLuhan Institute at the University of Toronto, has been working with new organizational models through his concept of the architecture of intelligence. We will discuss these ideas later in Chapter Eight.

7. Jacques Ellul labels this phenomenon as "self-augmenting" and describes its nature in several of his books, including *The Technological Society* (Toronto, Canada: Alfred A. Knopf, 1964); *The Technological Bluff* (Grand Rapids, Mich.: Wm. B. Eerdmans, 1990); and *The Technological System* (New York: Continuum, 1980).

8. Feedback loops are a central part of systems theory and research. Peter Senge's book *Fifth Discipline* (New York: Bantam Doubleday Dell, 1990) diagrams several common patterns. He lists a hierarchy of feedback loops that form the underlying dynamic of social interaction, positive and negative. Understanding the behavior of loops provides an alternative to linear cause-effect analysis.

9. George Gilder deals with the devaluation of tangible assets and the increasing valuation of intangible assets in two books: *Microcosm* (New York: Simon and Schuster, 1989) and *Telecosm* (New York: The Free Press, 2000). George Gilder is chairman of Gilder Publishing, a fellow at the Discovery Institute, and an author of several books on social, economic, and technological issues.

10. *Hyper-mediated* is a term to describe the degree of separation we have from the original sources of our consumption, information, and understanding.

11. Among other high-profile Arthur Andersen accounts that imploded are WorldCom, Global Crossings, and Adelphia.

12. S. Zuboff and J. Maxmin, *The Support Economy: Why Corporations Are Failing Individuals and the Next Episode of Capitalism* (New York: Viking, 2002), p. 356.

13. After the implosion of the high-tech industry, Time Warner repositioned itself and discussed the divestiture of AOL. Despite Time Warner's reversion, the tide is still toward convergence. Growing sciences like nanotechnology provide a more compelling metaphor of what is coming, but these are harder to grasp than some of the daily news events.

14. Keith H. Hammonds, "The Strategy of a Fighter Pilot," *Fast Company* (June 2002), Issue 59, www.fastcompany.com. "An effective combatant, Boyd reasoned, looks constantly for mismatches between his original understanding and a changed reality. In those mismatches lie opportunities to seize advantage." Boyd developed a mind-set for operating in this kind of environment, a continuous process he called OODA: observe, orient, decide, and act.

15. K. Boulding, *Evolutionary Economics* (Thousand Oaks, Calif.: Sage, 1981), p. 44: "Prediction of the future is possible only in systems that have stable parameters like celestial mechanics. . . . Evolutionary systems, however, by their very nature have unstable parameters. They are disequilibrium systems and in such systems our power of prediction, though not zero, is very limited because of the unpredictability of the parameters themselves." Kenneth Ewert Boulding (1910–1993) was a prolific scholar. His publications covered ethics, religion, and peace, along with contributions in macroeconomics and price theory.

16. R. Norton, "Unintended Consequences," in *The Concise Encyclopedia of Economics*, David R. Henderson (ed.), Liberty Fund, Inc., Library of Economics and Liberty, [http://www.econlib.org/library/Enc/UnintendedConsequences.html], April 2003.

17. Nicholas Martin, executive director of the American Iatrogenic Association, excerpt from the home page http://www.iatrogenic.org/index.html: "In 2000, a presidential task force labeled medical errors a 'national problem of epidemic proportions.'" Members estimated that the "cost associated with these errors in

lost income, disability, and health care costs is as much as $29 billion annually." That same year the Institute of Medicine released a historic report, "To Err Is Human: Building a Safer Health System." The report's authors concluded that forty-four thousand to ninety-eight thousand people die each year as a result of errors during hospitalization. They noted that "even when using the lower estimate, deaths due to medical errors exceed the number attributable to the eighth-leading cause of death." The addition of nonhospital errors may drive the numbers of errors and deaths much higher. As the authors note, the hospital data "offer only a very modest estimate of the magnitude of the problem since hospital patients represent only a small proportion of the total population at risk, and direct hospital costs are only a fraction of total costs."

18. D. Schwartz, *Who Cares? Rediscovering Community* (Boulder, Colo.: Westview, 1997).

19. Paul also dealt with the flip side of the coin, legalists (Judaizers), within the Galatian church. Several of the New Testament letters provide insight on the variety of tangents likely to rise in these times of change. The early church also had its share of celebrities and those claiming transcendent understanding (Gnostics).

Part One, Stopping Time

1. M. McLuhan, *Understanding Media* (New York: McGraw Hill, 1964), p. 9.

2. N. Postman, *Amusing Ourselves to Death: Public Discourse in an Age of Show Business* (New York: Penguin, 1985), p. 8.

3. W. Stringfellow, *An Ethic for Christians and Other Aliens in a Strange Land* (Nashville: Word, 1976).

4. J. Ellul, *Presence of the Kingdom and Technological Society* (New York: Seabury Press, 1948).

5. I use the invention of the printing press as the primary dividing line between oral and print culture. Print and manuscripts had

been in existence for several millennia prior to Gutenberg. We see evidence, for example, in Greek and Roman culture of print's influence in architecture, art, and law. However, it did not reach a tipping point (a point at which the balance of power between an oral worldview and print shifts) for social revolution until the printing press.

Chapter One, Oral Culture—Liturgical Church

1. One example is Genesis 11:7: "Come, let us go down, and there confound their language, that they may not understand one another's speech." The Hebrew word for understand is *shama* (word 08085 in Strong's Concordance), which means "to perceive by ear" or "have the power to hear." We find this same word used in Deuteronomy 6:4, "Hear, O Israel, the Lord your God is one Lord." By contrast, the Greek word *oida* (word 1492 in Strong's Concordance), which we translate as "understand" in 1 Corinthians 13:2, means "to perceive with the eyes" (KJV).

2. W. Ong, *The Presence of the Word* (New York: Simon and Schuster, 1967), p. 3.

3. "The expression of truth is felt as itself always an event. In this sense, the contact of an oral culture with truth, vague and evanescent though it may be by some literate standards, retains a reality that literate cultures [broadcast and computerized too] achieve only reflexively and by dint of great (self) conscious effort" (W. Ong, *Presence of the Word*, p. 33). This becomes more pronounced in a highly produced broadcast environment and the drive toward multimedia virtual reality in a computerized environment.

4. Genesis 15:10–21 describes God's covenant with Abraham: "The cutting in halves of the sacrifice spoke of the end of existing lives for the sake of establishing a new covenant. The sacred nature of this bond was attested to by the shedding of lifeblood. In this instance, only God passed between the pieces, indicating that it

was His covenant and He would assume responsibility for its administration" (C. Simpson, commentary, *New Spirit-Filled Life Bible* (Nashville: Thomas Nelson, 2002), p. 24.

5. Exodus 34:6–11 (NASB).

6. Jesus had several run-ins with the spiritual authorities. He confronted those who wanted to stone a woman caught in adultery by saying in John 8:7 (NASB), "He who is without sin among you, let him be the first to throw a stone at her." The Pharisees' attempt to have Jesus pronounce their righteousness was turned upside-down as Jesus told the parable of the good Samaritan. Perhaps most poignant is Mark 11:28, when the Pharisees attempt to get at the root of Jesus' authority. Jesus was not the product of the priestly lineage of Aaron or from among the seventy elders serving Moses (the Sanhedrin). When the Pharisees questioned his credentials, he asked them who authorized John the Baptist. They would not answer because it was a no-win question for them. After numerous encounters like these, "They were amazed at his teaching, because his message had authority" (Luke 4:32, NIV).

7. Romans 10:14–15 (NASB).

8. Psalm 5:6 (NASB): "You destroy those who speak falsehood; The LORD abhors the man of bloodshed and deceit."

9. "The Catholic doctrine of the efficacy of the sacraments suggests this sense of the word as something belonging to the world of physical power. . . . the efficacy of the sacraments in Catholic teaching is certainly more readily comprehensible to oral-aural man" (W. Ong, *Presence of the Word*, p. 279). The liturgical church, birthed in oral culture, assumed an intimately interconnected state of being and reflected it in its rituals.

10. We might feel the solemn conviction behind our vows to one another or even the thrill of witnessing God's answer to prayer. That sense, however, is distinct from Isaac's giving Jacob the blessing that designated his destiny or Esau's grief and panic when pleading for Isaac to recall his words. It is distinct from the relationship that Elisha had with his master, Elijah. Elijah knew he was going to die soon, another indication of that intimacy with the cycles of life; and Elisha asked for Elijah to bless him with a

double portion of the power God anointed him with. Peter told the cripple, "I do not possess silver and gold, but what I do have I give to you: In the name of Jesus Christ the Nazarene—walk!" (Acts 3:6, NASB). These were not elusive realities for those in oral cultures as they seem to be for us.

11. The church embraced expressing this connection through art and icon, whereas most Jewish sects found these to violate the second commandment (having no graven images).

12. J. Neusner, *Invitation to the Talmud* (New York: HarperCollins, 1973) p. 37.

13. K. LeMee, *Chant: The Origins, Forms, Practice and Healing Power of Gregorian Chant* (Sedona, Ariz.: Pharaoh Audiobooks, 1994).

14. K. LeMee, *Chant*.

15. The Catholic liturgy was performed in Latin until the 1960s, and few laypersons would understand what the priest said or sang.

16. The Benedictine Monks of Santo Domingo De Silos, *Chant*, compact disc, Angel Records, 1993.

Chapter Two, Print Culture–Reformation Church

1. W. Ong, *Presence of the Word*, p. 50.

2. W. Ong, *Presence of the Word*, p. 135.

3. "The modern age was much more the child of typography than it has commonly been made out to be" (W. Ong, *Presence of the Word*, p. 9).

4. This shifted perception created much of the theological debate around the "God Is Dead" movement and prompted books like Francis Schaeffer's *The God Who Is There* (Downers Grove, Ill.: Intervarsity Press, 1968).

5. F. Schaeffer, *How We Should Then Live: The Rise and Decline of Western Thought and Culture* (Wheaton, Ill.: Good News Publishing, 1983).

6. It would not take long for artists to adopt a more naturalistic worldview. Angels and even God no longer looked like symbols but idealized people. Perhaps another by-product of this visual rational approach is the subordination of means to achieve the end. Artists would use as models family, neighbors, and even lovers to portray biblical characters, in order to reach a greater level of realism.

7. "[T]he word literally locked in space—for at approximately the same time that alphabetic typography appears, painting is being swept by a revolution in its treatment of . . . perspective" (W. Ong, *Presence of the Word*, p. 8).

8. For a discussion of perspective in art, including pictures, see "Perspective as a Geometric Tool That Launched the Renaissance," The Smith-Ketwell Eye Research Institute, [http://www.ski.org/CWTyler_lab/CWTyler/Art%20Investigations/PerspectiveHistory/Perspective.BriefHistory.html].

9. W. Ong, *Presence of the Word*, pp. 63–64.

10. Aristotle's foundational premise is as follows:

All that is, is (A is A, law of identity)

Nothing can at the same time be and not be (A cannot be both A and not A, law of contradiction)

All must either be or not be (A must be either A or not A, law of the excluded middle)

From the European Society for General Semantics: Alfred Korzybski, *The Role of Language in the Perceptual Processes* (New York: The Ronald Press Company, 1951) [http://www.esgs.org/uk/ari.htm].

11. The modern church's war cry for reestablishing absolute truth traces back to a world in which A is A and a belief that the Bible is the complete and absolute word of God.

12. W. Ong, *Presence of the Word*, p. 229.

13. W. Ong, *Presence of the Word*, p. 126.

14. J. Mander, *Four Arguments for the Elimination of Television* (New York: Quill, 1978), p. 75.

15. Notice some of the encounters between Jesus and the Pharisees. For example, when one asked, "Is it lawful to pay taxes to Caesar?" Jesus asked a question in return, "whose picture is on this coin?" (Matthew 22:17–21, NASB).

16. Bill Bright formed Campus Crusade for Christ in 1967 to pursue the great commission in Matthew 28:19–20, focusing on college campuses. He wrote The Four Spiritual Laws as a tool of evangelism.

17. Orchestras not only represented a new expression of music but became a metaphor for organizational structures.

Chapter Three, Broadcast Culture–Celebration Church

1. Bob Dylan, "The Times They Are A-Changin'," 1964.
2. This conflict is portrayed in the movie *Pleasantville*. Gary Ross, New Line Cinema, 1998.
3. M. McLuhan, *The Medium Is the Message*, p. 16.
4. In some ways the battle between print and broadcast is like the continuing debate over who really won the Civil War. Even though it was fought and decided long ago, some remnants behave as if the war is still going on. There are also some eloquent defenders of the old confederacy. Authors like Neil Postman, Christopher Lasch, Chuck Colson, Francis Schaeffer, Jerry Mander, Jerzy Kosinski, and Alan Bloom describe the disintegration of the rational (print) foundations of civic life. These arguments are extremely persuasive and appealing, especially in the face of all of the problems and breakdowns in so-called traditional values. However, the arguments try to reclaim the myth that our golden age was the age of reason—the world that print created.
5. R. B. Fuller, *Operating Manual for Spaceship Earth* (Mattituck, N.Y.: Aeonian Press, 1969), p. 44.
6. N. Postman, *Amusing Ourselves to Death*, pp. 78–79.
7. B. Johnson, D. R. Hoge, and D. A. Luidens, "Barna Research Group LTD and Mainline Churches: The Real Reason for Decline," *First Things*, 31 (Mar. 1993): 13–18.
8. J. Kosinsky, *Being There* (Orlando: Harcourt Brace, 1973), p. 6.
9. "The painting is the result of split-second decision making and happenstance, choreography and chance. Each physical 'performance' was a unique, spontaneous, and unrepeatable event, but the final product was always subject to artistic will. 'I can control the flow of the paint,'" Pollock contended. 'There is no accident.'" The Smithsonian National Gallery of Art Web site, http://www.nga.gov/feature/pollock/process2.html.
10. Jerzy Kosinski and Robert C. Jones, *Being There*, Screenplay, 1979, Scene 123.
11. In an earlier era, individuals comfortable with right-brain culture would probably have been the prophets and poets of society.
12. The White House is obviously an extreme example. The movie

Network (Warner Brothers, 1976) portrays a similar environment: frenetic, fragmented, urgent, cutthroat, impersonal, and narcissistic. Again, this may be broadcast at its extreme worst, but it is also broadcast at its best. Why? Because it is the nature of the medium.

13. Colonel David Grossman describes the story of Carneal's shootings in his book *Stop Teaching Our Kids to Kill* (New York: Crown Publishing, 1999).

14. Spin is the art of influencing the interpretation of information to favor one's purpose.

15. L. Stahl, *Reporting Live* (New York: Simon and Schuster, 1999), pp. 209–211.

16. *The Truman Show* takes reality television to its logical conclusion. Truman Burbank is born on the set of a television show and is unaware that his home and town are nothing but studio props and that the friends and family in his life are actually actors. The movie plays out this plot to the point where he discovers the reality of his world.

17. These shows had simple sets and few props, and relied on the ad-lib interaction between the host and support cast (puppets, clowns, and side kicks). The September 1950 edition of *Time* magazine describes this early successful format as "The Chicago School."

18. Stuart K. Hine, hymn-writer, "How Great Thou Art," Manna Music, Valencia, Calif., 1953. Published in *Songs for a Gospel People* (1987).

Chapter Four, Digital Culture—Convergence Church

1. The virtual world allows you to design your own vacation, select a compatible mate, test your capabilities for a new job, choose a car to buy with the price, color, and features you select, explore hypothetical lifestyles and locate resources and individuals to help you accomplish almost anything you ask for. Pilots, astronauts, doctors, engineers, and the military train in virtual environments to better prepare for real-life situations. We are redesigning the fundamental properties of matter (through nan-

otechnology) and life (through genetic engineering)—and we are just beginning.

2. Open source: "In general, . . . any program whose source code is made available for use or modification by users, developers, or hackers" (www.netlingo.com). The Linux operating system, which competes with Microsoft Windows, is a good example of open-source software. One key distinction is that the software is free and the operating (or source) code for Linux is available to any software writer to add to or improve. By contrast, Microsoft's Windows is proprietary; no company can adapt it to its software, and users must pay Microsoft a license fee to use it. Microsoft's approach and size requires most of the industry to adapt around its proprietary applications (paradigms). Linux not only represents an alternative to Windows, it also reflects a philosophy and paradigm opposite to Microsoft's. Open source is, in a sense, the opposite of branding. Branding is the effort to condense the distinctions and the expectations of one's service or product into a phrase, a symbol, or an image.

3. Scribes could produce a copy of the Bible in two years; the printing press compressed the time to a few months.

4. Peter Senge wrote *The Fifth Discipline* and *The Fifth Discipline Fieldbook* (New York: Currency and Doubleday, 1994), providing a worldview of networked systems. Archetypes provide the grammar for understanding how these systems work and interact with one another.

5. Another archetype describes the phenomenon of outbreaks or epidemics, which share common traits. These dynamics have found applications in other fields like crime prevention and marketing. Some books even use the term *viral marketing*. Because networks seem to have similar characteristics, archetypes learned from one area can transfer to others.

6. W. Ong, *Presence of the Word*, p. 303.

7. The organization is called Smart Work and Referral Marketing (SWARM). The community has been in place since 1990, and it continues to grow in depth and strength. Although we started as a network of self-interest, we've developed a philosophy, methodology, criteria for belonging, applied technology, ongoing

education, strategies, means to help one another, facilitation, and accountability. For more information about SWARM, please visit http://www.millenniummmatrix.com.

8. D. Tapscot, *Growing Up Digital* (New York: McGraw-Hill, 1998), p. 7.

9. M. Montessori, *The Secret of Childhood* (New York: F.A. Stokes, 1939), p. 132.

10. The following introduction to the discussion forum for AmericanCatholic.org provides an example of setting the boundaries for participants: "Welcome to Conversation Corner, AmericanCatholic.org's online discussion forums. We want to hear what you think about events and issues facing Catholics today. While we welcome all opinions, we ask that you treat each other with respect and refrain from name-calling and vulgarities. We are striving for a healthy exchange of ideas and opinions that will help us all understand these issues better." http://www.americancatholic.org/forum/activeforums.asp

11. Philippians 2:12 (NIV).

12. These churches can also be large-scale multimedia theater structures that operate twenty-four hours a day. They might include omni-directional screens with multiple services taking place globally. The technical crew can capture earlier events and then reloop them into the setting to fit a particular context. Facilitators will replace leaders, and their role will be to weave the collective experience. Speakers can come forward to teach, preach, or express insight from God. These facilities can also have break-out rooms for people to retire for more individualized prayer or counseling. This is the other side of the digital coin that takes the multimedia, real-time, globally connected capabilities and pulls them all together. Even though potentially large in scale it is counter to main event gatherings in many respects. There are no set times to gather, the audience contributes in creating the collective experience, there are simultaneous activities taking place instead of a single point of focus, and families participate instead of dividing into the demographic groups.

13. Buildings will provide an accessible, flexible home for both the community of faith and the local community. Instead of attempt-

ing to embody the gospel story as cathedrals did, future facilities will have the means to offer an interactive journey for those who want to discover the roots of faith or the history of the congregation. Early prototypes are the Holocaust Museum in Washington, D.C., and the Newseum, which will be relocated to Washington, D.C. Disney has long made the making of an attraction part of its attractions. Many new restaurants are also allowing people to watch their food being prepared as part of the "entertainment." Part of the interest of Krispy Kreme is watching the endless row of donuts floating down their river of grease to be plucked hot and eaten on the spot. The secret here is bringing the back room onto the main stage.

I've seen churches create interactive children's environments with painted walls and animatronics (robots that look like creatures). Focus on the Family has an area that allows children to play and at the same time interact with the different animated characters from its shows. This combination of play and learning makes these facilities far more accessible to the congregation and flexible. Near Fort Lauderdale I visited Christ's Fellowship Church, which built a large youth center with recreation, a food bar, bandstand, computer area, and break-out rooms. Kids in this active facility create their own learning experiences, and facilitators help to shape the topics and issues they "buzz" around. Imagine too opening up music rehearsals to the public and inviting people to come up and play a part—like some of the shows at Disney World. Future facilities will also express the integration of faith communities and commerce. The point is not to consider the various activities to adopt but to consider how we integrate our facilities into community life.

14. Architecture also provides a powerful vehicle in shaping new attitudes for the future. In addition to some of the examples I gave earlier, I recommend observing places like Starbucks coffee shops and the Lettuce Entertain You and Pappas restaurants as examples for creating a tailored context and experience. The models that will help the church are not ecclesiastical; they are the places you and your kids enjoy going.

The Complete Millennium Matrix

1. W. Ong, *Presence of the Word*, p. 3.

2. W. Ong, *Presence of the Word*, p. 3.

3. Albert Einstein and Howard Eves, *Mathematical Circles Squared* (Boston: Prindle, Weber, & Schmidt, 1972).

4. The many different personality matrices that are available, such as Myers-Briggs and DISC, trace their roots back to the Greeks' four divisions of personality: sanguine, melancholy, choleric, and phlegmatic. Today's psychology has little similarity in method to that of the early Greeks, but the early Greek roots of modern analysis are evident. The DISC Web site at http://www.discinterconsult.com/disc/history.html provides some of the history behind personality profiles.

5. P. Davies, *The Mind of God* (New York: Simon and Schuster, 1992). This is just one of thousands of examples illustrating the shift from intimate relationship toward unlocking the laws of the universe.

6. ThankyouMusic, 2000.

7. "People in a hurry will imitate more readily than people at leisure. Hustling tends to produce uniformity. And in the deliberate fusing of individuals into a compact group, incessant action will play a considerable role" (E. Hoffer, *The True Believer*, New York: HarperCollins, 1951), thought 81, p. 96.

8. "Cyberia . . . where the limitations of time, distance and the body are meaningless." From Douglas Rushkoff, *Cyberia* (SanFrancisco: HarperSanFrancisco, 1994), p. 3.

9. "The important element in Greek tense is *kind of action*. This is its fundamental significance. 'The chief function of a Greek tense is thus not to denote time, but progress.' . . . The character of an action may be defined from [any of] three points of view: it may be continuous, it may be complete, or it may be regarded simply as occurring, without reference to the question of progress. There are, therefore, three fundamental tenses in Greek: the present, representing continuous action; the perfect, representing completed action; and the aorist (*aoristos*, without limits, undefined), representing indefinite action. 'These three tenses were first

developed irrespective of time.'" Future perfect tense is, therefore, complete action viewed from a point in future time. H. E.
Dana, Th.D., and Julius R. Mantey, Th.D., D.D., *A Manual Grammar of
the Greek New Testament* (Toronto, Canada: Macmillan, 1955), p. 178.

This concept was introduced to business in Stanley Davis's
book *Future Perfect* (Boulder, Colo.: Perseus, 1997), which suggests
that most business planning is conducted based on past events
projected into the future. Davis argues that results of this kind of
planning always lag behind the realities of the marketplace. He
introduces a method of planning based on a model of the future.
This model is used to pull the company forward instead of pushing the company from the past.

10. Derrick de Kerckhove developed the concept of an architecture of
intelligence. "Having lost faith in the notion of a material explanation for existence, these scientists have begun to look at the
ways reality conforms to their expectations, mirroring back to
them a world changed by the very act of observation. . . . An infinitely complex series of interdependencies, where the tiniest
change in a remote place can have system-wide repercussions"
(D. Rushkoff, *Cyberia*, p. 4).

11. J. Mander, "Four Arguments for the Elimination of Television"
(New York: Quill, 1978). See Mander's third argument and
specifically the sections beginning on p. 200 ("Television
Bypasses Consciousness") and p. 205 ("Television Is Sleep
Teaching").

12. "Computers are manipulators; they juggle items in space, quanti-
fied items only. What cannot be reduced to a spatial arrangement
. . . cannot be digested in computer language" (W. Ong, *Presence of
the Word*, p. 90).

13. Jesus presents several juxtaposed concepts in the Beatitudes.
"Blessed are the poor in spirit, for theirs is the Kingdom of heav-
en" (Matthew 5:3–12, NASB). Jesus proclaims that the last will
be first in the Kingdom of God (Matthew 20:16, NASB) and Paul
addresses the Corinthians by declaring that the foolishness of
Christ confounds the wisdom of the world (1 Corinthians 1:21,
NASB).

14. E. DeBono, *I Am Right—You Are Wrong: From This to the New Renaissance:*

From Rock Logic to Water Logic (New York: Penguin USA, 1992). Edward DeBono presents flowscaping as an alternative to flow-charting as a means of finding primary causes within dynamic environments. In other words flowcharts are used to map linear cause and effect relationships. But complex social or political situations, for example, cannot be mapped in simple cause-and-effect relationships. DeBono's book explains how his approach can aid in uncovering root causes.

15. A. N. Whitehead, *Science and the Modern World* (New York: Irvington, 1987, first published in 1926). One of Whitehead's contributions is the idea that reality, physical and metaphysical, is not simply static but a process. His idea of process introduced a new paradigm for viewing reality. I would summarize his shift by comparing the difference between viewing the world as a snapshot and as a movie strip.

16. P. Senge, *Fifth Discipline*.

17. "I believe that the existence of the classical 'path' can be pregnantly formulated as follows: The 'path' comes into existence only when we observe it." W. Heisenberg, in uncertainty principle paper, 1927. David Cassidy, *Uncertainty: The Life and Science of Werner Heisenberg* (New York: W.H. Freeman, 1992).

18. Our national economy offers a wonderful illustration of a complex system that currently defies understanding. So many components influence the economy: corporate results, monetary policy, fiscal policy, politics, global news, innovation, scandal, labor unions, real estate, investors, seasons, energy, technology, and so on. The most visible and understandable barometers of the economy have been the stock market and the Federal Reserve chairman, Alan Greenspan. Even these clearinghouses and influencers have been ineffective either predicting or influencing where our economy goes. This is the nature of the new epistemology for any number of intellectual disciplines.

19. "I would say that in my scientific and philosophical work, my main concern has been with understanding the nature of reality in general and of consciousness in particular as a coherent whole, which is never static or complete but which is an unend-

ing process of movement and unfoldment . . ." (D. Bohm, *Wholeness and the Implicate Order*, New York: Routledge, 1980, p. ix). On this stream one may see an ever-changing pattern of vortices, ripples, waves, splashes, and so on, which evidently have no independent existence. Rather, they are abstracted from the flowing movement, arising and vanishing in the total process of the flow. Such transitory subsistence as these abstracted forms may possess implies only a relative independence or autonomy of behaviour, rather than absolutely independent existence as ultimate substances (D. Bohm, *Wholeness and the Implicate Order*, p. 48).

20. Smart buildings use technology to monitor and manage utilites, security, and communication.

21. One example is Camille Utterback's installation called Liquid Time. Viewers walk up to a large video screen and see a "cubist"-like image of people crossing at an intersection. Utterback has collected 160 strips that change and morph depending on where the observer stands and how he or she moves.

Chapter Five, The Church in Transition

1. The music industry is a vivid example of a domain attempting to hold on to its treasures. Companies that create proprietary software and technology that does not integrate with others' are examples of strategies that used to work in a world of autonomous, hierarchically structured organizations.

2. For a list of ministries at Willow Creek go to http://www. willowcreek.org/ministries.asp.

3. "A communion reflects the unanimity and singularity of the Apostolic and Patristic Church, while encompassing both protestant and catholic traditions as well as embracing a multiplicity of expressions of worship and practice. In contrast to a denomification, a communion expresses the organic unity Jesus Christ originally established in His Body, the Church. Rather than emerging from divisions created by historic differences over doctrine and practice, a communion represents return to unity based on the recovery of the essential oneness of the ancient, medieval and

contemporary church." "Canons," 1st ed., adopted September 16, 2000, *CEEC Preamble* (found on the home page of the Communion of Evangelical Episcopal Churches Web site; http://www.theceec.org).

4. "For 113 years Vision New England, formerly known as the Evangelistic Association of New England, has been a cutting-edge ministry that brought believers and churches together for evangelism and renewal. Now the largest regional association in the country, more than 30 Vision New England ministry initiatives serve more than 5,000 churches in 80 denominations. As the region's leading resource for pastors and churches, Vision New England is an interdependent network of individual Christians and local churches who are committed to reaching New England through healthy churches." "About Vision New England" (found on the home page of Christianity.com; http://www.christianity.com).

5. The growth ethos within the church is no different than that in business, fueled to a great degree by a broadcast approach to relating to the world. Business is further along than the church in realizing a need to shift toward a strategy for retaining customers.

6. This may be the most socially important direction for the church to consider. Historians note that the United States's success with democracy was built on several generations of personal responsibility and community cooperation. Early generations needed these qualities to survive the harsh realities of the New World. Conversely, France did not have this social heritage; so when the French Revolution brought liberation, it quickly led to anarchy and totalitarianism. A new social structure for a digital new world must have time to develop naturally; otherwise, the revolution will lead to similar anarchy and totalitarianism. The church is better positioned than any other institution or community to lay this foundation. I believe it is the only institution that can salt this new era with the preserving qualities that allow a civil society.

7. P. F. Fagan, "The Real Root Causes of Violent Crime: The Breakdown of Marriage, Family, and Community," *The Heritage*

Foundation Backgrounder, March 17, 1995, p. 1026. The Web site information for Jammin Java is http://www.jamminjava.com.

8. J. Houston, "Myths for the Future: A Futurist Look at the Archetypes Which Guide Our Common Destiny," (Louisville, Colo.: Sounds True Inc., July 1995).

9. This is one of the primary themes in Neil Postman's book, *Amusing Ourselves to Death.*

10. R. Carson, *Silent Spring* (Boston: Houghton Mifflin, 1962).

11. F. Schaeffer, *The God Who Is There* (Colorado Springs, Colo.: Intervarsity Press, 1968).

12. U2 is a popular rock group and Bono is their lead singer. He has become a leading voice for dealing with the AID's epidemic in Africa and has won the respect of many world leaders for his political and social positions. Anne Lamott is a best-selling fiction writer and a convert to Christianity. She does not fit most of the Christian stereotypes and provides an appealing example for those who are interested in the Christian message but mistrust organized religion. George Gilder has been introduced earlier in the book. He has written several groundbreaking books about technology and its impact on culture and business. Christopher Locke is the author of *Cluetrain Manifesto* and *Gonzo Marketing* and consults with businesses that are trying to understand how to adapt to Internet technology and its culture. He challenges many of the current paradigms regarding company and customer relationships.

13. M. Vance, *Cultivating Company Culture Through Original Thinking* (Cleveland: Intellectual Equities Inc./Creative Thinking Association of America, 1993). Shared during a live seminar in Indianapolis.

14. C. Hamby, *Beyond Certainty* (Boston: Harvard Business Press, 1998).

15. D. Hock, *Birth of the Chaordic Age* (San Francisco: Berrett-Koehler, 1999).

16. During the 1980s, Robert Allen wrote several books on real estate investing and also provided training seminars. This quote came from *Creating Wealth* (Del Mar, Calif.: Challenge Systems, 1988), sound cassette.

17. S. Zuboff and J. Maxmin, *The Support Economy* (New York: Viking, 2002).

18. The early church also changed the world as it permeated through the Roman empire and outward to the Western world.

19. R. Probst, *The Office: A Facility Based on Change* (Elmhust, Ill.: Business Press, 1968), p. 33.

20. The Reverend Charles Simpson developed the concept of internal integrity leading to external integration. Charles Simpson has been a pastor, Bible teacher, and church planter for more than forty years and ministers extensively around the world. He has authored numerous books, served as contributor to *The Spirit-Filled Life Bible*, and is the senior editor of *One-to-One* magazine.

21. Information and decision capabilities are distributed through an organizational structure that looks like a web or a fishnet of relationships. This contrasts with most current organizations that centralize information and decision making into a hierarchy or pyramid structure.

22. I draw the *Titanic* metaphor from Christopher Locke, author of the iconoclastic books *Cluetrain Manifesto* (Boulder, Colo.: Perseus, 2000) and *Gonzo Marketing* (Boulder, Colo.: Perseus, 2002).

23. Quoted on the College of Charleston Web site at http://www.cofc.edu/~kdk/Einsteinquotes.htm.

Chapter Six, Trust Connections

1. One of my favorite chapters in Max DePree's book *Leadership Is an Art* (New York: Dell, 1989) is titled "The Millwright Was a Poet." It will stir your leadership passions. This is one of those chapters that will shape and inform all of your thoughts regarding leadership.

2. William McDonough is this building's architect. "I believe we can accomplish great and profitable things within a new conceptual framework—one that values our legacy, honors diversity, and feeds ecosystems and societies. . . . It is time for designs that are creative, abundant, prosperous, and intelligent from the start" (www. mcdonough.com).

3. M. DePree, *Leadership Is an Art*, p. xx.

4. P. F. Drucker (ed.), *Preparing Tomorrow's Business Leaders Today* (Upper

Saddle River, N.J.: Prentice Hall, 1969). Drucker writes on p. 87, "I would define modern entrepreneurship as anticipating the future requirements of society, and successfully meeting these needs with new, creative, and imaginative combinations of resources. The classical resources of land, labor, and capital are relatively less important today. The critical resources I would add are information, superior organization, talented and professionally trained people, and lastly, time itself."

5. D. Steinborn, "The Grafters," *Forbes*, Oct. 2003.

6. J. Collins, *Good to Great: Why Some Companies Make the Leap . . . and Others Don't* (New York: Harper Business, 2001), p. 22.

7. Some examples are Dan Kimball, *The Emerging Church* (Grand Rapids, Mich.: Zondervan, 2003); Carl F. George, *The Coming Church Revolution* (Grand Rapids, Mich.: Revell, 1994); Leith Anderson, *Dying for Change* (Minneapolis: Bethany 1990); Jim Peterson, *Church Without Walls* (Colorado Springs, Colo.: Navpress, 1992); and George Barna, *The Second Coming of the Church* (Nashville: Word, 1998).

8. The Vatican home page for English is found at http://www. vatican.va/phome_en.htm. Catholic Online is the largest nonprofit online network supporting the communication objectives of the Catholic Church. It is found at http://www. catholic.org.

9. The Presbyterian Church USA site is found at http://www.pcusa.org/; the Presbyterian Church of America site at http://www.pcanet.org/; the United Methodist Church site at http://www.umc.org/index.asp; the Lutheran Church Missouri Synod site at http://www.lcms.org/; and the Southern Baptist Convention site at http://www.sbc.net.

10. The Willow Creek Community Church site is http://www. willowcreek.org/default.asp; the Saddleback site is http://www. saddleback.com/home/today.asp; and the McLean Bible Church site is http://www.mcleanbible.org/home_flash.asp.

11. The Mars Hill site is http://www.marshillchurch.org/; the Cedar Ridge Community Church site is http://www.crcc.org/; the Emergent Village site is http://www.emergentvillage.org/;

The Ooze site is http://www.theooze.com/main.cfm; and the Kaleo Fellowship site is http://www.kaleo.us.

12. The National Clergy Support Network, a group devoted to helping "needy pastors," reported on findings from a 1991 survey of one thousand U.S. pastors conducted by the Fuller Institute of Church Growth. Among the troubling findings:

80 percent of pastors believe their pastoral ministry has negatively affected their families.

75 percent reported a significant stress-related crisis at least once in their ministry.

50 percent felt unable to meet the demands of the job.

90 percent felt inadequately trained to cope with ministry demands.

70 percent have a lower self-image than when they began their professions.

50 percent had considered leaving the ministry within the three months prior to completing the survey.

J. P. Winds and G. R. Rendle, *The Leadership Situation: Facing American Congregations* (Alban Institute Special Report, 2001).

13. L. Crabb, *Connecting* (Nashville: Word, 1997).

14. D. Schwartz, *Who Cares: Rediscovering Community* (Boulder, Colo.: Westview Press, 1997).

15. J. Naisbitt, *Megatrends: Ten New Directions Transforming Our Lives* (New York: Warner, 1982).

16. This vision has also led to reaching out in innovative ways to the underserved minority communities. Dr. Anderson has adopted a concept called congregational nursing, developed at Duke University. Here is an excerpt from the Duke University School of Nursing at http://www.nursing.duke.edu/academics/hnm/what.html: "At its core, congregational nursing is about transforming human relationships, about employing the disciplines of nursing and ministry to help people live in relationship with one another . . . about living in their families and their faith community, in a morally grounded way that creates wholeness and heals brokenness."

17. Natural time is the opposite of "programmed" time in which you meet to discuss an issue or study the Bible.

18. Some of the multilevel marketing companies have learned this secret and have thrived with only soap and vitamins to offer. Multilevel marketing is a legal means of selling products through a network of distributors. It has a pyramid structure, and distributors earn revenue through their direct sales and through bonuses and commissions from the sales of distributors they recruit.

   The interesting phenomenon that energizes many of these organizations is not the products or the promises of wealth but the sense of community they create. Relationships seem to provide the greater cohesion for these millennial companies.

19. S. Zuboff and J. Maxmin, *The Support Economy*, p. 12.

20. Read Fred Wiersema and Michael Treacy's book, *The Discipline of Market Leaders: Choose Your Customers, Narrow Your Focus, Dominate Your Market* (Reading, Mass.: Addison-Wesley, 1995) to understand why organizations do not seem to be able to do it all—at least well.

21. Taken from the Web site *Management* at http://management.about. com/cs/generalmanagement/a/Pareto081202.htm?terms= pareto., p. 28.

22. Jack Reis and John Trout made an earlier and similar argument in their best-selling book *Positioning* (New York: McGraw Hill, 1981).

23. S. Zuboff and J. Maxmin, *The Support Economy*, p. 359.

24. Information about Chaordic Commons and its mission statement can be found at http://www.chaordic.org.

25. Taken from Web site www.houston.indymedia.org/news/ 2002/12/6005.php/

26. L. Tischler, "He Struck Gold on the Net (Really)," *Fast Company*, (June 2002), www.fastcompany.com.

27. The medium of radio is a key factor to Keillor's effectiveness. Radio is an oral-aural experience, which makes it distinct from television.

Chapter Seven, Growing Vital Relationships

1. These can be found in towns such as Reston, Virginia, and Southlake, Texas; and they are popping up all over the country.

2. It is interesting to note that companies are now hiring "plants," individuals who hang out at bars or walk the streets and essentially put on an act to endorse a product. This is called "Buzz marketing" and it attempts to create an "un-promotion" promotion. Gerry Khermouch, with Jeff Green, "Buzz Marketing," *Business Week*, July 2001.

3. This symptom is epitomized in recent strategies to close the back door. These churches are not blind to the problem. They rightly want people to stay in order to build a community, but they have gotten the sequence backward. Community becomes a strategy, a means to retain the numbers, instead of the end or the purpose from the very outset. That inversion seems to be an inherent trap that many churches focused on numerical growth succumb to.

4. I call these franchise churches to communicate their intention to replicate the structure, content, and feel of the mother church.

5. I recommend reading Wiersema and Treacy's book *Discipline of Market Leaders* (Chapter Six, note 20). This book will provide a great awakening for church leaders who think they can excel both in large-event formats and intimate community. The underlying premise explains the structural characteristics that allow an organization to excel in one area but exclude it from being able to excel in others. The implications of focusing on core strengths rather than trying to be all things to all people seems clear in business (at least on paper).

6. Neil Howe and William Straus define kids born after 1982 (next-geners) as "millennials" in their book *Millennials Rising: The Next Generation of American* (New York: Knopf, 2000).

7. Sometimes these lawsuits get covered by the news services, but they are usually visible only to the church and the neighborhoods being affected. You can go to the Internet search engine Google and type in "+litigation+zoning 'church'" and find dozens of references covering zoning lawsuits with churches. The Becket Fund Web site at www.becketfund.org listed more than forty. Some are probably well justified and some not. In either case, the number of suits should cause leaders and congregations to ask deeper questions about the means they chose for achieving growth.

8. If you are or have been part of a church that has moved to another community to accommodate growth then you are aware of the congregation's disruption, the calculated trade-off by leaders of losing some in order to attract more, and the fixed focus leaders communicate on the future mission and vision with little thought to the effect on the community left behind.

9. Even though I hear and read about con artists, sexual predators, and people portraying pseudo personalities, I find that the younger generation I interact with is more astute about these kinds of deceptions. People who have integrated the Internet into their lives tend to be more discerning about what they download, who they get information from, and who they share with. People like myself, who use the computer a lot but have not grown up with it, tend to be more naïve and susceptible to being taken advantage of. But we are learning quickly.

10. M. Albom, *Tuesdays with Morrie: An Old Man, A Young Man, and Life's Greatest Lesson* (Derry, N.H.: Broadway Books, 2002).

11. Henri Nouwen, a Catholic priest who was highly influential during the 1970s into the 1990s, is another example of a servant apprentice. He moved to the L'Arche Daybreak community in Toronto during the 1980s to live and serve those with developmental disabilities. He became friends with Adam Arnett, a resident who could not speak and required a great deal of personal attendance. Here is an excerpt from the Henri Nouwen Literary Centre Web site *Lives Lived: Henri J. M. Nouwen* by Carolyn Whitney-Brown, *The Globe and Mail*, Oct. 2, 1996: "He developed a deep friendship with Adam Arnett (1961–1996), a man who never spoke a word, who taught Henri to slow down (briefly!), to be physically present, and to trust love that could grow without words." Nouwen tells Adam's story in the book *Adam: God's Beloved* (Orbis, 1997).

12. M. Gladwell, *The Tipping Point: How Little Things Can Make a Big Difference* (New York: Little, Brown, 2000), p. 141.

13. J. Collins, *Good to Great: Why Some Companies Make the Leap . . . and Others Don't* (New York: HarperBusiness, 2001), pp. 164–187. A flywheel is a device that looks like a large wheel and transfers the energy it receives to make the wheel turn into a consistent output of energy. Jim Collins uses this analogy to draw attention to

the effect of many small focused efforts that eventually translate into enough momentum to create sustained change.

14. W. Berry, *A Continuous Harmony: Essays Cultural and Agricultural* (Orlando: Harcourt Brace, 1972). Chapter available at http://www.msu.edu/~kikbradl/little.html.

15. J. Collins, *Good to Great*, p. 179.

16. "We are going to have to rebuild the substance and the integrity of private life in this country. We are going to have to gather up the fragments of knowledge and responsibility that we have parceled out to the bureaus and the corporations and the . . . specialists" (W. Berry, *A Continuous Harmony*, see Web site listed in note 14).

17. I highly recommend two books by Larry Crabb: *Connecting: A Radical New Vision* (Nashville: Word, 1997) and *The Safest Place on Earth: Where People Connect and Are Forever Changed* (Nashville: Word, 1999).

18. Promise Keepers is an organization that emerged during the 1990s with a message challenging men to live up to their commitments and promises to their families and others by dedicating their lives to serving God.

19. I've paraphrased the opening verses of this psalm to bring the word picture closer to our experience.

20. The quotation is from Jeanne Houston's audiobook *Myths for the Future* (Louisville, Colo.: Sounds True, 1995).

21. 1 Corinthians 13 is challenging not only because it describes love but also because it reveals the shallowness of one's own relational connections. Love gives me the ability to connect directly with Christ within another, but I too often compromise and am content to connect with that person's death shroud instead. Patience is the key, the antidote to our full-speed-ahead culture.

22. J. Houston, *Myths for the Future*.

23. Accountability groups are typically small and made up of individuals who aid each other in keeping their commitments or goals expressed openly to one another. Trust and confidentiality are key elements that members provide so that failures and successes can be safely expressed along with correction and encouragement.

Chapter Eight, Convergence

1. The idea of a living church is borrowed from Arie de Guess's book *The Living Company* (Boston: Longview, 1997).
2. De Guess, *Living Company*, p. 4.
3. C. Locke, *Gonzo Marketing*.
4. Boards of directors, boards of elders, and similar governing bodies are presently insufficient and not structured to provide this kind of input. Recent corporate and ministry scandals bear this out. Too often the board members' limited awareness of daily activities and their circular friendships make them blind to potential problems. This is not a governing function but an ecological issue. It has to do with protecting and nurturing the spiritual environment.
5. H. Campbell, "Community.dot.com: A Look at Networked Community and Generation X," paper presented at the Connecting with Absent Friends Conference, St. John's College, Durham, September 2000, p. 7.
6. "If you want to take your first baby step towards entering the market conversation, . . . replace brochures with ways to ignite . . . dialogue" (C. Locke, *Cluetrain Manifesto*, p. 94).
7. D. Siegel, *Futurize Your Enterprise—Business Strategy in the Age of the E-Customer* (New York: John Wiley & Sons, Inc., 1999), p. 23.
8. Metcalfe's Law is named after Robert Metcalfe, founder of 3Com Corporation and designer of the Ethernet protocol for computer networks. It states that "the usefulness, or utility, of a network equals the square of the number of users." For example, the Internet reached critical mass in 1993, when roughly 2.5 million host computers were on the network, and by November 1997, the Internet contained approximately 25 million host computers (Netlingo). (Netlingo is a dictionary of Internet terms and can be found at www.netlingo.com.)
9. According to Netlingo (see note 8), "The Internet represents an extraordinary opportunity to converse with people all over the world; online communities provide a framework in which to exchange ideas and information, build relationships, and interact."

10. A small and growing core get it. Some of the pioneers developing the virtual ethos in business, culture, and church are people like Christopher Locke, David Siegel, Dan Tapscott, John Hagel III, Derrick de Kerckhove, and Heidi Campbell. All of these thinkers are still developing a vision or picture of this new world.

11. M. McLuhan, *Understanding Media*, p. 23.

12. Relational linkages tie pieces of information together based on their relative relationship to other pieces of information instead of by more traditional linear, logical, or chronological means. Edward DeBono developed an ideation process based on this model, which he called flowscaping. James Burke's historical overviews provide another example. Edward DeBono is author of over sixty-seven books related to creativity and business. His Web site is www.debonogroup.com. James Burke is an author, historian, host of the documentary series *Connections*, and a Smithsonian Associate.

13. J. Burke, *The Knowledge Web: From Electronic Agents to Stonehenge and Back—And Other Journeys Through Knowledge* (New York: Simon and Schuster, 1999).

14. Community Christian Church located in Naperville, Illinois, is addressing this issue with its concept of the "Big Idea": "Have you ever gone to church on Sunday, listened to the message and wished you could keep that idea fresh in your mind throughout the week? Well, the Big Idea is CCC's way of helping you do just that. We have one Big Idea every week in all our celebration services and our small groups. For the adults, the teaching pastor will present the Big Idea for the week and our creative team will reinforce this weekly theme with the use of musical theatre, drama, video, or dance. The Big Idea not only connects Small Groups and celebration services together, it also connects ministries and attendees of all ages! On Sunday, your children will be learning about the same topic that you are hearing in service in a creative, age-appropriate fashion. On Sunday nights, your students will address the same Big Idea in the kind of atmosphere and aggressive fashion that teens love. And we also present the Big Idea of our Tuesday night Support & Recovery ministry event, called Celebrate the Journey. The Big Idea is church-wide. . . . it's really big!" You can find this at http://www.communitychristian.org.

15. "[MUD]: A multi-user simulation environment, usually text-based. It incorporates an object-oriented programming language that participants use to construct their own characters and worlds. Some worlds are purely for fun and flirting, but others are used for serious software development, educational purposes, and all that lies in between. A significant feature of most MUDs is that users can create things that stay after they leave and that can be further developed in their absence, thus allowing a world to be built gradually and collectively." Definition found at www.netlingo.com.

16. Some of the newer museum designs are creating "journeys" that build or create a simulated environment, taking participants not only through the story but into past contexts and mind-sets. The Holocaust Museum in Washington, D.C., is one such example. Interactive architecture is reemerging on many fronts. Interactive architecture will encompass several emerging capabilities: sensors, lasers, thin profile screens, high resolution digital images, and a variety of other technologies to create simulated experiences eventually tailored to and responsive to the individual.

17. Virtual space is a destination on the Internet that facilitates the movement and fulfillment of people's thoughts and intentions.

18. D. de Kerckhove, *The Intelligence of Architecture* (San Francisco: Chronicle Books, 2001), p. 7. The author is the director of the McLuhan Program in Culture and Technology and a professor in the department of French at the University of Toronto. He was an associate of the Centre for Culture and Technology from 1972 to 1980 and worked with Marshall McLuhan for over ten years as translator, assistant, and coauthor.

19. Joe Pereira, then Director of Global Planning and Design, both provided the tour of Monsanto in 1998 and edited my recounting of the event.

Appendix

1. Robert Probst, *The Office: A Facility Based on Change* (Elmhurst, Ill.: Business Press, 1968), p. 14.

The Author

M. Rex Miller is married and the father of three children. He has a successful twenty-five-year career in sales and executive management. Rex is a futurist and the creator of the SWARM (Smart Work and Referral Marketing) Network, a business development approach based on the strategies of tightly aligned corporate coalitions. He consults for business and non-profit organizations and is on the board of Lamar Boschman Ministries.

Rex graduated from the University of Illinois with a degree in theology and communications. As an undergraduate he was initiated into the Sigma Chi fraternity and was active in campus ministry. Since college he has remained active in church leadership. He is a member of the United States Professional Tennis Association and the National Eagle Scout Association. Rex has been a youth leader, tennis coach, Boy Scout master, and lay pastor. His interests include camping, tennis, music, photography, and researching future trends. Rex has had a lifelong focus on mentoring relationships and a professional focus developing healthy organizational cultures.

Index

Blur, 2
Blurring, of private and public, 67–68
Bob's Market, 172, 173
Body of Christ, in digital culture, 88–89
Bohm, D., 181
Bohmian worldview, 108
Bono, 128, 179
Boulding, K., 7, 239
Boyd, J. R., 7
Brain function, 38, 65–66, 106, 123–124
Brain, The (file management system), 233, 234
Branding, in broadcast culture, 174–175
Bright, B., 244
Broadcast culture: architecture in, 73–74, 113; art in, 63–65, 113–114; branding and, 174–175; church in, 60–61, 70–75, 96–102; church Web sites and, 150–153; economics in, 116–118; knowledge in, 104–110; leadership in, 149, 154; mall mentality in, 172–174; problems of, 120–121; society in, 69, 110–112; television and, 54–60, 67–68; thinking process in, 65–67; time concepts in, 103, 104–105; trade-offs in, 61–62
Broken-windows theory, 186, 187–188, 193
Burke, J., 208–209, 264
Business clubs, 214
Buzz marketing, 260

C

Cage, J., 64
Call to faith, 50
Campbell, H., 204
Campus Crusade for Christ, 244
Carneal, M., 66–67, 84
Carson, R., 128
Cathedrals, 31–33, 52, 53, 215
Catholic Church: AmericanCatholic.org and, 248; call to faith and, 50; cathedrals and, 52, 53; efficacy of sacraments in, 242; lead-to-serve model and, 154; liturgy and, 29, 96, 243; parish model of, 213–214; Protestant schism and, 49
Catholic Online, 150
CATIA software, 80
Cause, and disconnect with effect, 185–186
Celebration church. See Broadcast culture; Churches
Celera Genomic, 80
Change, in digital culture, 77, 134

Chant, 30–31, 114
Chant (recording), 31
Chaordic Commons, 166
Chaordic reality, 130
Chaos theory, 108, 238
Charity, 126–127, 134, 191–192, 196–197
Chicago Children's Museum Web site, 235
Child development, in digital culture, 84
Chinn, E., 2
Christian business centers, 214
Churches: in broadcast culture, 60–61, 70–75, 96–102; in digital culture, 86–94, 96–102, 124–127, 174–178; disconnects within, 182–188; growth and, 60–61, 125, 175–178, 182–183, 211–214, 254; lessons for, 132–135; in oral culture, 27–34, 96–102; in print culture, 48–53, 96–102, 174; Web sites and, 150–153, 205–208
Churchill, W., 149
Circumcision, as sign of inclusion, 28
Clergy, problems of, 258
Clinton, B., 148, 149
Closure, in print culture, 63–65
Cohesion, in digital culture, 134
Collaboration, in digital culture, 135, 164–167
Collaborative ethos, 86
Collective memory, 110
Collins, J., 147, 148, 186, 187, 194
Commerce, and convergence, 126–127, 134
Commitment, 22–23, 47, 82–83, 111, 230
Communal living, 83
Communication tools, 15–17, 78–81, 119–120, 137–141
Communications theory, 16
Communion, 25, 29, 45
Communion of Evangelical Episcopal Churches, 125
Community: basis for, 112; convergence and, 126–127, 134; disconnect removal and, 182–188; federation model for churches and, 177–178; human-scaled communities and, 180; ingredients for, 188–197; Internet and, 204–208; in living church, 203–204; in oral culture, 28–29; restoration of morality and, 180–182
Community Christian Church, 213, 264
Complexity, and new millennium, 5
Computer Aided Three Dimension Interactive Application, 80
Computers, 76–80, 84–85

Concert model, of church experience, 173–174
Confession, and repentance, 194–195
Congregational nursing, 258
Connection (Crabb), 155
Context, 123–124, 163–164, 186–187
Contextual composition, 114–115
Contextual songs, in convergence church, 90–91
Continuity, and leadership skills, 163–164
Contract. *See* Commitment
Convergence, 6–7, 126–127, 134, 198–222
Convergence church. *See* Churches; Digital culture; Living church
Conviction, 71, 98
Core competencies, 165
1 Corinthians 4:16, 196
1 Corinthians 8:9, 181
1 Corinthians 10:27–31, 25
1 Corinthians 12, 89
1 Corinthians 13, 262
2 Corinthians 3:6, 37
Covenant, 230: confession and, 194–195; fellowship and, 190–191; Herman Miller, Inc. and, 146; in oral culture, 22–23, 111; reclaiming concept of, 189–190; relational accountability and, 192–193; as relationship, 167; service as servant and, 195–196
Covenetwork, 167
Crabb, L., 155, 188
Cubism, 42, 62
Cyber-punk project Web site, 236
Cyberculture, catalogue of, 236
Cyberia, 250

D

David, King, 28
Davies, P., 101
Davis, S., 2
De Kerckhove, D., 238, 251
De Tocqueville, A., 182
DeBono, E., 264
Decision making, and fighter pilots, 7, 239
"Deck of cards" organization, 232–233
Declaration of Independence, 45, 46
Defense Advanced Research Projects Agency, 212
Democracy in America (de Tocqueville), 182
Democracy, in United States, 182, 254
DePree, D., 145–146

Depth, hunger for in digital era, 131–132
Detachment, 46–47
Deuteronomy 6:12, 105
Dialectic instruction, 47–48, 107–108
Dialogue, and right brain, 38
Dictionary.com Web site, 230, 231
Digital communications, 119–120, 159–161
Digital culture: architecture in, 91–92, 113, 215–218; art in, 113–114; blindness in, 121–123; church in, 86–94, 96–102, 124–127, 174–178; church Web sites and, 152–153, 205–208; communication tools and, 78–81, 137–141; economics in, 116–118; essence in, 85–86; framework for, 136–137; knowledge in, 104–110; leadership in, 124, 145–170, 199–200; lessons for churches in, 132–135; need for understanding of, 135–136; role models and, 178–180; skills of, 123–127; society in, 82–85, 110–112; spiritual hungers of, 127–132; time concepts in, 77–78, 103, 104–105. *See also* Living church
Digital language, 76–77
Dilbert (comic strip), 128–129, 190
Ding Dong School (television program), 69
DISC Web site, 250
Discipleship, 23–24, 158–159
Discipline of Market Leaders, The (Wiersema and Treacy), 165
Disconnects, as obstacles to community, 182–188
Divine Milieu: An Essay on the Interior Life (Teilhard de Chardin), 86
"Doom Loops," 187
Drucker, P., 147
Duke University School of Nursing, 258
Dylan, B., 54, 128

E

Earl, L., 126–127
Early childhood education, in digital culture, 84
Economics, in four cultures, 116–118
Education, 45, 50, 84–85
Edutainment, 69, 84
Effect, and disconnect with cause, 185–186
Efficiency, and spiritual dryness, 131
80/20 principle, 165
Einstein, A., 138
Einsteinian worldview, 108

Identity, sense of, 106–107
Immediacy, and new millennium, 7
Impartational leadership, 145–170, 199–200
Inclusion, process of in oral culture, 28–29
Influence, basis of, 111
Instruction, in print culture, 47–48
Intangibility, and new millennium, 6
Integration, external, 256
Integrity, and community, 187–188
Intellect, 40
Intentional communities, 83, 247–248
Interactive assemblies, 90
Interactive digital media, 85–86
Interactive dynamics, 168–169
Interactive-relational environment, 230
Interconnection, and new millennium, 4–5
Internal integrity, 256
Internet, 85, 204–208, 209, 212, 218. *See also*
    Web sites
Isaac, sacrifice of, 25, 27–28

J
James 2:23, 101
James 5:16, 195
Jammin Java, 126
Japan, spiritual dryness in, 127
Jazz model, of church experience, 174
Jesus: authority of, 27; as master, 24; morality
    and, 181; oral culture and, 19–22; spiritual
    authorities and, 242; teaching and, 33–34;
    and unity of word and being, 34
Jewish community, 214
John 1:1, 19
John 1:14, 23
John 8:32, 194
John 10:4, 145
John 14:6, 23, 29, 109
John 15:5, 198
John 15:13, 195
John 17:16–17, 86
Judaizers, 240
Jung, C., 103

K
Kaleo Fellowship, 152–153
Keillor, G., 169, 210–211
Kelling, G., 186
Kennedy, J. F., 149
2 Kings 6:15–17, 170
Knitworks, 206–207
Knowledge, 36–37, 104–110, 183–184

Knowledge Web, The (Burke), 208–209
Kosinski, J., 62
Krispy Kreme, 249
Kuhn, T., 10, 120

L
Lamott, A., 128, 179–180
L'Arche Daybreak community, 261
Last Supper, 45
Latin liturgy, in Catholic Church, 243
Lead-to-serve model, 154–157
Leadership: comparison of, 110; continuity
    and, 163–164; impartational nature of,
    145–170; in living church, 199–200; ser-
    vice as servant and, 195–196; trends of in
    digital age, 124
Leadership and the New Science (Wheatley), 181
Leadership Is an Art (DePree), 146
Learning, 23–24, 47–48, 69, 83–85, 109
Left-brain thinking, 38, 65–66, 123–124
Lettuce Entertain You, 249
"Level 5" leaders, 148–149, 157–158
Lincoln, A., 148–149
Linear-sequential environment, 230
Linux software, 167–168, 247
Liquid Time, 253
Literacy, effects of, 37–38
Liturgical church. *See* Oral culture
Liturgy. *See* Worship
Liu, B., 172
Living church: characteristics of, 199–218;
    Monsanto parable and, 219–222
Living museums, 234
Living word, 24–26, 39–40
Locke, C., 128, 202
Logic, 42, 107–108
Love, reclaiming of, 191–192
Luke 4:36, 27
Luke 6:45, 97
Luke 7:47, 180
Luke 10:25–37, 181–182
Luke 10:29, 171
Luke 10:30–37, 33
Luke 10:41, 131
Luke 16:10, 186
Luther, M., 44

M
Madonna and child depictions, 41
Magic Eye Web site, 229
Mall mentality, in broadcast culture, 172–174